STUDY GUIDE

Gerald V. Booth
University of Windsor

Heather E. Metcalfe
University of Windsor

SOCIOLOGY

Fourth Canadian Edition

John J. Macionis
Linda M. Gerber

Prentice
Hall

Toronto

ISBN 0-13-042139-1

Acquisitions Editor: Jessica Mosher
Executive Developmental Editor: Lise Dupont
Production Editor: Susan Adlam
Production Coordinator: Wendy Moran
Cover Design: Lisa Lapointe

3 4 5   06 05 04 03

Printed and bound in Canada.

Prentice
Hall

CONTENTS

CHAPTER 1 — The Sociological Perspective

I CHAPTER OUTLINE

I. **The Sociological Perspective**
    A. Seeing the General in the Particular
    B. Seeing the Strange in the Familiar
    C. Individuality in Social Context

II. **The Importance of Global Perspective**

III. **Applying the Sociological Perspective**
    A. Sociology and Social Marginality
    B. Sociology and Social Crisis
    C. Benefits of the Sociological Perspective
    D. Applied Sociology

IV. **The Origins of Sociology**
    A. Science and Sociology
    B. Social Change and Sociology
        1. A New Industrial Economy
        2. The Growth of Cities
        3. Political Change
    C. Marginal Voices
    D. Canadian Sociology: Distinctive Touches

V. **Sociological Theory**
    A. The Structural-Functional Paradigm
    B. The Social-Conflict Paradigm
        1. Feminism
    C. The Symbolic-Interaction Paradigm
    D. Applying the Perspectives: The Sociology of Sport
        1. The Functions of Sports
        2. Sports and Conflict
        3. Sports as Interaction

VI. **Summary**
VII. **Critical Thinking Questions**
VIII. **Applications And Exercises**
IX. **Sites To See**

II LEARNING OBJECTIVES

- To understand how perspective is shaped and becomes the basis for "reality."

- To be able to define sociology and understand the basic components of the sociological perspective.

- To be able to provide examples of the way in which social forces affect our everyday lives.

- To understand the significance of the research on suicide done by Emile Durkheim, showing the impact of social forces on individual behaviour.

- To recognize more about ourselves as Canadians through global comparisons and to see how Canada fits into the rest of the world.

- To understand how the socially marginal and those undergoing social change experience sociological vision.

- To recognize how sociological thinking can impact upon our daily lives.

- To recognize how sociological thinking affects social policy decisions.

- To be able to identify important historical factors in the development of sociology.

- To be able to identify and understand the differences between the three major theoretical paradigms used by sociologists.

- To be able to provide illustrative questions raised about society using each of the theoretical paradigms.

- To be able to differentiate between sociological observations and stereotypical statements.

III CHAPTER REVIEW

Much of the behaviour that people exhibit in society is highly predictable. For the most part people conform to a set of social expectations, whether they are explicitly identified or not. The scenario outlined to begin this chapter illustrates how something as simple as males and females holding hands appears to operate according to a set of unwritten rules. Sociology helps us to comprehend the social forces which influence behaviour patterns.

THE SOCIOLOGICAL PERSPECTIVE

Sociology is defined as the systematic study of human society. Sociology as a discipline is guided by a distinctive perspective. The qualities of this perspective are outlined, with illustrations for each being presented.

Seeing the General in the Particular

Sociologist Peter Berger refers to the fact that sociologists see general social patterns in the behaviour of particular individuals. In fact each chapter in the text will illustrate how social forces shape our lives. Age, gender and social class, for example, are seen to have a remarkable impact upon behaviour and life chances. While not erasing our uniqueness as individuals, social forces touch our lives in many unseen, yet significant ways such as the behaviour of Canadian "peacekeepers" in Somalia who responded to cultural imperatives in the commission of atrocities.

Seeing the Strange in the Familiar

This is the process of detaching oneself from "familiar" individualistic interpretations of human behaviour and the acceptance of the initially "strange" notion that behaviour is a product of social forces.

Students will typically respond to a question about their own attendance at a university in a personal way while, in social reality, factors such as family income, age, race and government funding influence the choice. As we step back from "particular" choices and focus on "general" patterns our understanding is enhanced as we see how our lives are linked to others and to the society.

Individuality in Social Context

In a society which emphasizes individuality we are often reluctant to admit that our lives are predictable and patterned. Even suicide, a seemingly very personal act, can be seen to be affected by social forces. The research by Emile Durkheim on suicide clearly shows how impersonal social forces affect personal behaviour. Records of suicide in central Europe during the last part of the 19th century were found by Durkheim to show certain social categories as having higher suicide rates than others. It was found that the degree of *social integration*, or how strongly a person is bound to others by social ties, had a significant influence on the patterns of suicide rates. Figure 1-1 (p. 6) provides rates of suicide over time in Canada for males and females.

THE IMPORTANCE OF GLOBAL PERSPECTIVE

Although many academic disciplines have incorporated a global perspective such an inclusion is especially important to the sociological perspective since our basic understanding is that where we are placed within some social construct (including global constraints) affects our experiences as people. Comparative data indicate that Canada is a very wealthy nation where, most people enjoy material abundance. In fact, Table 1-1 (p. 10) shows Canada as the best place to live in the world, according to the United Nations Human Development Index. Although many of our citizens experience relative poverty it is not the abject poverty felt by most of the globe's peoples. The **Global Sociology** box "The Global Village: A Social Snapshot of Our World" (p. 8) indicates the nature of international distribution of income, food and education. As well the **Window on the World Global Map** titled Economic Development in Global Perspective (p. 9) clearly outlines the differences in international economic development and the consequent impacts on people's lives. Quite clearly globalization has led to increasing interconnectedness which has enabled us to see ourselves and examine ourselves and perhaps learn more about ourselves in the light of other nation's experiences.

APPLYING THE SOCIOLOGICAL PERSPECTIVE

Encountering people who are different from us reminds us of the power of social forces but two additional situations further stimulate a sociological outlook.

Sociology and Social Marginality

Social marginality or being an "outsider" enhances sociological thinking. Aboriginals, women, gay people, those with disabilities and the aged are used to illustrate how certain socially significant characteristics can place people on the "outside" of social life, and make them more aware of social patterns others take for granted.

Sociology and Social Crisis

Secondly, social crisis can enhance sociological thinking. C. Wright Mills has suggested that historical periods characterized by massive change have resulted in increased sociological awareness. The massive unemployment of the depression years, for example, could be seen as a product of social forces and not individual ineptitude. Conversely, sociological thinking itself can foment social change rather than simply result from it.

Benefits of the Sociological Perspective

Four general benefits of using the sociological perspective are reviewed. These include:

1. It challenges familiar understandings about ourselves and others, so that we can critically assess the truth of commonly held assumptions.
2. It allows us to recognize both opportunities we have and the constraints that circumscribe our lives.
3. It empowers us as active members of our world through the grasp of our "sociological imagination", the capacity to comprehend the interplay between personal life and societal forces.

4

4. It helps us to recognize human diversity and to begin to understand the challenges of living in a diverse world.

Applied Sociology

Sociological training provides not only a useful perspective for hundreds of jobs in the public and private sectors of the workforce, but also the particulars of sociological research can be applied to program evaluation, public information gathering and analysis and the provision of research analysis for public and private agencies. Such analysis, for example, has influenced the policy decisions taken on medical care, bilingualism and biculturalism and aboriginal affairs, among many others.

THE ORIGINS OF SOCIOLOGY

While "society" has been a topic of thought and discussion since the beginning of human history, sociological thinking is a recent historical phenomenon. The discipline of sociology is relatively young, and itself emerged as a product of particular social forces. Auguste Comte coined the term *sociology* in 1838 during a period of rapid social transformation.

Science and Sociology

Emile Durkheim pointed out in the latter part of the 19th century that the great philosophers from antiquity through the first half of the 19th century, using only philosophical and theological perspectives in their studies, concentrated on the qualities of imaginary "ideal" societies rather than on the analysis of what society was really like. Sociology was born when focus was given to understanding how society actually operates.

Auguste Comte argued that the key to achieving this was to use the scientific approach in studying society. He divided the history of the study of society into three distinct eras, which he labelled the *theological*, the *metaphysical*, and the *scientific*. The latter he called *positivism*, or the path to understanding the world based on science.

Even today, most sociologists in North America accept the importance of the scientific perspective but there is a recognition that human behaviour may never conform to rigid "laws of society."

Social Change and Sociology

Three key factors are identified as reshaping society during the 17th and 18th centuries. These include:

➤A New Industrial Economy

Rapid technological changes of the 18th century brought people in great numbers to work in factories, thus breaking down established patterns of social life.

➤The Growth of Cities

As factories spread across Europe, drawing people out of the countryside seeking employment due to the changing nature of the economy, this massive influx of people into cities created many social problems. The crises which emerged stimulated the development of the sociological perspective.

➤Political Change

The rapid economic and urban growth created a context for change in political thinking. Traditional notions of Divine Law were being replaced by ideas of individual liberty and freedom. Such rights are now enshrined in the Canadian Charter of Rights and Freedoms.

Sociological thinking prospered in those societies where change was greatest and led Comte, Marx and many others to examine the social forces which impacted so greatly on individual lives.

Marginal Voices

While Comte, Durkheim and Marx are accepted as giants of sociology, other voices have been muted. Because women were regarded as inferior in a male-dominated society their sociological works were essentially ignored. Harriet Martineau in Britain and Jane Addams in the United States were accomplished sociologists but did not receive the attention they deserved. Nor did W. E. B. Dubois, a black sociologist during a period when blacks were treated as socially inferior. Sociology itself is a response to the set of social conditions which exist at any time in a society.

Canadian Sociology: Distinctive Touches

Sociology began in Canada and the United States in the early part of the twentieth century but the traditions differ because of Canada's two major cultures and linguistic communities. A European influence was historically obvious in both French Canadian sociology and the University of Toronto where the focus was on political and economic issues while at McGill the American approach to social problems and community studies was in evidence. The works of Harold Innis on Canadian economic development, Marshall McLuhan on the impact of electronic communications, and John Porter on inequality are noted for their influence on Canadian sociology.

SOCIOLOGICAL THEORY

While the sociological perspective provides us with a unique vantage point from which to observe our social world, theory helps us to meaningfully organize and explain the linkages between specific observations we make. A *theory* is a statement of how and why specific facts are related. There are a number of research methods available to researchers which are used to evaluate whether a theory is supported by facts. The basis upon which sociologists choose to study particular issues is a "road map" or *theoretical paradigm*, *"a basic image of society that guides thinking and research.*

There are three principal theoretical paradigms used by sociologists. Each theory focuses the researcher's attention on particular types of questions about how society is organized, and each provides a different explanation about why certain patterns are found in society.

The Structural-Functional Paradigm

This paradigm is a framework for building theory guided by the assumption that society is a complex system whose parts work together to promote stability. The two basic components of this paradigm are *social structure*, or relatively stable patterns of behaviour, and *social functions,* which refer to consequences for the operation of society as a whole. Structural functionalists often liken society to the human body, with different parts of society being interdependent, much like the various organs of the body. Early structural-functionalists included Spencer, Durkheim and Comte. As sociology developed in the United States during the 20th century, researchers Talcott Parsons and Robert K. Merton further applied and developed the thinking of these early social scientists. Merton differentiated between what he called *manifest functions*, or consequences of social structure recognized by people within a society, and *latent functions*, which are unrecognized or unintended consequences of social structure. Merton further points out that elements of social structure may be functional for one aspect of society and not for others. There may be undesirable effects on the operation of society, or *social dysfunctions*. In critically evaluating this paradigm, it is pointed out that it is a conservative approach to the study of society which tends to ignore tension and conflict in social systems, often brought about by inequalities based upon social class, race, ethnicity and gender.

The Social-Conflict Paradigm

This paradigm is a framework for building theory based on the assumption that society is a complex system characterized by inequality and conflict which generate social change. Power and privilege are distributed unequally by social class, race, gender and age and often these inequalities are reinforced in various societal institutions such as education. "Streaming (the placement of students in academic and non-academic programs) for example, often has less to do with talent than social background. A past government effort to reduce streaming in Ontario schools has been overturned by the present government.

Karl Marx, the major proponent of this paradigm, sought not only to understand society but to change it for the better. Perhaps this activism is what attracts many feminist sociologists to this approach as they critically assess the constraints on women's lives in Canada. Critics, however, suggest that this paradigm ignores evidence of social unity and compromises objectivity in the pursuit of political goals.

The Symbolic-Interaction Paradigm

The first two paradigms discussed focus on a *macro-level* orientation, meaning a concern with large-scale patterns that characterize society as a whole. An alternative approach is to take a *micro-level orientation*, meaning a concern with small- scale patterns of social interaction in specific settings. This third paradigm, *symbolic interactionism*, is a theoretical framework based on the assumption that society is continuously recreated as human beings construct reality through interaction. The symbolic-interactionist paradigm was greatly influenced by the work of Max Weber, a German sociologist of the late 19th and early 20th centuries. In the United states, during the 20th century, the work of George Herbert Mead, Erving Goffman, George Homans and Peter Blau were instrumental in the development of this paradigm. Mead's work on socialization, Goffman's work on *dramaturgical analysis*, Garfinkel's creation of ethnomethodology and Homans' and Blau's development of *social-exchange analysis* are discussed in later chapters.

In critically analysing this view it must be stressed that the focus is on how individuals personally experience society. This approach does not allow us to examine the impact of larger social structures on people's lives.

Each of the paradigms provides a unique perspective for the development of greater understanding of society. Table 1-2 (p. 21) reviews the orientation, image of society, and illustrative questions representative of each of the three major theoretical paradigms and those emerging.

Applying the Perspectives: The Sociology of Sport

Sports in North America are discussed as an indispensable part of social life. The question becomes, what insights can the sociological perspective provide us concerning sports?

➤The Functions of Sports

The structural-functional paradigm reveals many functional and dysfunctional consequences which sports have for society. For example sports promote the pursuit of success but university student athletes are often primarily athletes and secondarily students.

➤Sports and Conflict

The social-conflict paradigm provides an analysis of sports focusing upon the social inequalities within sports at all levels of competition. Male and female inequalities are addressed, as well as racial inequalities in professional sports.

➤Sports as Interaction

The symbolic-interactionists view sports as ongoing processes and not merely as a "system." The individual perceptions of specific participants concerning the reality, as each experiences it, becomes the focus.

No one paradigm is better than another in analysing sports, or any other aspect of society. The sociological perspective is enriched by the controversy and debate brought about through the application in research of these different paradigms.

Reining in the Cowboys in Outer Space

The **Applying Sociology** Box (p. 19) discusses the problematic relationships between people of divergent cultures in a 110 day simulated space mission. In the absence of naturally emergent norms, planners for space stations will be required to devise workable codes of conduct.

Sociology. Nothing More Than Stereotypes?

The **Controversy and Debate** Box (pp. 23) indicates that while sociology employs generalizations, these are more than simple stereotypes applied unfairly to whole categories of people. Sociological statements are not applied indiscriminately to all individuals in a category, they are supported by facts, and they are stated within a framework of fair-minded pursuit of the truth.

KEY CONCEPTS

Define each of the following concepts on separate paper. Check the accuracy of your answers by referring to the key concepts in the text as well as by referring to italicized definitions located throughout the chapter.

global perspective
high-income countries
latent functions
low-income countries
macro-level orientation
manifest functions
metaphysical stage
micro-level orientation
middle-income countries
positivism
seeing the general in the particular
seeing the strange in the familiar
scientific stage

social-conflict paradigm
social dysfunctions
social functions
social structure
sociological imagination
sociology
stereotype
structural-functional paradigm
symbolic-interaction paradigm
theological stage
theoretical paradigm
theory

STUGY QUESTIONS

✎ True-False

1. **T** F   Sociologists suggest that society acts differently on various categories of people.

2. T **F**   People's personal choices have little to do with societal social forces.

3. T **F**   Durkheim suggested that categories of people with strong social ties will have high suicide rates.

4. **T** F   In a global village of 1000 people representing all the planet's population citizens from the People's Republic of China would be 600 strong.

5. T **F**   Although sociology promotes intellectual growth, it has had little impact on social policy in Canada.

6. **T** F   Positivism is the belief in science as a means to understand the world.

7. T **F**   Sociology flowered in societies where change was greatest.

8. **T** F   Latent functions refer to social processes which appear on the surface to be functional for society, but which are actually dysfunctional for society.

9. T **F**   Placement of students into academic streams is based solely on their academic abilities.

10. T **F**   The symbolic-interaction and social conflict paradigms both operate from a micro-level orientation.

✎ Multiple-Choice

1. While we usually think of post-secondary education as a personal choice, which of the following items are social factors which influence educational choice?

    (a) age   (d) all of the above
    (b) family income   (e) a and b above
    (c) ethnicity

2. Middle income countries are defined as nations characterized by _____ .

    (a) industrialization in which most people enjoy abundance.
    (b) limited industrialization and high personal income.
    (c) limited industrialization, moderate personal income and marked social inequality.
    (d) limited industrialization and moderate personal income
    (e) little industrialization in which severe poverty is the rule.

3. The concept developed by C. Wright Mills which suggests that political action can result from an understanding of the social forces which shape our lives is

    (a) hypothesis testing
    (d) perspective
    (b) positivism
    (e) sociological imagination
    (c) consciousness raising

4. While sociology may be linked to intellectual growth in students there are also many applied opportunities in Canadian society. Which of the following are examples?

    (a) criminal justice system
    (b) Royal Commission on Fresh Water Applications
    (c) evaluation research
    (d) a and b above
    (e) a and c above

5. Positivism is the idea that _____ ,rather than any other type of human understanding, is the path to knowledge.

    (a) human nature
    (d) optimism
    (b) religion
    (e) intuition
    (c) science

6. The Canadian sociologist who gained world renown for his insights into the impacts of electronic communication on culture, politics and personal identities was

    (a) John Porter
    (d) Marshall McLuhan
    (b) Herbert Spencer
    (e) Peter Berger
    (c) Harold Innis

7. Consequences of social structure which are largely unrecognized and unintended are called:

    (a) latent functions
    (d) paradigms
    (b) manifest functions
    (e) social dysfunction
    (c) social marginality

8. The structural-functional paradigm tends to gloss over _____ in its focus on social integration.

    (a) research
    (d) a and b above
    (b) inequality
    (e) b and c above
    (c) conflict

9. Who said "The philosophers have only interpreted the world in various ways; the point, however, is to change it."?

    (a) Peter Berger
    (d) Herbert Spencer
    (b) Max Weber

(e) George Herbert Mead

(c) Karl Marx

10. Sociologists who view society as a mosaic of subjective meanings and variable responses are guided by the

(a) conflict approach

(d) structural-functional approach

(b) symbolic-interactional approach

(e) none of the above

(c) social Darwinism

✎ Fill-In The Blank

1. The systematic study of human society is the general definition for _Sociology_

2. We begin to think sociologically, according to Berger, when we see the _general_ in the _particular_

3. C. Wright Mills suggested that times of _Social Crisis_ foster widespread sociological thinking.

4. In today's cost conscious environment where the effectiveness of programs is a major concern, many sociologists find employment conducting __ research. _evaluation_

5. Auguste Comte asserted that scientific sociology was a result of a progression throughout history of thought and understanding in three stages, the _Theological_, _metaphysical_ and _Scientific_.

6. The development of sociology as an academic discipline was shaped within the context of three revolutionary changes in Europe during the 17th and 18th centuries. These included

_____ , _____ , and _____ .

7. A statement of how and why specific facts are related is a _Theory_ .

8. A fundamental image of society that guides sociological thinking and research is called a __ _Theoritical paradigm_

9. Feminist sociology has led to the development of a new field in universities called _Women Studies_

10. An exaggerated generalization that one applies to all people in a given category is called a _Stereotype_ .

Definition and Short-Answer

1. Using the perspective of a sociologist, explain how individuals come to study at universities.

2. Discuss Emile Durkheim's explanation of how suicide rates vary between different categories of people. Explain how this research demonstrates the application of the sociological perspective.

3. Of what value is global awareness to sociological thinking?

4. What three key societal changes during the 17th and 18th centuries were significant for the emergence of sociology as a scientific discipline?

5. How is Canadian sociology distinctive from American society?

6. What are the four basic benefits of using the sociological perspective?

7. What are the three major theoretical paradigms used by sociologists? Identify the key questions raised by each.

8. Discuss Merton's concept of social dysfunction and provide an example.

9. Discuss the contributions to sociology made by the following theorists: Robert K. Merton, Karl Marx, and Emile Durkheim.

10. Discuss how the various sociological theoretical paradigms apply to an analysis of sport.

Answers To Study Questions

True-False

1. T (p. 3)	6. T (p. 13)
2. F (p. 6)	7. T (pp. 14-15)
3. F (p. 6)	8. F (p. 18)
4. F (p. 8)	9. F (p. 19)
5. F (p. 11)	10. F (p. 20)

Multiple-Choice

1. d (pp. 5-6)	6. d (p. 16)
2. d (p. 7)	7. a (p. 18)
3. e (p. 11)	8. e (p. 18)
4. e (pp. 11-12)	9. c (pp. 19-20)
5. c (p. 13)	10. b (p. 21)

Fill-In

1. sociology (p. 3)
2. general, particular (p. 3)
3. social crisis (p. 10)
4. evaluation (p. 12)
5. theological, metaphysical, and scientific (p.13)
6. rise of the industrial economy, growth of cities, and political changes (pp. 13-15)
7. theory (p. 16)
8. theoretical paradigm (p. 17)
9. women's studies (p. 20)
10. stereotype (p. 23)

ANALYSIS AND COMMENT

Go back through the chapter and write down in the spaces below key points from each of the following boxes.

GLOBAL SOCIOLOGY

"The Global Village: A Social Snapshot of Our World."

_____

_____

_____

_____

APPLYING SOCIOLOGY

"Reining in the Cowboys in Outer Space."
Key Points:

_____

_____

_____

_____

CONTROVERSY AND DEBATE

"Is Sociology Nothing More Than Stereotypes?"
Key Points:

_____

_____

_____

_____

SUGGESTED READINGS
Classic Sources

C. Wright Mills. 1959. *The Sociological Imagination*. New York: Oxford University Press.
This classic elaborates on the benefits of learning to think sociologically and links this perspective to the possibilities for social activism.

Peter Berger. 1963. *An Invitation to Sociology*. Garden City, N.Y.: Anchor Books.
Berger's readable classic account of the sociological perspective highlights its value for enhancing human freedom.

Contemporary Sources

Lynn McDonald. 1994a. *The Early Origins of the Social Sciences*. Montreal: McGill-Queen's University Press;
Lynn McDonald. 1994b. *The Women Founders of the Social Sciences*. Ottawa: Carleton University Press.
These books discuss the history of sociology.

Janet Mancini Billson and Bettina J. Huber. 1993. *Embarking Upon a Career with an Undergraduate*
This classic book looks at Canada from a social-conflict or political economy perspective.

Mary O'Brien. 1981. *The Politics of Reproduction*. London: Routledge and Kegan Paul.
Meg Luxton. 1981. *More Than a Labour of Love*. Toronto: Women's Press.
Dorothy Smith. 1987. *The Everyday World as Problematic*. Toronto: University of Toronto Press.

Degree in Sociology. **2nd ed. Washington, D.C.: American Sociological Association.**
This publication describing career possibilities in sociology is available for U.S.$8.50 from the American Sociological Association, 1722 N Street N.W., Washington, D.C. 20036; (202) 833-3410.

Canadian Sources

Marlene Shore. 1987. *The Science of Social Redemption: McGill, the Chicago School, and the Origins of Social Research in Canada*. **Toronto: University of Toronto Press.**
 Robert J. Brym and Bonnie J. Fox. 1989. *From Culture to Power: The Sociology of English Canada*. **Don Mills, Ontario: Oxford University Press.**
Harry H. Hiller. 1987. *Society and Change: S.D. Clark and the Development of Canadian Sociology*. **Toronto: University of Toronto Press.**
These three books provide an introductory overview of the history of sociology in Canada.

Ann Hall et al. 1991. *Sport in Canadian Society*. **Toronto: McClelland and Stewart.**
Helen Lenskyj. 1986. *Out of Bounds: Women, Sport, and Sexuality*. **Toronto: Women's Press.**
Barry D. McPherson et al. 1989. *The Social Significance of Sport: An Introduction to the Sociology of Sport*. **Champaign, Ill.: Human Kinetics Books.**
These three books provide a sociological analysis of sports.

Everett Hughes. 1943. *French Canada in Transition*. **Chicago: University of Chicago Press.**
S.D. Clark. 1966. *The Suburban Society*. **Toronto: University of Toronto Press.**
These books examine aspects of Canadian society from a structural-functional perspective.

John Porter. 1968. *The Vertical Mosaic: An Analysis of Class and Power in Canada*. **Toronto: University of Toronto Press.**
These books are written by three Canadian feminist sociologists.

Rex Lucas. 1971. *Minetown, Milltown, Railtown: Life in Canadian Communities of Single Industry*. **Toronto: University of Toronto Press.**
W. Shaffir. 1974. *Life in a Religious Community: The Lubavitcher Chassidim in Montreal*. **Toronto: Holt, Rinehart and Winston.**
These books provide some examples of sociology done from a symbolic-interaction perspective.

Roy Turner, ed. 1974. *Ethnomethodology: Selected Readings*. **Harmondsworth, U.K.: Penguin.**
This book is a good introduction to ethnomethodology.

Elliott Layton. 1986. *Hunting Humans: The Rise of the Modern Multiple Murderer*. **Toronto: McClelland and Stewart.**
An analysis of multiple murderers.

Global Sources

Mike Featherstone. 1991. *Global Culture: Nationalism, Globalization and Modernity*. **Newbury Park, Calif.: Sage.**
Roland Robertson. 1992. *Globalization: Social Theory and Global Culture*. **Newbury Park, Calif.: Sage.**
These two books provide a sophisticated overview of the process of globalization. The first, a collection of two dozen essays, explains the importance of global thinking to members of our society. The second offers one analyst's reflections on the meanings of globalization for our society as well as for sociology.

CHAPTER 2

I CHAPTER OUTLINE

I. **The Basics of Sociological Investigation**
      A. Science as One Form of Truth
      B. Common Sense versus Scientific Evidence

II. **Science: Basic Elements and Limitations**
      A. Concepts, Variables, and Measurement
         1. Reliability and Validity of Measurement
         2. Relationships Among Variables
      B. The Ideal of Objectivity
         1. Max Weber: Value-Free Research
      C. Some Limitations of Scientific Sociology (Positivism)
      D. A Second Framework: Interpretive Sociology
      E. A Third Framework: Critical Sociology
      F. Gender and Research
      G. Women as Methodologists
      H. Research Ethics

III. **The Methods of Sociological Research**
      A. Testing a Hypothesis: The Experiment
         1. The Hawthorne Effect
         2. An Illustration: The Stanford County Prison
      B. Asking Questions: Survey Research
         1. Population and Sample
         2. Questionnaires and Interviews
         3. Surveys at Work: The Case of Anti-Semitism in Quebec
      C. In the Field: Participant Observation
         1. An Illustration: Street Corner Society
      D. Using Available Data: Secondary and Historical Analysis
         1. Content Analysis
         2. Historical Research: Open for Business
      E. Technology and Research
      F. The Interplay of Theory and Method

IV. **Putting It All Together: Ten Steps in Sociological Investigation**

V. **Summary**

VI. **Critical Thinking Questions**

VII. **Applications And Exercises**

VIII. **Sites To See**

IX. **CYBER.SCOPE**

II LEARNING OBJECTIVES

- To understand the requirements fundamental to using sociological investigation.

- To understand how the different ways of knowing facts affect what is considered "true."

- To become familiar with the basic elements of science and how they are used in sociological investigation namely concepts, variables, measurement and relationships between variables.

- To understand the limitations of scientific sociology or positivism.

- To recognize the importance of interpretive sociology which focuses on the meanings people attach to their social world.

- To understand critical sociology where the focus is on the need to change society, not simply to study it.

- To understand the origins of special efforts to investigate the lives of women and the perspectives which have been used in those efforts.

- To begin to view ethical considerations involved when studying people.

- To become familiar with the major research methods used by sociologists, and to be able to compare and contrast the various procedures involved in each.

- To be able to discuss the relative advantages and disadvantages for each of the different research methods.

- To be able to discuss each of the examples of sociological research provided in the text, including research design used, variables identified and studied, findings, and interpretations.

- To be able to recognize how technology has impacted upon research methodology.

- To be able to relate theory and method.

- To be able to identify and describe each of the ten steps in carrying out a research project using sociological investigation.

- To be able to assess the impact of the Information Revolution on people's lives and on the discipline of sociology.

In the opening scenario students gather data from federal ridings in order to comprehend voting behaviour in Canada. But this is only one example of the process of sociological investigation which can vary from information gathered from questionnaires to participation in groups one wishes to understand. Research can strive to be "objective" or offer a prescription for change. Table 2-1 (p. 28) shows the usefulness of questionnaire data for evaluating changes in attitude over time.

THE BASICS OF SOCIOLOGICAL INVESTIGATION

There are two basic requirements identified as underlying sociological investigation:

    1. Look at the world using the sociological perspective.
    2. Be curious and ask questions.

A fundamental issue being raised in this chapter concerns how we recognize information as being true. The requirements identified above are only the beginning of learning about the process of studying society using sociology. The focus now is on how sociologists find answers to questions about society.

Science as One Form of Truth

How do we come to know something to be true? Four ways of knowing are identified. These include: faith, recognition of expertise, agreement through consensus, and science. *Science* is the basis of sociological investigation, and is defined as a logical system that bases knowledge on direct, systematic observation. Science is based on *empirical evidence*, meaning evidence that we can verify using our senses.

Common Sense versus Scientific Evidence

Six common sense statements considered to be true by many Canadians are identified in the text but scientific evidence is presented which contradicts these "truths". For example, the accuracy of the statement that most poor people ignore opportunities to work is seriously questioned by empirical evidence that the majority of the poor in Canada are children, single-parent mothers or the aged.

As a scientific discipline, sociology can provide us with a framework to critically evaluate the many kinds of information we are exposed to, and enable us to more systematically consider the assumptions we are making about social life.

SCIENCE: BASIC ELEMENTS AND LIMITATIONS

Many sociologists approach the study of society in the same way as natural scientists investigate the physical world. The elements of positivism are presented, along with its limitations and alternatives.

Concepts, Variables, and Measurement

Sociologists use concepts to identify elements of society. A *concept* is a mental construct that represents a part of the world, inevitably in a somewhat simplified form. For example, terms like family, society, and social class are concepts sociologists use to help orient us to our social world. A *variable* is a concept whose value changes from case to case. For example, social class varies with some people being identified as middle-class and others as working-class, etc. *Measurement* is the process of determining the value of a variable in a specific case. Sociological variables, however, can be measured in many different ways, leaving the measurement developed somewhat arbitrary. Social class, for example, might be measured by income, education, occupation or all three.

Since sociologists collect data on thousands or even millions of people, they make use of statistical measures such as averages to simplify the description.

Operationalzing a variable means to specify exactly what is to be measured in assigning a value to a variable. As mentioned earlier, social class can be measured using education, income, occupation or any combination.

➢Reliability and Validity of Measurement

Careful and specific operationalization is critical, but there are two other important issues concerning the measurement of variables to be considered. First, there is the issue of *reliability*, or the quality of consistency in measurement. For example, does a person taking several different math achievement tests score equivalently on each? If not, one or more of the tests are not reliable. The second issue is that of *validity*, or the quality of measuring precisely what one intends to measure. The question here is, is the measurement device really measuring what it purports to measure? For example, are math tests truly measuring math skills and knowledge, or are they possibly measuring some other quality in a person like obedience to rules?

➢Relationships Among Variables

Sociological investigation enables researchers to identify *cause and effect* relationships among variables. In cause and effect relationships we are saying one variable *(independent)* causes a change or effect in another variable *(dependent)*. Determining real cause and effect is a difficult and complex process. While variables may be *correlated*, meaning that two or more variables are related or change together in some way, it does not necessarily mean that one causes the change in the other(s). The concept *spurious correlation* refers to an apparent, although false, association between two (or more) variables caused by some other variable. Figure 2-1 (p. 33) outlines an example using the variables population density, income level, and juvenile delinquency.

Using scientific *control*, meaning the ability to neutralize the effect of one variable in order to assess the relationships among other variables, researchers can check for spuriousness.

In summary, to conclude that a cause and effect relationship exists, at least three conditions must be established:

1. A correlation exists between the variables
2. The independent variable precedes the dependent variable in time
3. No evidence exists that a third variable is responsible for a spurious correlation between the two variables

The Ideal of Objectivity

Researchers make every effort to neutralize their personal biases and values. Complete neutrality *(objectivity)* is seen as an ideal rather than as a reality in science, and is defined as a state of personal neutrality in conducting research. Max Weber argued that research may be *value-relevant*, or of personal interest to the researcher, but the actual process of doing the research must be *value-free*. One way biases are controlled is through *replication*, or repetition of research by others in order to assess its accuracy. The research process itself may limit access to particular kinds of data. Although there are no guarantees of objectivity, the process of research does offer the probability of self correction of bias.

Some Limitations of Scientific Sociology

In the application of the logic of science to our social world several important limitations must be recognized:

1. Sociologists can rarely make precise determinations of cause and effect because of the complexity of human behaviour.
2. The presence of the researcher can affect the behaviour of the people being studied.
3. Social patterns are constantly changing over place and time.
4. Objectivity is very difficult because sociologists are themselves part of the social world they are studying.

A Second Framework: Interpretive Sociology

Interpretive sociology doesn't just record behaviour, it attempts to determine the meanings actors attach to their behaviour and the behaviour of others. Weber's concept of *verstehen* or "understanding" provides the foundation for interpretive sociology where reality is seen as something constructed by people and where qualitative information gathered in interaction with people allows us to best understand how they make sense of their everyday world.

A Third Framework: Critical Sociology

Critical sociology rejects the notion of value-freedom and suggests that all research is value driven or political. Karl Marx, the founder of critical sociology, suggests that the point is not to study the world, but change it so the less advantaged have their life chances improved. Table 2-2 (p. 37) describes how the scientific, interpretive and critical approaches are attached to major theoretical paradigms.

Gender and Research

Values associated with gender influence research. Dangers to sound research that involve gender include: androcentricity, overgeneralizing, gender blindness, double-standards, and interference.

Women as Methodologists

Feminist scholars suggest that special efforts must be made to study women's condition in society, recognizing explicitly their usual position of subordination to men. They reject Weber's value-free orientation and suggest that mainstream methodology is simply supportive of patriarchy. Feminists are concerned to allow the subjects of research to participate in agenda establishment.

Such an approach is seen by conventional sociologists as more politics than science and Lynn McDonald, in a recent analysis of the role of women in the early development of sociology, suggests that feminists are missing much of what women have contributed to research methodology. Harriet Martineau and Florence Nightingale were conducting sophisticated research in the 1800s, a time when few men but Durkheim were actually gathering empirical data.

The **Applying Sociology** Box (p. 36) examines the works of Dorothy Smith, Meg Luxton and Susan Wendell as critical and interpretive examples of how women's lives are ordered within a capitalist and patriarchal society. Smith illustrates how farm women's lives changed as the farm moved to cash production and their labours benefited only their husband-owners, especially at divorce when they were unable to claim any portion of the farm property. Luxton's research demonstrates how women's and children's lives in a single industry town revolve around the needs of the husband/father in relation to his employment. Wendell shows how disabled women are marginalized in a society which idealizes strong bodies and personal independence. None of these studies is concerned with objective operationalization of concepts but rather with subjective interpretation of exploitation and injustice with a view towards equitable change.

Research Ethics

Yet another issue concerns how research affects the people being studied. The American Sociological Association and various Canadian funding agencies have a set of formal guidelines for the conduct of social research, including technical competence, fair mindedness, disclosure of findings, safety and privacy for subjects, accurate presentation and disclosure of the sources of support. A debate still exists over the use of deception in research but generally speaking, researchers will obtain informal consent and carefully think through their responsibility to protect subjects from harm. The **Social Diversity Box** (p. 40) indicates the guidelines for research established for the Royal Commission on Aboriginal Peoples whose mandate was to do extensive research and establish baseline data on aboriginal life in Canada. The guidelines are concerned primarily with the protection of community interests.

THE METHODS OF SOCIOLOGICAL RESEARCH

A *research method* is defined as a systematic plan for conducting research. Four of the most commonly used methods are introduced, each with particular strengths and weaknesses for the study of social life.

Testing a Hypothesis: The Experiment

Experiments study cause and effect relationships under highly controlled conditions. This type of research tends to be explanatory. Experiments are typically designed to test a specific *hypothesis*, or an unverified statement of a relationship between variables. The ideal experiment involves three steps leading to the acceptance or rejection of the hypothesis. The three steps are: measurement of the dependent variable, exposure of the dependent variable to the independent variable, re-measurement of the dependent variable. The separation of subjects into *control* and *experimental* groups is a powerful technique of control.

➤The Hawthorne Effect

The issue of the awareness of subjects being studied and how this affects their behaviour is important. Distortion in research caused by such awareness is called the *Hawthorne effect*, so labelled after a company in which an experiment was done on work productivity, and behaviour changed simply because of experimenter attention rather than the introduction of the experimental variable.

➤An Illustration: The Stanford County Prison

Philip Zimbardo's classic study focuses on the structural conditions in prisons. The hypothesis being tested was that the character of prison itself, and not the personalities of the prisoners or guards, is the cause of prison violence. Twenty-four volunteers, deemed to be physically and emotionally healthy, were divided into two groups, prisoners and guards and participated in this mock prison experiment which was scheduled to run for two weeks. Because of the stress created and the inhumane behaviour produced the experiment had to be cancelled within a week.

Asking Questions: Survey Research

A *survey* is a research method in which subjects respond to a series of items in a questionnaire or interview. It is the most widely used of the research methods. Surveys can be used to do explanatory research, but are most useful for descriptive research, or research focussing on having subjects describe themselves or some social setting.

➤Population and Sample
A *population* is defined as the people who are the focus of research. Generally, contacting all members of a population is impossible, so samples are taken from the population to be studied. *Samples* are a part of a population selected to represent the whole.

The most critical issue concerns how a researcher knows the sample truly is representative of the population, meaning, does the sample reflect the qualities present in the population? *Random selection* techniques are used to help ensure the probability that inferences made from the results of the sample actually do reflect the nature of the population as a whole. Table 2-3 (p. 45) identifies the accuracy of a large sample in representing population characteristics.

➤Questionnaires and Interviews

Selection of the subjects is only one step in a survey. Another step requires the researcher to develop a specific plan for asking questions and recording answers. Two general techniques are used: questionnaires and interviews.

A *questionnaire* is a series of questions presented to subjects. Two basic types of questions asked have *open-ended* and *closed-ended* formats. Generally, surveys are mailed to subjects who are asked to complete a form and return it. This technique is called a self-administered survey. A low response rate renders this technique problematic.

An *interview* is a series of questions administered personally by a researcher to respondents. This strategy has advantages, including more depth and high rates of completion but also involves the disadvantages of extra time and expense, and the influence of the researcher's presence on the subjects' responses.

For both questionnaires and interviews, how the questions are asked is extremely important; poor questions will lead to poor research results and conclusions.

➤Surveys at Work: The Case of Anti-Semitism in Quebec

Sniderman et al., used an existing survey to test the hypothesis that French Canadians are more anti-Semitic than English Canadians. The authors find evidence to support the hypothesis but note that most Québecois, as is the case with other Canadians, are not anti-Semitic.

In the Field: Participant Observation

Participant observation is a method in which researchers systematically observe people while joining in their routine activities. The approach is very common among cultural anthropologists who use *fieldwork* as the principal method to gather data in the form of *ethnographies*. Sociologists refer to the same activities as the *case study* approach when doing exploratory research. This is a very valuable approach when there is not a well defined understanding of the social patterns being investigated.

Participant observation has two sides, the participant and observer, sometimes referred to as the insider-outsider roles and these can come into conflict with one another. Field notes, or the daily record kept by researchers, will reveal not only the conclusions of the researcher, but also the experience of the research itself. Such participant observation is classified as a form of *qualitative research*, or research based heavily on researcher impressions. Surveys, on the other hand, are examples of *quantitative research*, emphasizing the analysis of numerical data.

➤**An Illustration: Street Corner Society**

In the 1930s, William F. Whyte conducted what was to become one of the classic participant observation studies. He sought to study a poor, Italian, urban neighbourhood of Boston (which he called Cornerville) to determine the true social fabric of the community. His work reveals the conflict between the roles of participant and observer, involvement and detachment. The role of a *key informant* is highlighted as part of this research process indicating the strengths of assistance in entr⅃ and the weakness of the introduction of bias.

Using Available Data: Secondary and Historical Analysis

Secondary analysis is a research method in which researchers utilize data collected by others. Advantages of this approach are the considerable saving of time and money, and the typically high quality of data available from agencies such as Statistics Canada. Problems, however, are also involved, including the possibility that data was not systematically gathered, or not directly focussed on the interests of the researcher. Durkheim's research on suicide is an example of secondary analysis with possible classification problems.

➤**Content Analysis**

Content analysis entails the counting or coding of the content of written, aural or visual materials such as television programming or newspapers. This method has a long history in sociology including the renowned ***Polish Peasant in Europe and America*** where Thomas and Znaneicki used diaries and letters written to and from Polish immigrants to the United States, to describe their adjustment processes.

➤**Historical Research: Open for Business**

An historical study by Gordon Laxer, ***Open for Business: The Roots of Foreign Ownership in Canada,*** examines the reasons for the high level of dependence on foreign ownership. He rejects the usual arguments of geographical closeness to the United States and Canada's relative lack of technological development and focuses instead on the relative weakness of organized farmers' movements which have been found elsewhere to protect countries against economic penetration and exploitation of the land and other resources. Because of weak agrarian policies, then, Canada was ripe for branch plant development.

Table 2-4 (p. 49) reviews the applications, advantages and limitations of the four major methods discussed.

Technology and Research

Personal computers and the Internet have transformed the research process giving researchers remarkable technical competence and a rapidly expanding source of information. Soon the Internet will provide faculty and students with instant access to current information which, in the past, would have taken years to reach libraries.

The **Exploring Cyber-Society Box** (p. 50) elaborates on the changes to research function accompanying computer development. From constant re-entry of computer cards to mainframes

24

and the tedious re-typing of journal papers we have moved to sophisticated, continuous analysis of data on personal computers and the production of journal articles by electronic transfer of information.

The Interplay of Theory and Method

The obtaining of facts is not the final goal of science. Beyond facts is the issue of the development of theory, or combining facts into meaning. Two processes of logical thought are used by scientists. ***Deductive logical thought*** is reasoning that transforms general ideas into specific hypotheses suitable for scientific testing. Zimbardo's prison research is a good example of this type of thinking. ***Inductive logical thought*** involves reasoning that builds specific observations into general theory.

PUTTING IT ALL TOGETHER:
TEN STEPS IN SOCIOLOGICAL INVESTIGATION

The general guidelines for conducting sociological research follow these steps:

1. What is your topic?
2. What is known already?
3. What, exactly, are your questions?
4. What will you need to carry out the research?
5. Are there ethical concerns?
6. What method(s) will you use?
7. How will you record your data?
8. What do the data tell you?
9. What are your conclusions?
10. How can you share what you have learned?

Can People Lie With Statistics

The **Controversy and Debate** box (p. 51) warns us of the possibility of being misled by researchers. The choice of which data to use, how to interpret it and how to present that data rests with the researcher. The possibility always exists that the researcher will make sure that the data "fit" with his or her hypothesis.

KEY CONCEPTS

Define each of the following concepts on separate paper. Check the accuracy of your answers by referring to the text as well as referring to italicized definitions located throughout the chapter.

cause and effect	measurement
concept	objectivity
content analysis	operationalizing a variable
control	participant observation
control group	population
correlation	qualitative research
critical sociology	quantitative research
deductive logical thought	questionnaire
dependent variable	reliability
empirical evidence	replication
experiment	research method
experimental group	sample
Hawthorne effect	science
hypothesis	secondary analysis
independent variable	spurious correlation
inductive logical thought	survey
information revolution	validity
interpretive sociology	variable
interview	

CYBER.SCOPE

The Industrial Revolution has given way to the Information Revolution where computers and other related information technologies enhance our capacity to work with ideas, rather than create things and allow us to communicate our ideas in "virtual reality" rather than in a particular physical space.

The three major sociological paradigms will continue to spark sociological imagination about how cyberspace impacts behaviour patterns and sociological research will be enhanced by improved communication among researchers throughout the world.

STUDY QUESTIONS

 True-False

1. (T) F   Bibby has found that between 1975 and 1995, Canadian attitudes toward homosexuality have become increasingly accepting.

2. (T) F   In the mid-1990s close to 5 million Canadians were living below the poverty line.

3. T (F)   Valid measurement means getting the same result again and again, even if it is not a correct measurement.

4. (T) F   When two variables are correlated they are said to demonstrate a cause and effect relationship.

26

5. (T) F   Max Weber argued that people involved in scientific research must strive to be value-free.

6. T (F)   Because researchers are known to be objective their presence ordinarily does not affect the behaviour patterns of the people they are studying.

7. T (F)   Interpretive sociology differs from scientific sociology in that it tends to rely on qualitative data.

8. (T) F   Feminist researchers ground their research in the assumption that women generally experience subordination.

9. (T) F   Gordon Laxer's study found that the demise of Canadian economic independence was a function of the weakness of agrarian and populist nationalism.

10. (T) F   The first step in the scientific research process should be to determine what research design will be used to obtain the data.

✎ Multiple-Choice

1. Science, as a way of knowing, relies on

(a) the wisdom of experts   (d) general concensus
(b) faith   (e) common sense
(c) empirical evidence

2. Specifying exactly what one intends to measure in assigning a value to a variable is

(a) measurement   (d) validity
(b) reliability   (e) correlation
(c) operationalizing a variable

3. Measuring what one intends to measure is the quality of measurement known as:

(a) reliability   (d) control
(b) operationalization   (e) objectivity
(c) validity

4. When two variables are related to each other but only through the existence of another variable, the relationship is said to be

(a) a reliable measure
(b) a valid measure
(d) a spurious correlation

(d) empirically sound
(e) average

5. Several limitations of scientific sociology are reviewed in Chapter 2. Which of the following is _not_ identified as a limitation involved in sociological research?

(a) Human behaviour is exceedingly complex.
(b) We all react to the world around us, so the mere presence of researchers may affect the behaviour that is being studied.
(c) Social patterns are constantly changing.
(d) Because sociologists are part of the social world they study, objectivity in social research is especially difficult.
(e) Few quantitative techniques are appropriate for sociologists to utilize in their analysis of data.

6. Which of the following is **not** a characteristic of interpretive sociology?

(a) It focuses upon the meanings people attach to their social world.
(b) It focuses upon what people do.
(c) It sees reality as being socially constructed
(d) It tends to rely on qualitative data.
(e) It focuses on subjective thoughts and feelings.

7. Dorothy Smith notes that the condition of approximate equality between men and women in the farming community changed as the economic unit moved to:

(a) share-cropping
(b) proximate justice

(c) cash production
(d) none of the above

8. What theoretical paradigm is most clearly linked with the critical methodological approach?

(a) Social-conflict
(b) Structural-functional
(c) Social-exchange

(d) Symbolic-interaction
(e) None of the above

9. The prison research conducted by Philip Zimbardo is an example of the use of which research method?

(a) survey
(b) case study
(c) participant-observation

(d) experiment
(e) secondary analysis

10. In the study by Paul Sniderman anti-Semitism in Quebec was found to be culturally supported by:

    (a) a history of discrimination in France   (d) normative conformity
    (b) normative prejudice   (e) authoritarian personality types
    (c) nationalism

11. William F. Whyte was fortunate in his study of "Cornerville" to locate somebody to help him gain entree to the community. "Doc" is called a

    (a) observer-participant   (d) qualitative worker
    (b) "helper"   (e) none of the above
    (c) key informant

12. If a researcher begins a sociological investigation with general ideas about the world which then are used to produce specific hypotheses suited for scientific testing, the process is known as:

    (a) inductive logical thought   (d) deductive logical thought
    (b) a qualitative methodology   (e) speculative reasoning
    (c) empirical analysis

$$\frac{6}{12} = 50\%$$

✎ Fill-In The Blank

1. ___Science___ is a logical system that bases knowledge on direct, systematic observation.

2. A ___Variable___ is a concept whose value changes from case to case.

3. In a cause and effect relationship, the variable which causes the change in the variable is called the _dependent / independent_ variable.

4. The state of personal neutrality in conducting research is referred to as _Objectivity_

5. In the mid 1800s _Florence nightingale_ noted that crime, suicide, mortality, accident, marriage and poverty levels could be predicted with exact precision.

6. The ___Control___ group is the group which typically receives a "placebo".

7. A ___Sample___ is a part of a population that represents the whole.

8. In ___qualitative___ research the investigator gathers impressionistic, not numerical, data.

29

9. In _Secondary_ analysis a researcher utilizes data collected by others.

10. By choosing particular data from their study and interpreting it in a particular way, researchers can be said to ___lie___ with statistics.

Definition and Short-Answer

1. What are the two requirements which underlie the process of sociological investigation?

2. What are the four "ways of knowing" discussed in the text? Please describe and provide an illustration for each.

3. What are the three factors which must be determined to conclude that a cause and effect relationship between two variables may exist?

4. What must the sociological researcher do to be ethically sound?

5. Review Max Weber's points concerning objectivity in science.

6. Margaret Eichler points out five dangers to sound research that involve gender. Please identify and define each.

7. Define the concept "hypothesis." Further, write your own hypothesis and operationalize the variables which you identify.

8. What are the twin roles of the research involved in participant observation?

9. What are the basic steps of the sociological research process? Please briefly describe each step in the process.

10. Discuss the impact of the Information Revolution on Canadian society.

Answers to Study Questions

True-False

1. T (p. 28)
2. T (p. 29)
3. F (p. 31)
4. F (p. 32)
5. T (p. 33)
6. F (p. 35)
7. T (p. 36)
8. T (p. 38)
9. T (p. 48)
10. F (p. 51)

= 60%

Multiple Choice

1. c (p. 29)
2. c (p. 31)
3. c (p. 31)
4. c (p. 32)
5. e (pp. 34-35)
6. b (p. 35)

7. c (p. 36)
8. a (p. 37)
9. d (p. 41)
10. d (p. 45)
11. c (p. 47)
12. d (pp. 49-50)

= 50%

Fill-In

1. science (p. 29)
2. variable (p. 31)
3. dependent/independent (p. 31)
4. objectivity (p. 33)
5. Florence Nightingale (p.39)

6. control (p. 41)
7. sample (p. 42)
8. qualitative (p. 46)
9. secondary (p. 47)
10. lie (p. 51)

ANALYSIS AND COMMENT

Go back through the chapter and write down in the spaces below key points from each of the following boxes.

APPLYING SOCIOLOGY

Feminist Research: Critical and Interpretive Examples.
Key Points:

_____
_____
_____
_____
_____

SOCIAL DIVERSITY

Conducting Research With Aboriginal Peoples.
Key Points:

_____
_____
_____
_____
_____

EXPLORING CYBER-SOCIETY

From Card Punching to Number Crunching: Technological Advances in Research.
Key Points:

_____

_____

_____

_____

_____

CONTROVERSY AND DEBATE

"Can People Lie With Statistics?"
Key Points:

_____

_____

_____

_____

_____

CYBER.SCOPE

"Welcome To The Information Revolution."
Key Points:

_____

_____

_____

_____

_____

SUGGESTED READINGS

Classic Source

Alvin Gouldner. 1970. *The Coming Crisis in Western Sociology.* New York: Aveon Books.
In this volume, Alvin Gouldner provided one of the earliest and best efforts to evaluate the place of values and politics in sociological research.

Feminist Research

Dorothy Smith. "The Social Construction of Documentary Reality." *Sociological Inquiry*, Vol. 44, No. 4: 257–68, 1974.
Dorothy Smith. 1987. *The Everyday World as Problematic: A Feminist Sociology.* Toronto: University of Toronto Press.
Winnie Tomm, ed. 1989. *The Effects of Feminist Approaches on Research Methodologies.* Calgary: Calgary Institute for the Humanities.
Lynn McDonald. 1994b. *The Women Founders of the Social Sciences.* Ottawa: Carleton University Press.
These books provide an historical and feminist antidote to the concerns of contemporary feminists about traditional, positivist social science research

Floyd J. Fowler, Jr. 1993. *Survey Research Methods.* Newbury Park, Calif.: Sage.
This book is filled with technical detail about implementing sociology's most widely used method of investigation.

Harriet Zuckerman, Jonathan R. Cole, and John T. Bruer, eds. 1991. *The Outer Circle: Women in the Scientific Community.* New York: Norton.
There is a widespread notion that sex discrimination in the scientific community has all but disappeared: However, the articles in this edited volume tell a different story.

Global Sources

Gerardo Marín and Barbara VanOss Marín. 1991. *Research with Hispanic Populations.* Newbury Park, Calif.: Sage.
This book explores the meaning of Hispanic ethnicity and its implications for sociological research.

Melvin L. Kohn. 1989. *Cross-National Research in Sociology.* Newbury Park, Calif.: Sage.
Global research offers valuable insights into other societies as well as our own way of life. This provocative paperback includes seventeen essays on global research.

CHAPTER 3

Culture

I CHAPTER OUTLINE

- To understand the sociological meaning of the concept culture.

- To understand the experience of culture shock.

- To understand the relationship between human intelligence and culture.

- To understand the relationship between culture, society, nation and state.

- To know the components of culture and to be able to provide examples of each.

- To understand how cultural differences can lead to misunderstandings.

- To explain the current state of knowledge about whether language is uniquely human.

- To understand that Aboriginal languages in Canada are in danger of extinction.

- To understand the Sapir-Whorf hypothesis.

- To be able to identify the major Canadian values and to recognize their interrelationships with one another and with other aspects of our culture.

- To comprehend the differences between American and Canadian values.

- To be able to provide examples of the different types of norms operative in a culture.

- To understand the impact of technology on culture, and the production of virtual culture.

- To explain how subcultures and countercultures contribute to cultural diversity.

- To be able to explore the nature of multiculturalism in Canada.

- To be able to differentiate between ethnocentrism and cultural relativism.

- To be able to compare and contrast analyses of culture using structural-functional, social-conflict, cultural materialism, sociobiological, and constraint paradigms.

III CHAPTER REVIEW

WHAT IS CULTURE?

Culture is defined as the values, beliefs, behaviour, and material objects that constitute a people's way of life. The scenario addressed at the beginning of the chapter suggests some common Canadian cultural values but enormous differences as well. Indeed when people travel between societies or even within their own, they can experience *culture shock*, a personal disorientation that can come from encountering an unfamiliar way of life.

Sociologists differentiate between *non-material culture*, the intangible creations of human society, and *material culture*, the tangible products of human society.

Sociologically, culture is viewed in the broadest possible sense, referring to everything that is part of a people's way of life. Our lives become meaningful to us through culture. Our lifestyles are not determined by *instincts*, or biological forces, as is true in large degree for other species. We are the only species whose survival depends on what we learn through culture, rather than by what we are naturally given through biology.

Culture and Human Intelligence

The primate order among mammals, of which our species is a part, emerged some 65 million years ago. Humans diverged from our closest primate relatives some 12 million years ago; however, our common lineage remains apparent. This includes, hands that precisely manipulate objects, ability to walk upright, great sociability, affective and long-lasting bonds for child-rearing and protection.

Fossil records indicate the first creatures with clearly human characteristics lived about 2 million years ago, which is relatively recent in terms of evolutionary time. Our species, *homo sapiens* (meaning thinking person) evolved 250,000 years ago and creatures which look much like us a mere 40,000 years ago. Civilization based on permanent settlements has existed only for the last 12,000 years.

Human culture and biological evolution are linked but over evolutionary time, instincts have gradually been replaced by "mental power," enabling us to actively fashion the natural environment. This shift from instinct to culture has allowed great human diversity to be created.

Culture, Nation, State and Society

While *culture* is shared values, ideas and artifacts, a *nation* is a people who share a culture, usually within a *state*, a political entity with designated borders. *Society* is the organized activities of people within that nation or state. Multicultural Canada may be said to contain many nations. The continuing challenge is to build a federal nation which supercedes the others.

Although there are many cultures and nations globally, distinctions have declined with increased global contact.

THE COMPONENTS OF CULTURE

Even though considerable cultural variation exists, all cultures share five components: symbols, language, values, norms, and material objects.

Symbols

A *symbol* is anything that carries a particular meaning recognized by people who share a culture. Symbols, often taken for granted, are the means by which we make sense of our lives.

Symbols vary widely globally and even within a given society. The **Global Sociology** box (pp. 78-79) indicates how gestures that may be viewed positively in one culture may be seen as an insult in another.

Language

The significance of language for human communication is vividly illustrated by the story of Helen Keller recounting the moment she acquired language and a symbolic understanding of the world, through the help of her teacher Ann Sullivan. *Language* is a system of symbols that allows members of a society to communicate with one another. The process by which culture is passed, through language, from one generation to the next is our most important form of *cultural transmission*. As the **Applying Sociology** Box (p. 65) makes clear, the loss of Aboriginal languages means a serious loss to world culture. We are very familiar with the link between language and culture in Canadian society as the debate over Bill 101 in Québec makes amply clear. Language is rooted in oral cultural tradition. Only in the last five thousand years did humans invent writing and even in countries like Canada many people have limited literacy skills. Language is our linkage to cultural pasts and the generation of ideas for the future.

➤Is Language Uniquely Human?

While virtually all nonhuman animal communication seems largely rooted in instinct, there is some scientific evidence to suggest certain other animals have at least a rudimentary ability to use symbols. Research with chimps has found them capable of attaching words to objects and creating simple sentences. While they lack the physical ability to form sounds of human speech, and are unable to transmit what they learn to others, it appears they do "experience" culture to some degree.

➤Does Language Shape Reality?

Two anthropologists, Edward Sapir and Benjamin Whorf, have argued that language is more than simply attaching labels to the "real world." They reject the view that language merely describes a single reality. The *Sapir-Whorf hypothesis* holds that we know the world only in terms of our language. Language then determines our cultural reality.

Values and Beliefs

Values are defined as the standards by which people assess desirability, goodness and beauty; they are broad principles which underlie *beliefs*, specific statements that people hold to be true. They are learned through socialization and help shape how we perceive our surroundings and how our personality develops. Indeed they provide the cultural capital by which we evaluate our future possibilities.

Although in our diverse society few cultural values are shared by everyone, there are several central values which are widely accepted in Canadian society. As Lipset has suggested in the **Social Diversity** box (p. 67) while Americans value freedom and individual initiative Canadians stress conformity and obedience to the law. The Canadian tendency to emphasize the good of the collectivity over the good of the individual has resulted in social programs such as universal medicare. Futurist Roger Sauvé has recently identified substantial value differences between the U.S. and Canada

➤Values: Inconsistency and Conflict

In a society characterized by cultural diversity and rapid social change, cultural values can be inconsistent and even contradictory. On the one hand Canadians espouse equality and on the other they degrade people because of their race, gender, or sexual orientation. Even long standing traditions such as ice-hockey lose their value importance as other nations begin to play the game better than we do.

Norms

Norms are defined as rules that guide behaviour. They can be *proscriptive*, mandating what we should not do, or *prescriptive,* stating what we should do. They can change over time, as illustrated by norms regarding sexual behaviour. Some are meant to apply to all situations and all people, while others apply to only certain people and vary situation to situation.

➤Mores and Folkways

Norms vary in their degree of importance. *Mores* distinguish between right and wrong while *folkways* distinguish between right and rude.

➤Social Control

Norms provide for conformity. *Sanctions* are positive and negative responses to the behaviour of people that reward conformity and punish deviance. They are an important part of our cultural system of *social control*, or the various means by which members of society encourage conformity to cultural norms. Through socialization we internalize cultural norms and impose constraints on our own behaviour. The "breaking" of an internalized norm results in *guilt* and *shame*.

"Ideal" and "Real" Culture

Values and norms are not descriptions of actual behaviour, but rather reflect how we believe members of a culture should behave. Therefore, we distinguish between *ideal culture* or social patterns mandated by cultural values and norms, and *real culture* or social patterns that only approximate cultural expectations.

Material Culture and Technology

Material and nonmaterial culture are very closely related. *Artifacts*, or tangible human creations, express the values of a culture. For instance, the Yanomamo value militaristic skill, and devote great care to making weapons while Canadians value independence and build highways for our automobiles.

Material culture also reflects a culture's ***technology***, which is the application of cultural knowledge to the task of living in a physical environment. Technology is the link between culture and nature. While we, in Canada, attempt to manipulate our natural environment, most technologically "simple" cultures attempt to adapt to their natural worlds. Also, advances in technology can create both positive and negative effects for the quality of life. The Old Order Mennonites in Ontario, for example, shun modern technological conveniences while their communities flourish.

New Information Technology and Culture

The industrial society is giving way to the information society where the focus is on the creation, processing and application of information. As the **Exploring Cyber-Society** Box (p. 71) makes clear, cultural symbols in the past were transmitted from generation to generation. Heroes were real people, then long dead. In the emerging Cyber-society cultural symbols are created electronically by a small elite and the heroes are not real but virtual. Today's youngsters hear little of Alexander Graham Bell or Maurice Richard but know intimately the Power Rangers and the Teletubbies.

CULTURAL DIVERSITY: MANY WAYS OF LIFE IN ONE WORLD

Cultural variety in Canada is described as a "patchwork quilt" or mosaic. We are a land of many peoples.

High Culture and Popular Culture

High culture refers to patterns associated with a society's elite while popular culture refers to patterns widespread among a society's entire population. Sociologists tend to be uncomfortable with the implicit ranking of patterns of culture since the evaluation is more often a product of power and prestige than of inherent superiority or inferiority.

Subculture

Sociologists define ***subculture*** as cultural patterns that set apart some segment of a society's population. Subcultures can be based upon age, ethnicity, residence, sexual orientation, occupation and many other factors. Ethnicity is perhaps the most recognized dimension with which to identify cultural diversity. While ethnicity is often a source of pleasing diversity the conflict which has erupted in the former Yugoslavia illustrates the sources of tension and outright violence. The cultural diversity in Canada is not without disadvantage as subcultural groups are distinguished by hierarchy as well as variety.

Multiculturalism

Canadian society is officially multicultural, a society that encourages ethnic or cultural heterogeneity. Historically a European (primarily English) style of life was identified as ideal but with massive immigration from non-European societies Canada moved away from Eurocentrism to multiculturalism. A debate rages on, however, about the usefulness of this concept for Canadian society. Proponents suggest a multicultural perspective will help us develop a more meaningful understanding of our past, present, and global interdependence while strengthening academic achievement of all our children. Those opposed suggest that multiculturalism promotes divisiveness rather than cohesiveness and denies children access to the knowledge that will enable them to compete.

Counterculture

A *counterculture* is defined as a cultural pattern that strongly opposes those which are widely accepted in a society. Members of countercultures are likely to question the morality of the majority group and engage in some form of protest activities. Although countercultures are not as predominant now as in the 1960s we currently experience militaristic groups who reject the legitimacy of the political system and sometimes engage in extreme violence such as the bombing of the Oklahoma City federal building in 1995.

Cultural Change

Cultural change is continuous, and change in one area is usually associated with change in others. Family life in Canada, for example, has changed as more women work, some delay entry into marriage and more, once married, decide to divorce.

These system-wide connections are described in the concept of *cultural integration* but it is also recognized that some cultural elements change faster than others leaving an inconsistency called *cultural lag*.

Cultural change is set in motion by three different causes; invention, discovery and diffusion.

Ethnocentrism and Cultural Relativity

Ethnocentrism is the practice of judging another culture by the standards of one's own culture. It creates a biased evaluation of unfamiliar practices. The evaluations of cultural variations in the maintenance of personal space or bathroom practices are illustrations of this concept. *Cultural relativism* is the practice of judging a culture by its own standards. The issue of cultural sensitivity related to international business ventures is amusing but there are some cultural practices which are deeply disturbing, such as child labour in various parts of the world, which suggests that perhaps there are some universal standards we could identify as necessary rather than accepting any behaviour within the context of cultural relativity.

A Global Culture?

The recent flow of goods, information and people between societies seems to have led to similarities in various cultural patterns worldwide. However, rural areas remain largely unaffected, not many citizens of poorer societies can afford the goods from elsewhere and a question yet remains whether people everywhere attach the same meaning to cultural entities.

40

THEORETICAL ANALYSIS OF CULTURE

We attempt to understand culture using several theoretical paradigms.

Structural-Functional Analysis

Drawing on the philosophical doctrine of *idealism*, this approach holds that core values bind members of society together in an integrated system. While core values may differ between societies there appear to be *cultural universals*, found in every culture of the world. The limitations of this approach include an underestimation of culture conflict and a downplaying of the extent of change in society.

Social-Conflict Analysis

The focus among researchers using this paradigm is the social conflict generated by inequality among different categories of people in a culture. The question of why certain values are dominant in a culture rather than some others is central to this view. Karl Marx, using the philosophical doctrine of *materialism*, argued that the way we deal with the material world (i.e., through capitalism) powerfully affects all other dimensions of our culture. A limitation of this perspective is an underestimation of the extent of integration in society.

Cultural Materialism

Rooted in the natural sciences, this paradigm emphasizes that human culture is significantly shaped by the natural environment. *Cultural materialism* is defined as a theoretical paradigm that explores the relationship of human culture to the physical environment.

Marvin Harris' analysis of India's sacred cow provides an informative illustration of the application of this approach. Limitations of this perspective involve an oversimplification of the connections between cultural and physical forces and a lack of applicability to technologically sophisticated societies who extensively manipulate the natural environment.

Sociobiology

Sociobiology is a theoretical paradigm that seeks to explain cultural patterns as a product, at least in part, of biological causes. This view poses an interesting challenge to the sociologist's focus on culture as the dominant force in human life.

Sociobiologists argue that Charles Darwin's theory of natural selection applies to human evolution as it does to all other species.

Controversy exists concerning the application of Darwin's insights to humans. Sociobiologists focus on the existence of certain cultural universals as evidence that culture is determined to a significant degree by biology. For example the *double standard* in sexuality is found, according to Kinsey, in all peoples and makes sense as a biological imperative. The most efficient reproductive strategy for males is promiscuity while the best strategy for females is the selection of one male who will contribute to their child's survival.

Sociobiology has been criticized as historically supporting racism and sexism and certainly there is little in the way of definitive proof that biological characteristics explain the roots of human culture. Perhaps sociobiology will help us understand why some cultural patterns are more common than others but it appears that most human behaviour is learned within a system of culture.

Culture as Constraint

Over the course of human evolution, culture has become our means of survival but it has also become the burden of limited choices and isolation from others in our pursuit of success. The **Controversy and Debate** box (p. 83) describes the terrible consequences of a cultural appetite for information about celebrities that culminated in the death of Princess Diana..

Culture as Freedom

While being dependent on culture and constrained by our particular way of life, the capacity for creating change, or shaping and reshaping our existence, appears limitless. Culture is a liberating force to the extent we develop an understanding of its diversity and the opportunities available within it for change and autonomy.

KEY CONCEPTS

Define each of the following concepts on separate paper. Check the accuracy of your answers by referring to the key concepts section in the text as well as referring to italicized definitions located throughout the chapter.

beliefs	cultural universals
counterculture	culture
cultural integration	culture shock
cultural lag	discovery
cultural materialism	diffusion
cultural relativism	ethnocentrism
cultural transmission	Eurocentrism
folkways	popular culture
high culture	real culture
ideal culture	Sapir-Whorf hypothesis
invention	social control
language	sociobiology
material culture	subculture
mores	symbols
multiculturalism	technology
nonmaterial culture	values
norms	

STUDY QUESTIONS

 True-False

1. T F   Nonmaterial culture is the intangible world of ideas created by members of a society.

2. T F   The personal disorientation a person feels when moving from one society to another is referred to as social shock.

3. T. F   Bill 101 in Quebec is designed to protect the English language in that province.

4. T F   The Sapir-Whorf hypothesis states that people perceive the world through the cultural lens of a language.

5. T F   The enforcement of norms always depends directly on the reactions of others.

6. T F   Popular culture refers to patterns of behaviour that distinguish a society's elite.

7. T F   Critics of multiculturalism contend that it fuels the "politics of difference."

8. T F   The practice of judging any culture by its own standards is referred to as ethnocentrism.

9. T F   Jokes are found in all cultures, acting as a relatively safe means of releasing social tensions.

10. T F   The structural-functionalist perspective argues that values are shaped by a society's system of economic production.

11. T F   Marvin Harris uses the cultural materialism perspective to help explain the existence of India's "sacred cow" belief.

12. T F   Humans are the <u>only</u> creatures who experience alienation.

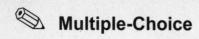 **Multiple-Choice**

1. The personal disorientation that comes from encountering an unfamiliar way of life is called
    _____ .

    (a) cultural relativism   (d) cultural schizophrenia
    (b) ethnocentrism   (e) cultural shock
    (c) non-material culture

2. Studying fossil records, scientists have concluded that the first creatures with clearly human
    characteristics existed about _____ years ago.

    (a) 2 million   (d) 40 million
    (b) 12,000   (e) 60,000
    (c) 10 million

3. Symbols, a component of culture, can:

    (a) vary from culture to culture   (d) give rise to conflict
    (b) allow people to make sense of their lives   (e) all of the above
    (c) change over time

4. A system of symbols that allows members of a society to communicate with one another is
    the definition of:

    (a) values   (d) cultural relativity
    (b) language   (e) cultural transmission
    (c) norms

5. Standards by which members of a culture distinguish the desirable from the undesirable,
    what is good from what is bad, the beautiful from the ugly, is the definition for:

    (a) norms   (d) mores
    (b) beliefs   (e) sanctions
    (c) values

6. Specific statements that people hold to be true are

    (a) standards   (d) norms
    (b) values   (e) sanctions
    (c) beliefs

7. According to Lipset the differences in value structure between Americans and Canadians are deeply rooted in the past. The key event which differentiates them is:

(a) the French in North America   (c) slavery
(b) the climate   (d) the American War of Independence

8. When Mark Twain suggested that human beings "are the only animals that blush...or need to" he was referring to the cultural creation of

(a) norms   (d) mandate
(b) guilt   (e) artifacts
(c) social control

9. The old adage "Do as I say, not as I do" illustrates the distinction between:

(a) "ideal" and "real" culture   (d) folkways and mores
(b) subcultures and countercultures   (e) cultural integration and cultural lag
(c) symbols and language

10. The new Information Society is characterized by

(a) the creation, processing, storing, and application of information
(b) cultural symbols which are intentionally created
(c) virtual culture
(d) all of the above
(e) a and b above

11. Inconsistencies within a cultural system resulting from the unequal rates at which different cultural elements change are termed:

(a) cultural lag   (d) counterculture
(b) culture shock   (e) cultural relativity

12. Which of the following are reasons given for the spread of a global culture?

(a) the flow of goods   (d) a and b above
(b) the flow of communication   (e) all of the above
(c) global migration

13. The theoretical paradigm that focuses upon universal cultural traits is:

(a) cultural ecology   (c) structural functionalism
(b) cultural materialism   (d) social-conflict

45

14. The philosophical doctrine of materialism is utilized in the analysis of culture by proponents of which theoretical paradigm?

    (a) sociobiologists (d) cultural ecologists
    (b) structural-functionalists (e) social-conflict
    (c) symbolic-interaction

15. Although culture is the human strategy for survival, it can also be limiting in the following ways.

    (a) It leads us to repeat troubling patterns like racial prejudice.
    (b) It leads to the experience of alienation.
    (c) In an electronic age culture is manipulated for the pursuit of profits.
    (d) all of the above
    (e) none of the above

✎ Fill-In The Blank

1. The tangible products of human society are referred to as _____.

2. The concept _____ is derived from the Latin meaning "thinking person."

3. Human beings learn to live their lives through _____ rather than biological inheritance.

4. A _____ is anything that carries a particular meaning recognized by members of a culture.

5. The Canadian tendency to emphasize the good of the _____ has resulted in the creation of social programs such as universal medical care.

6. _____ are rules that refer to a society's standards of proper moral conduct.

7. _____ _____ is defined as the various means by which members of society encourage conformity to cultural norms.

8. _____ is a social policy in Canada designed to encourage ethnic or cultural heterogeneity.

9. The spread of cultural traits from one society to another is called _____.

10. A theoretical paradigm that focuses upon the interrelationship of human culture and the physical environment is _____.

Definition and Short-Answer

1. Discuss the research presented in the text concerning the uniqueness of language to humans. Make specific reference to the research involving the chimp Kanzi in your discussion.

2. What is the Sapir-Whorf hypothesis? Provide an example.

3. How do the value systems differ in Canada and the United States?

4. What is the relationship between technology and culture?

5. How has the concept of multiculturalism impacted upon Canada.

6. Three causes of cultural change are identified in the text. Identify these and provide an illustration for each.

7. Discuss the dangers inherent for a society or for humankind in both ethnocentrism and cultural relativity.

8. Define the philosophical doctrine of "idealism."

9. Define the philosophical doctrine of "materialism." How does this doctrine fit into the conflict theory of society?

10. How do cultural materialists explain the relationship between culture and the physical environment? Using Marvin Harris' analysis of the existence of the sacred cow in India describe this perspective.

11. What are the basic premises of the sociobiological approach to understanding human behaviour and what are the most common critiques of the approach?

Answers to Study Questions

True-False

1. T (p. 60)	7. T (p. 74)
2. F (p. 60)	8. F (p. 76)
3. F (p. 65)	9. T (p. 80)
4. T (p. 66)	10. F (p. 80)
5. F (p. 69)	11. T (pp. 80-81)
6. F (p. 72)	12. T (p. 82)

Multiple Choice

1. e (p. 60)	9. a (p. 69)
2. a (p. 60)	10. d (pp. 70-71)
3. e (pp. 62-63)	11. a (p. 75)
4. b (p. 63)	12. e (p. 77)
5. c (p. 66)	13. c (p. 80)
6. c (p. 67)	14. e (p. 80)
7. d (p. 67)	15. e (p. 82)
8. b (p. 69)	

Fill-In

1. material culture (p. 60)	6. mores (p. 69)
2. homo sapiens (p. 61)	7. social control (p. 69)
3. culture (p. 62)	8. multiculturalism (p. 73)
4. symbol (p. 62)	9. diffusion (p. 75)
5. collectivity (p. 67)	10. cultural materialism (p. 80)

ANALYSIS AND COMMENT

Go back through the chapter and write down in the spaces below key points from each of the following boxes.

APPLYING SOCIOLOGY

"Aboriginal Languages in Danger of Extinction"
Key Points:

_____

_____

_____

_____

SOCIAL DIVERSITY

"Canadians and Americans: What Makes Us Different?"
Key Points:

_____

_____

_____

EXPLORING CYBER-SOCIETY

"Here Comes Virtual Culture."
Key Points:

_____

_____

_____

_____

GLOBAL SOCIOLOGY

"Travellers Beware! The Meaning of Gestures in Other Societies"
Key Points:

_____

_____

_____

CONTROVERSY AND DEBATE

"The Paparazzi: Villains or Our Eyes to the World?"
Key Points:

_____

_____

_____

SUGGESTED READINGS
Classic Sources

Napoleon A. Chagnon. 1992. *Y͇anomamö: The Fierce People.* **4th ed. New York: Holt, Rinehart and Winston.**
Napoleon Chagnon's updated account of the Y͇anomamö offers fascinating insights into a culture very different from our own. It is also a compelling tale of carrying out fieldwork in an unfamiliar world.

Margaret Mead. 1928. *Coming of Age in Samoa: A Psychological Study of Primitive Youth for Western Civilization.* **New York: Wm. Morrow.**
Margaret Mead, perhaps the best-known student of culture, carried out this study of the Samoan Islands, which demonstrates the variability of cultural systems.

Contemporary Sources

Seymour Martin Lipset. 1990. *Continental Divide: The Values and Institutions of the United States and Canada.* **New York: Routledge.**
This book compares the cultures of Canada and the United States.

Anastasia M. Shkilnyk. *A Poison Stronger Than Love: The Destruction of an Ojibwa Community.* **New Haven, Conn.: Yale University Press.**
Shkilnyk's book offers a telling description of the devastating effect of the state on the Grassy Narrows band in northern Ontario. The band was forced to relocate from its reserve to a narrow strip of land in order to facilitate the provision of some modern amenities such as a school, electricity, improved housing, and social services.

S. Crean and M. Rioux. 1983. *Two Nations.* **Toronto: James Lorimer.**
S. Ramcharan. 1982. *Racism: Non-Whites in Canada.* **Toronto: Butterworths.**
P.S. Li and B.S. Bolaria., eds. 1984. *Racial Minorities in Multicultural Canada.* **Toronto: Garamond Press.**
Mel Watkins. 1977. *Dene Nation: The Colony Within.* **Toronto: University of Toronto Press.**
Pierre Vallières. 1971. *White Niggers of America.* **Toronto: McClelland & Stewart.**
W. Clement. 1975. *The Canadian Corporate Elite: An Analysis of Economic Power.* **Toronto: McClelland and Stewart.**
S.M. Crean. 1976. *Who's Afraid of Canadian Culture?* **Don Mills, Ont.: General Publishing.**
R. Mathews. 1983. *The Creation of Regional Dependancy.* **Toronto: University of Toronto Press.**
These books describe cultural, class, regional, and racial divisions within Canadian society.

M. Patricia Marchak. 1975. *Ideological Perspectives on Canada.* **Toronto: McGraw-Hill Ryerson.**
R. Breton, J.G. Reitz, and V.F. Valentine. 1980. *Cultural Boundaries and the Cohesion of Canada.* **Montreal: Institute for Research in Public Policy.**
G. Caldwell and E. Waddell. 1982. *The English of Quebec: From Majority to Minority Status.* **Quebec: Institut québecois de recherche sur la culture.**
R.J. Bryan and R.J. Sacouman. 1979. *Underdevelopment and Social Movements in Atlantic Canada.* **Toronto: Hogtown Press.**
These books give a description of Canadian ideology, culture, and values, see the following.

D.H. Clairmont and D.W. Magill. 1974. *Africville: The Life and Death of a Black Community.* **Toronto: University of Toronto Press.**
See this book for a classic Canadian community study.

Global Sources

Mike Featherstone, ed. 1990. *Global Culture: Nationalism, Globalization, and Modernity.* **London: Sage.**
These two dozen essays explore various ways in which a global culture is emerging.

Joana McIntyre Varawa. 1990. *Changes in Latitude: An Uncommon Anthropology.* **New York: Harper & Row.**
This fascinating book describes how a woman from Hawaii past midlife traveled to Fiji on vacation only to find a new home, a new husband, and a host of new challenges.

Craig Storti. *The Art of Crossing Cultures.* **Yarmouth, Minn.: Intercultural Press, 1990.**
This brief book explores the excitement as well as the difficulties of cross-cultural experience.

CHAPTER 4

| Society |

I CHAPTER OUTLINE

I.   **Gerhard and Jean Lenski: Society and Technology**
          A. Hunting and Gathering Societies
          B. Horticultural and Pastoral Societies
          C. Agrarian Societies
          D. Industrial Societies
          E. Post-Industrial Societies
          F. The Limits of Technology
II.   **Karl Marx: Society and Conflict**
          A. Society and Production
          B. Conflict in History
          C. Capitalism and Class Conflict
          D. Capitalism and Alienation
          E. Revolution
III.   **Max Weber: The Rationalization of Society**
          A. Two World Views: Tradition and Rationality
          B. Is Capitalism Rational?
          C. Weber's Great Thesis: Protestantism and Capitalism.
          D. Rational Social Organization
          E. Rationality and Bureaucracy
              1. Rationality and Alienation
IV.   **Emile Durkheim: Society and Function**
          A. Structure: Society Beyond Ourselves
          B. Function: Society as System
          C. Personality: Society in Ourselves
              1. Modernity and Anomie
          D. Evolving Societies: The Division of Labour
V.   **Critical Evaluation: Four Visions of Society**
              1. What holds societies together?
              2. How have societies changed?
              3. Why do societies change?
VI.   **Summary**
VII.   **Critical Thinking Questions**
VIII. **Applications and Exercises**
IX.   **Sites To See**

II LEARNING OBJECTIVES

- To give answers to the questions: "What forces divide a society or hold it together?", "How do societies differ?", "How and why do societies change?", and "Are societies getting better or worse?"

- To be able to differentiate between the four "visions" of society discussed in this chapter.

- To explain the sociocultural evolution from hunting and gathering societies to industrial societies as developed by Gerhard and Jean Lenski.

- To contrast the different types of societies described by the Lenskis on the basis of their historical period, productive technology, population size, settlement pattern and social organization.

- To explain the model of society based on conflict and change developed by Karl Marx.

- To be able to discuss the perspective of Marx on the concepts of capitalism, communism, revolution, alienation, and materialism.

- To explain the role of rationality in modern society developed by Max Weber.

- To be able to identify Weber's qualities of rationality in modern society.

- To describe Emile Durkheim's functional view of society, including his analyses of the influence of social facts and the role of the division of labour in society.

- To imagine how the Lenskis, Marx, Weber and Durkheim would comprehend societal changes wrought by the Information Revolution.

III CHAPTER REVIEW

The preface to this chapter addresses the basic issues of what holds a society together and what are the forces which divide it. Canada is 130 years old yet is still characterized by a fragile national unity.

The concept *society* refers to people who interact within a defined territory and who share a culture. In this chapter four separate visions of society are discussed; each addresses questions which concern forces that shape human life. The visions include: (1) Gerhard and Jean Lenskis' focus on the importance of technology, (2) Karl Marx's understanding of the key role social conflict plays in society, (3) Max Weber's illustration of the significance of human ideas, and (4) Emile Durkheim's analysis of the patterns of social solidarity.

GERHARD AND JEAN LENSKI: SOCIETY AND TECHNOLOGY

Until about 10,000 years ago the hunting and gathering type of society was the only one in existence. Comparing present day hunting and gathering type societies with modern technologically "advanced" societies raises many interesting questions. The Lenskis analyze human society using the *sociocultural evolution* approach which focuses on the process of social change that results from gaining new cultural information, particularly technology. The greater the amount of technological information a society has, the more it can manipulate the physical environment and the faster it can change. Five general types of society are distinguished by using the Lenskis' work.

Hunting and Gathering Societies

Hunting and gathering societies are defined as those which use simple technology to hunt animals and gather vegetation. Only a very small number of such societies are still in existence today. Typical characteristics of people using this subsistence strategy include small bands of people, a nomadic lifestyle over large territories, specialization based only on age and sex, and only a few positions of leadership. Social organization tends to be simple and equal, being organized around the family. Life expectancy at birth is relatively low, however in environments with ample food supplies the quality of life is good, with some leisure time.

Horticultural and Pastoral Societies

Approximately 10-12,000 years ago plants began to be cultivated. *Horticultural* societies are those that use hand tools to cultivate crops. This strategy first appeared in the Middle East and later, Latin America and Asia and through diffusion spread throughout the rest of the world. Some societies combine horticulture with hunting and gathering strategies.

In regions where horticulture was impractical societies based on *pastoralism* emerged. These societies livelihood was based on the domestication of animals. Both horticultural and pastoral societies tend to have a more complex social organization and have increased specialization. *Material surpluses* become possible with these lifestyles, and this is often linked to greater social inequality. These societies, given their increased technological development, are more productive than hunting and gathering societies. However, the Lenskis suggest this was often accompanied by the practices of slavery and warfare.

Agrarian Societies

Agrarian societies emerged about 5,000 years ago and are based on *agriculture*, or the technology of large-scale farming using plows powered by animals or more powerful sources of energy. Technological change during this period was so dramatic that the Lenskis have argued it was the era of the "dawn of civilization." The use of the plow increased soil fertility as well as made agriculture more efficient. This also greatly increased the surplus of food available. Increased task specialization made the barter system obsolete and money was developed as a standard of exchange. The power of the elite greatly increased, supported by religious beliefs and the expanding political power structure, and men gained dominance over women unlike the previous horticultural period where women were primary providers of food.

Industrial Societies

Industrialism is the technology that powers sophisticated machinery with advanced sources of energy. The muscle power of humans and animals are no longer the basis of production and tools and machinery become more complex and efficient. Figure 4-1 (p. 91) shows the increasing rate of technological innovation during the 19th century, bringing about vast social changes. A major shift occurring was from production within families to production within factories. Occupational specialization became even more pronounced and cultural values became more heterogeneous.

In the twentieth century the automobile, the airplane and electronic communications have made a large world seem small, while the computer has ushered in the Information Revolution which threatens to change the way we relate to one another. Industrialism, in time, leads to prosperity and a decrease in political, social and economic inequality.

Post-Industrial Societies

An extension of the Lenski's analysis can be applied to post-industrialism, where technology supports an information based economy. Industrial work declines; workers who process information increase. Information flows are worldwide and the pace of change so staggering that cultural lag is experienced as notions of property are still based upon things rather than information. Table 4-1 (p. 94-95) summarizes how changes in technology have impacted upon population size, settlement patterns and social organization.

The Limits of Technology

While technology has relieved many human problems it has created others. Our sense of community has diminished while the fear of nuclear war has increased. As well our appetite for resources and the way we use them is endangering the environment of the planet.

KARL MARX: SOCIETY AND CONFLICT

Marx's thinking focused on a fundamental contradiction of industrial society. How could vast social inequality exist given the new industrial technology with its phenomenal productive capability? The central focus of Marx's work was on the idea of *social conflict*, which means struggle between segments of society over valued resources. For Marx, the most significant type of social conflict results from the manner in which society produces material goods.

Society and Production

Marx designated a very small part of the population as *capitalists*, or those who owned factories and other productive enterprises. Their goal was profit. The vast majority of people however were termed the *proletariat*, meaning those who provided the labour necessary for the operation of factories and other productive enterprises. Labour is exchanged by these people for wages. Fundamental conflict exists between the competing needs of these two groups who draw wages and profits from the same pool of funds.

Marx's analysis of society followed the philosophical doctrine of *materialism* in asserting that the system of producing material goods can shape all of society. He labelled the economic system the *infrastructure* and all other social institutions as the *super structures*. Figure 4-2 (p. 97) illustrates this philosophical viewpoint.

Marx believed capitalism promoted *false consciousness*, or the belief that the shortcomings of individuals, rather than society, are responsible for many of the personal problems people have.

Conflict in History

Marx understood historical change in society as operating in both gradual evolutionary and rapid revolutionary processes. He believed early hunting and gathering societies to be represented by communism, or the equal production of food and other material as a common effort shared more or less equally by everyone. He saw horticultural, pastoral, agrarian, and industrial societies as based on systems of inequality and exploitation. The concepts *bourgeoisie* (French, meaning "of the town") is discussed further within the framework of social history during the period of industrialization. Industrialization also produced the proletariat who he thought might form a unified class across national boundaries, setting the stage for confrontation.

Capitalism and Class Conflict

Marx viewed all social history as one of *class conflict*, or the struggle between social classes over the distribution of wealth and power in society. Social change involved workers first becoming aware of their shared oppression and then organizing and acting to address their problems. The process involved replacing false consciousness with *class consciousness*, or the recognition by workers of their unity as a class in opposition to capitalists and, ultimately, to capitalism itself.

Capitalism and Alienation

For Marx, *alienation* meant the experience of isolation resulting from powerlessness. Workers themselves are a mere commodity. Four ways industrial capitalism alienates workers are identified: (1) alienation from the act of working, (2) alienation from the products of work, (3) alienation from other workers, and (4) alienation from human potential, and these act as a barrier to social class unity.

Revolution

Marx viewed revolution as the only way to change the nature of society. The type of system he saw as replacing industrial capitalism was socialism, which he believed was a more humane and egalitarian type of productive system.

MAX WEBER: THE RATIONALIZATION OF SOCIETY

Weber made many contributions to sociology, perhaps more than any other sociologist. One of the most significant was his understanding about how our social world differs from societies of early times. His work reflects the philosophical approach of *idealism* which emphasizes the importance of human ideas in shaping society. New ways of thinking, not merely technology and materialistic relationships were the major force in social change. A conceptual tool used by Weber in his research was the concept *ideal-type*, defined as an abstract statement of the essential characteristics of any social phenomenon.

Two World Views: Tradition and Rationality

Weber differentiated between two types of societies in terms of how people thought. The first is characterized by *tradition*, or sentiments and beliefs about the world that are passed from generation to generation. The other is characterized by *rationality*, or deliberate, matter-of-fact calculation of the most efficient means to accomplish any particular goal. This process of change from tradition to rationality he termed the *rationalization of society*, denoting the change in the type of thinking characteristic of members of society. Industrialization was an expression of this process. The **Global Map** (p. 101) shows that personal computers are utilized intensively in the high-income countries and infrequently in low-income countries.

Is Capitalism Rational?

Weber saw industrial capitalism as the essence of rationality while Marx did not, citing its failure to meet basic human needs.

Weber's Great Thesis: Protestantism and Capitalism

Weber points out that industrial capitalism developed where Calvinism was widespread. This is discussed as an example of how the power of ideas shapes human social development. A central doctrine of this religion was *predestination*, creating visions of either damnation or salvation, but in the hands of God not the people. Anxious to know their fate people looked for signs of God's favour. Some reassurance was to be found in personal success and achievement. This success was accelerated through the acceptance of technological innovation. As religious fervour weakened, a "work" ethic replaced the "religious" ethic.

Rational Social Organization

Weber believed rationality shaped modern society in various ways. This included: (1) creating distinctive *social institutions*, or major spheres of social life organized to meet basic human needs, (2) large-scale organizations, (3) specialized tasks, (4) personal discipline, (5) awareness of time, (6) technical competence, and (7) impersonality.

Rationality and Bureaucracy

While traditional societies had large scale organizations, they were not based on rationality. Modern day society becomes characterized by a type of social organization called *bureaucracy*. Weber viewed this as the clearest expression of a rational world, especially within the capitalist market economy.

➤**Rationality and Alienation**

Weber, like Marx, was critical of modern society, but for different reasons. For Weber, economic inequality was not the major problem, rather dehumanization and alienation were what troubled society most. Weber saw individuality being constricted by modern rationality expressed through increasingly rigid rules.

EMILE DURKHEIM: SOCIETY AND FUNCTION

Durkheim suggests that society is both beyond us and a part of us.

Structure: Society Beyond Ourselves

Central to the work of Durkheim is the concept of *social fact*, any part of society that is argued to have an objective existence apart from the individual and is therefore able to influence individual behaviour. Examples are the cultural values and norms of a society. Society is something more than the sum of its parts and it has the power to shape our thoughts and tug at our conceptions of morality.

Function: Society as System

Function is another concept important in the understanding of Durkheim's view of society. The significance of social facts is to be discovered in the functional contribution to the general life of society, not in the experience of individuals. His perspective leads us to view the functional consequences of any social phenomenon, even crime for example.

Personality: Society in Ourselves

According to Durkheim, society exists not only beyond us, having a life of its own, but also within us. Personalities are built through the internalization of social facts. Suicide, discussed in chapter 1, illustrates this point. Individuals who are poorly regulated suffer the highest rates of suicide.

➤**Modernity and Anomie**

While modern society provides great personal freedom, the lack of regulation often leads to *anomie*, where little moral guidance is provided.

Evolving Societies: The Division of Labour

Durkheim differentiated between two types of solidarity which have characterized societies over history. For most of history human societies were dominated by a collective conscience, or moral consensus. Durkheim termed this *mechanical solidarity*, meaning social bonds, common to pre-industrial societies, based on shared moral sentiments. Likeness was the rule in society. As this type declined it was replaced by *organic solidarity*, or social bonds, common to industrialized societies, based on specialization. So Durkheim saw history in terms of a growing *division of labour*, or specialized economic activity. Durkheim, like Weber and Marx had concern about modern society and its effect on the individual. The dilemma for Durkheim was the fact that the positive benefits of modern society, such as technical advances and personal freedoms, were accompanied by diminishing morality and the danger of anomie.

CRITICAL EVALUATION: FOUR VISIONS OF SOCIETY

The concluding section focuses on the questions raised at the beginning of this chapter using each of the four visions provided by the Lenskis, Marx, Weber, and Durkheim. These questions include:

➢**What Holds Societies Together?**

The Lenskis would answer by focusing on cultural patterns. Marx argued that only through cooperative productive enterprise could a united society develop. Weber saw unity created through a society's distinctive world view. Durkheim focussed on the factor of social integration.

The **Controversy and Debate** box (p. 107) asks if our society is getting better? Despite the progress Canada has experienced in improved education, huge technological change, increase in average income and increase in life expectancy in the last century, the level of optimism by Canadians has been declining for the last twenty-five years. Objectively family incomes have recently increased only slightly, divorce rates have increased while marriage rates have declined and there is a perception that the crime rate is increasing even though it isn't. Despite these concerns, most Canadians claim to be happy. Perhaps the theorists who have been examined in this Chapter have some answers. The Lenskis suggested that technology was no panacea and Marx, Weber and Durkheim in various ways decried the increase in individualism at the cost of a sense of community. Perhaps that is what Canadians are experiencing now.

The **Exploring Cyber Society** box (p. 106) offers us the opportunity to imagine what Durkheim, Weber and Marx would think of the information society. Durkheim would probably note the increased specialization in the division of labour while Weber might celebrate the decline of rigid bureaucratic rules as factories become less important. Marx would likely identify a new elite, those who possess symbolic skills, and a new underclass, those with few.

The **Applying Sociology** Box (p.96) suggests that sociological concepts and sociological theories can be used in a "thought experiment" to design a society which will serve our needs better.

➤How Have Societies Changed?

The sociocultural evolution model used by the Lenskis focuses on technology in answering this question. Marx's conflict approach focuses on historical differences in the productive system. And, while Weber focussed on characteristics of human thought, Durkheim concentrated on how societies differ in terms of how they are bound together.

➤Why Do Societies Change?

The Lenskis see change occurring through technological innovation. Marx saw class struggles as the "engine of history." Weber's idealist approach focussed on how ideas contribute to social change. Finally, Durkheim believed the expanding division of labour was the main force behind the increasing complexity of society.

KEY CONCEPTS

Define each of the following concepts on a separate paper. Check the accuracy of your answers by referring to the key concepts section in the text as well as referring to italicized definitions located throughout the chapter.

Agriculture	organic solidarity
Alienation	pastoralism
Anomie	post-industrialism
Capitalists	proletariat
Class consciousness	rationalization of society
Class conflict	rationality
Division of labour	social conflict
False consciousness	social fact
Horticultural society	social institutions
Hunting and gathering society	society
Ideal-type	sociocultural evolution
Industrialism	tradition
Mechanical solidarity	

STUDY QUESTIONS

 ## ✎ True-False

1. (T) F As used sociologically, the concept of society refers to people who interact with one another within a defined territory and who share a culture.

2. T (F) The greater the amount of technological information a society has, the slower is the rate at which it changes.

3. T (F) Hunting and gathering societies disappeared from this planet in the middle of the 20th century.

4. T F Pastoral societies use a technology based upon the domestication of animals.

5. T F Agrarian societies were characterized by greater amounts of specialization than horticultural societies.

6. T F Industrial societies transformed themselves more in a century than they had in thousands of years before.

7. T F Our legal notions about "what is property" have changed rapidly because of the Information Revolution.

8. T F The most significant form of social conflict for Marx involved clashes between social classes that arise from the way a society produces material goods.

9. T F Durkheim argued that the significance of social facts is discovered not in the experience of individuals, but in the functional contributions they have for the general life of society itself.

10. T F Organic solidarity characterizes pre-industrial societies.

11. T F Unlike Marx and Weber, Durkheim was relatively optimistic about industrialization and the development of modern society.

Multiple-Choice

1. Gerhard and Jean Lenski focus on which factor as a major determinate of social change?

(a) human ideas   (d) social solidarity
(b) technology   (e) religious doctrine
(c) social conflict

2. Hunting and gathering societies have few formal leaders but most recognize a _____, a spiritual leader.

(a) hunter   (d) venerate
(b) kaska   (e) none of the above
(d) shaman

60

3. A settlement of several hundred people who used hand tools to cultivate plants, was family-centered, and existed about 10,000 years ago is:

   (a) a hunting and gathering society   (d) a pastoral society
   (b) a horticultural society   (e) an agrarian society
   (e) a traditional society

4. Industrialism engenders

   (a) more prosperity   (d) all of the above
   (b) a reduction in kin ties   (e) a and b above
   (e) a decline in inequality

5. Technology that supports an information-based economy is called _____.

   (a) hunting and gathering   (d) industrial
   (b) agrarian   (e) post-industrial
   (c) horticultural

6. Although technology has generally improved life the twenty-first century will likely still be dealing with the technologically produced problems of

   (a) lower life expectancy   (d) a and b above
   (b) a damaged environment   (e) b and c above
   (c) establishing peace

7. Marx contends that one institution dominates all others when it comes to steering the direction of a society. It is the

   (a) educational institution   (d) economic institution
   (b) political institution   (e) family institution
   (c) mass media

8. Marx's concept of the "bourgeoisie" is a word derived from French meaning:

   (a) to be exploited   (d) to be revolutionary
   (b) to be alienated   (e) to be above the law
   (c) to be of the town

9. In order for exploited classes to take political action to improve their situation, Marx proposed they must:

(a) become aware of their shared oppression
(b) organize to take collective action
(c) replace false consciousness with class consciousness
(d) all of the above

10. Max Weber's analysis of society reflects the philosophical approach known as:

(a) materialism
(b) idealism
(c) cultural ecology
(d) egalitarianism
(e) radicalism

11. Weber argued that modern society is characterized by:

(a) conflict
(b) harmony
(c) indecision
(d) ambiguity
(e) rationality

12. If the classical scholars were alive to evaluate the impact of the Information Revolution on Canadian society which one would likely identify a new elite who possessed symbolic skills?

(a) Emile Durkheim
(b) Max Weber
(f) Leo Tolstoy
(d) Karl Marx
(e) Gerhard Lenski

Fill-In The Blank

1. Hunting and gathering societies rarely form _permanent_ settlements.

2. Marx referred to those who own the means of production as the _Capitalists_, and those who provide the labour for its operation as the _proletariat_.

3. The recognition by workers of their unity as a class in opposition to capitalists, Marx called _Class Consciousness_

4. As a result of powerlessness workers experience _Alienation_ in Marx's theory of social conflict.

5. Max Weber demonstrated the importance of _ideas_ in shaping social change and development.

6. An abstract description of a social phenomenon on the basis of its essential characteristics Weber called an _ideal type_

62

7. Any part of society that is argued to have an objective existence apart from the individual Durkheim called a _Social_ _fact_ .

8. _anomie_ refers to a condition in which society provides individuals with little moral guidance.

9. Social bonds, common in industrial society, based on specialization, Durkheim called _organic_ _solidarity_.

10. Weber contended that modern societies were held together by a distinctive, shared _world_ _view_ .

Definition and Short-Answer

1. How do the Lenskis define sociocultural evolution?

2. What are the basic types of societies identified by the Lenskis? What are the basic characteristics of each?

3. What do our authors mean by the "limits of technology"?

4. What is the meaning of the philosophy of materialism?

5. How does Marx understand the role of social conflict through history?

6. According to Marx, what are the four ways in which industrial capitalism alienates workers?

7. According to Weber, what are the roots of rationality in modern society?

8. For Weber, what are the components of rational social organization?

9. What is the meaning of the term "social fact" as discussed by Durkheim?

10. Define the two types of solidarity according to Durkheim?

Answers to Study Questions

True-False

1. T (p. 87)   7. F (p. 93)
2. F (p. 88)   8. T (p. 94)
3. F (p. 88)   9. T (p. 104)
4. T (p. 89)   10. F (p. 105)
5. T (p. 90)   11. T (p. 105)
6. T (p. 91)

Multiple-Choice

1. b (p. 87)	7. d (p. 94)
2. c (p. 89)	8. c (p. 96)
3. b (p. 89)	9. d (p. 97)
4. d (pp. 91-92)	10. b (p. 99)
5. e (p. 92)	11. e (p. 99)
6. e (p. 93)	12. d (p. 106)

$\dfrac{6}{12} = 50\%$

Fill-In

1. permanent (p. 88)	6. ideal type (p. 99)
2. capitalists/proletariat (p. 94)	7. social fact (p. 103)
3. class consciousness (p. 97)	8. anomie (pp. 104-105)
4. alienation (p. 97)	9. organic solidarity (p. 105)
5. ideas (p. 99)	10. world view (p. 105)

ANALYSIS AND COMMENT

Go back through the chapter and write own in the spaces below key points from each of the following boxes.

APPLYING SOCIOLOGY

"Can Sociology Help Us Design a Better Society?"
Key Points:

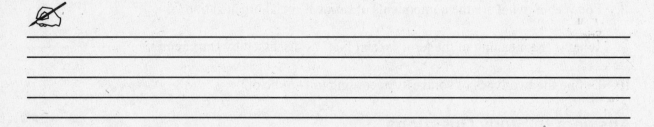

_____

_____

_____

_____

_____

EXPLORING CYBER-SOCIETY

"The Information Revolution. What Would Durkheim (and Others) Think?"
Key Points:

_____

_____

_____

_____

CONTROVERSY AND DEBATE

"Is Our Society Getting Better or Worse?"   What do you think?
Key Points:

_____

_____

_____

_____

_____

SELECTED READINGS

Classic Sources

Robert C. Tucker, ed. 1978 *The Marx-Engels Reader*. 2nd. Ed. New York: W. W. Norton.
This is an excellent source of essays by Karl Marx and Friedrich Engels.

Max Weber. 1995 (orig. 1904-5). *The Protestant Ethic and the Spirit of Capitalism*. Los Angeles: Roxbury Press.
Perhaps Max Weber's best-known study is his analysis of Protestantism and capitalism.

Emile Durkheim. 1964; orig. 1893. *The Division of Labour in Society*. New York: The Free Press.
This is Durkheim's major contribution to our understanding of modern societies.

Contemporary Sources

Gerhard Lenski, Patrick Nolan, and Jean Lenski. 1995. *Human Society: An Introduction to Macrosociology*. 7th ed. New York: McGraw-Hill. 1995.
A comprehensive account of Gerhard and Jean Lenski's analysis of human societies is found in this textbook.

Irving Louis Horowitz. 1993. *The Decomposition of Sociology*. New York: Oxford University Press.
A well known sociologist argues that the discipline, fraught with political, theoretical, and methodological divisions, is on the decline.

Michael S. Serrill. 1995. "A Nation Blessed, A Nation Stressed." *Time*, November 20, 20-43.

Global Source

Uta Gerhardt, ed. 1993. *Talcott Parsons on National Socialism*. Hawthorne, N.Y.: Aldine de Gruyter.
This book explains how an outstanding theorist applied his research to the Allied effort in World War II and the structuring of a democratic postwar Germany.

Canadian Sources

S. D. Clark. 1942. *The Social Development of Canada*. Toronto: University of Toronto Press.
Wallace Clement. 1974. *The Canadian Corporate Elite: An Analysis of Economic Power*. Toronto: McClelland and Stewart.
Dennis Forcese. 1980. *The Canadian Class Structure*. 2nd. Ed. Toronto: McGraw-Hill Ryerson.
John Porter. 1965. *The Vertical Mosaic*. Toronto: University of Toronto Press
This brief sampling of some classics in Canadian sociology focuses on the structure and development of Canadian society.

CHAPTER 5

Socialization

I CHAPTER OUTLINE

I. **Social Experience: The Key to Our Humanity**
    A. Human Development: Nature and Nurture
        1. Charles Darwin: The Role of Nature
        2. The Social Sciences: The Role of Nurture
    B. Social Isolation
        1. Effects of Social Isolation on Nonhuman Primates
        2. Effects of Social Isolation on Children

II. **Understanding the Socialization Process**
    A. Sigmund Freud: The Elements of Personality
        1. Basic Human Needs
        2. Freud's Model of Personality
        3. Personality Development
    B. Jean Piaget: Cognitive Development
        1. The Sensorimotor Stage
        2. The Preoperational Stage
        3. The Concrete Operational Stage
        4. The Formal Operational Stage
    C. Lawrence Kohlberg: Moral Development
    D. Carol Gilligan: Bringing in Gender
    E. George Herbert Mead: The Social Self
        1. The Self
        2. The Looking-Glass Self
        3. The I and the Me
        4. Development of the Self
    F. Erik H. Erikson: Eight Stages of Development

III. **Agents of Socialization**
    A. The Family
    B. Schooling
    C. The Peer Group
    D. The Mass Media

IV. **Socialization and the Life Course**
    A. Childhood
    B. Adolescence
    C. Adulthood
        1. Early Adulthood
        2. Middle Adulthood
    D. Old Age
    E. Dying
    F. The Life Course: An Overview

V.   **Resocialization: Total Institutions**
VI. **Summary**
VII. **Critical Thinking Questions**
VIII. **Applications and Exercises**
IX. **Sites to See**

- To understand the "nature" versus "nurture" debate regarding socialization.

- To explain the effects of social isolation on humans and other primates.

- To identify the key components in Sigmund Freud's model of personality.

- To identify and describe the four stages of cognitive development in the theory of Jean Piaget.

- To understand both Lawrence Kohlberg's theory of moral development and Carol Gilligan's critique.

- To comprehend whether males and females are different with respect to aggressive behaviour.

- To explain the contributions of George Herbert Mead to the understanding of the process of socialization.

- To understand Erik Erikson's eight stages of development.

- To be able to compare and contrast the theories of Freud, Piaget, Mead, Kohlberg, Gilligan and Erikson concerning socialization and human development.

- To compare and contrast the agents of socialization (family, schooling, etc.) in terms of their effects on an individual's socialization experiences.

- To compare and contrast the modes of socialization in childhood, adolescence, adulthood, and old age.

- To understand the power of the mass media to shape our understanding of the social world.

- To describe the social experience of life within a total institution.

III CHAPTER REVIEW
SOCIAL EXPERIENCE: THE KEY TO OUR HUMANITY

We are told the story of Anna, a young girl who was raised in a context devoid of meaningful social contact. Kingsley Davis, a sociologist, studied the six year old girl, and described her as being more an object than a person. What Anna had been deprived of was *socialization*, or lifelong social experience by which individuals develop human potential and learn the patterns of their culture. Socialization is the foundation of *personality*, referring to a person's fairly consistent pattern of thinking, feeling, and acting. In Anna's case, personality just did not develop.

Human Development: Nature and Nurture

➤Charles Darwin: The Role of Nature

Naturalists during the mid 19th century, applying Charles Darwin's theory of evolution, claimed that all human behaviour was instinctive. Although this is no longer a dominant view the thinking is still with us as people, for example, talk about "born criminals."

➤The Social Sciences: The Role of Nurture

Social scientists reject much of the biological argument and see human nature itself as shaped by cultural context.

Psychologist John Watson challenged the naturalistic perspective and developed an approach called behaviourism, claiming that all human behaviour was learned within particular social environments. The work of anthropologists illustrating the great cultural variation existing around the world supports Watson's view.

Contemporary social scientists do not argue that biology plays no role in shaping human behaviour. At the very least, human physical traits are linked to heredity. Also, certain characteristics such as intelligence, potential to excel in music and art, and personality characteristics seem to be influenced by heredity. The current position on this issue is that nature and nurture are not so much in opposition as they are inseparable.

Social Isolation

For obvious ethical reasons research on the effects of social isolation has been limited to the study of animals. A few rare cases, like Anna's, of human isolation have been investigated.

➤Effects of Social Isolation on Nonhuman Primates

Classic research by Harry and Margaret Harlow using rhesus monkeys has illustrated the importance of social interaction for other primates besides humans. Using various experimental situations with artificial "mothers" for infant monkeys they determined that while physical development occurred within normal limits, emotional and social growth failed to occur. One important discovery was that monkeys deprived of mother-infant contact, if surrounded by other infant monkeys, did not suffer adversely. This suggested the importance of social interaction in general rather than specifically a maternal bond. A second conclusion was that monkeys who experienced short-term isolation (3 months or less) recovered to normal emotional levels after rejoining other monkeys. Long-term separation appears to have irreversible negative consequences.

➤Effects of Social Isolation on Children

The cases of Anna, Isabelle, and Genie, all of whom suffered through years of isolation and neglect as young children are reviewed. Each case suggests that while humans are resilient creatures, extreme social isolation results in irreversible damage to normal personality development.

UNDERSTANDING THE SOCIALIZATION PROCESS

Sigmund Freud: The Elements of Personality

While trained as a physician, Freud's most important contribution was the development of psychoanalysis and the study of personality development.

➤Basic Human Needs

Freud saw biological factors having a significant influence on personality, though he rejected the argument that human behaviour reflected simple biological instinct. He conceived instincts as general urges and drives. He claimed humans had two basic needs or drives; *eros*, a need for bonding and *thanatos*, which related to a drive for death.

➤Freud's Model of Personality

Freud's perspective combined both these basic needs and the influence of society into a unique model of personality. He argued the personality is comprised of three parts. One is the *id*, rooted in biology and representing the human being's basic needs, which are unconscious and demand immediate satisfaction. Another, representing the conscious attempt to balance innate pleasure-seeking drives of the human organism and the demands of society, he labelled the *ego*. Finally, the human personality develops a *superego* which is the operation of culture within the individual which ultimately defines, for the individual, moral limits.

➤Personality Development

There is basic conflict between the id and the superego which the ego must continually try to manage. If the conflict is not adequately resolved personality disorders result. The controlling influence on drives by society is referred to as *repression*. Often a compromise between society and the individual is struck, where fundamentally selfish drives are redirected into socially acceptable objectives. This process is called *sublimation*.

Id-centred children feel good only in a physical sense but after three or four years, with the gradual development of the superego they can begin to evaluate their behaviour by cultural standards.

While being controversial, Freud's work highlights the internalization of social norms and the importance of childhood experiences in the socialization process and the development of personality.

Jean Piaget: Cognitive Development

A prominent psychologist of the 20th century, Piaget's work centred on human *cognition*, or how people think and understand. He was concerned with not just what a person knew, but how the person knows something. He identified four major stages of cognitive development which he believed were tied to biological maturation as well as social experience.

➤**The Sensorimotor Stage**

The *sensorimotor stage* is described as the level of human development in which the world is experienced only through sensory contact. This stage lasts for about the first two years of life. The understanding of symbols does not exist during this period. The child experiences the world only in terms of direct physical contact.

➤**The Preoperational Stage**

The *preoperational stage* was described by Piaget as the level of human development in which language and other symbols are first used. This stage extends from the age of two to the age of six. Children continue to be very egocentric during this time, having little ability to generalize concepts.

➤**The Concrete Operational Stage**

The third stage in Piaget's model is called the *concrete operational stage* and is described as the level of human development characterized by the use of logic to understand objects or events. This period typically covers the ages of seven to eleven. Cause and effect relationships begin to be understood during this period. The ability to take the perspective of other people also emerges.

➤**The Formal Operational Stage**

The fourth stage is the *formal operational stage* and is described as the level of human development characterized by highly abstract and critical thought. This stage begins about age twelve. The ability to think in hypothetical terms is also developed.

Some critics suggest that the model may not fit traditional societies and that, even in our own society, as many as a third of adults do not reach the final stage.

Laurence Kohlberg: Moral Development

Kohlberg used Piaget's theory as a springboard for a study on moral reasoning. He suggests a *preconventional stage* based on pain and pleasure, a *conventional stage* (in the teenage years) where right and wrong is understood within cultural norms and a *postconventional stage* where abstract critique of the social order is possible.

Kohlberg's theory may not apply equally well in all societies and it would appear that many North Americans do not reach the final stage of moral development. As well his research subjects were all boys.

Carol Gilligan: Bringing in Gender

Gilligan, as a response to the gender limited work of Kohlberg, concludes that males and females make moral judgements in different ways. Males use a *justice perspective*, it's wrong if the rules define it that way. Females use a *care and responsibility perspective*, it's wrong if it damages relationships. Her recent research on self-esteem demonstrates that female self-esteem begins to slip during adolescence, as they encounter more authority figures who are men.

The **Applying Sociology** Box (p. 119) suggests that men and women may not be very different with respect to the expression of violence.

George Herbert Mead: The Social Self

Our understanding of socialization owes much to the work of Mead. His analysis is often referred to as *social behaviourism* where he focuses on mental processes.

➤**The Self**

Mead understood the basis of humanity to be the *self*, a dimension of personality composed of an individual's self- conception. For Mead, the self was a totally social phenomenon, inseparable from society. The connection between the two was explained in a series of steps, the emergence of the self through social experience, based on the exchange of symbolic intentions, and occurring within a context in which people take the role of the other, or take their point of view into account during social interaction.

➤**The Looking-Glass Self**

The process of taking the role of the other can be understood using Charles Horton Cooley's concept of the *looking-glass self*. This term focuses on the ideas that a person's self-conception is based on the response of others, perhaps explaining Gilligan's observations on the loss of self-esteem of young women.

➤**The I and The Me**

The capacity to see oneself has two components, namely: (1) the self as subject by which we initiate social action and (2) the self as object, concerning how we perceive ourselves from the perspective of others. The subjective part of the self Mead labelled the "I". The objective aspect Mead called the "Me". All social interaction is seen as the continuous interplay of these two aspects of the self.

➤**Development of the Self**

Mead minimized the importance of biology in personality development, the key was social experience. Mead saw infants as responding to others only in terms of imitation. As the use of symbols emerges the child enters a *play* stage, in which role-taking occurs. Initially, the roles are modelled after significant others, especially parents. Through further social experience children enter the *game* stage where the simultaneous playing of many roles is possible. The final stage involves the development of a *generalized other,* or widespread cultural norms and values used as a reference in evaluating ourselves.

Figure 5-1 (p. 121) illustrates the development of the self as a process of gaining social experience. Although Mead's work is criticized as being radically social he helps us to understand the importance of symbolic interaction to the development of self.

Erik H. Erikson: Eight Stages of Development

Erikson offers a broader view of socialization, suggesting that personality continues to change throughout life. His eight stages begin in infancy and end in old age.

Some are critical of the apparent rigidity of the model but it does force us to examine the influence of agencies of socialization other than the family.

AGENTS OF SOCIALIZATION
The Family

The family is identified as the most important agent of socialization. The process of socialization within this institution is both intentional and unconscious. While parenting styles vary, the most important aspect in parent-child relations seems to be *attention* paid by parents to their children. The family is the initial source for transmission of culture to the child.

From an early age children learn from their families that social class exists and that it is associated with different behaviour patterns.

Schooling

It is within the context of school that children begin to establish contact with people from a diversity of social backgrounds. The expressed objective purpose of the school experience is the imparting of knowledge, math, reading, etc. However, there exists a *hidden curriculum* which also teaches children important cultural values such as achievement and punctuality.

It is within the educational environment that evaluations are made of children based on universal standards on *how they perform* instead of *who they are.* Schooling is critical for obtaining the knowledge and skills necessary for adult roles but the limitations of gender schema are also reinforced.

The Peer Group

Peer group socialization typically occurs outside the context of adult supervision. A *peer group* is defined as a social group whose members have interests, social position, and age in common. Some research provides evidence suggesting that the conflict between parents and their adolescent children is more apparent than real. A major feature operative during adolescence is referred to as *anticipatory socialization*, or the process of social learning directed toward gaining a desired position.

The Mass Media

The *mass media* are impersonal communications directed to a vast audience. This includes television, newspapers and radio but television has become the dominant medium such that children spend more hours watching television than they do in school or in interacting with their parents. The message includes class, gender and racial biases but, on the other hand, the producers tend to be more liberal than the average Canadian or American. Figures 5-2, 5-3 and 5-4 demonstrate the pervasiveness of T.V. viewing and the **Social Diversity** box (p. 126) discusses the portrayal of racial minorities and women in television productions. While historically minority groups and women were under-represented and portrayed stereotypically, there has been massive change in the last few years so that minorities and women play a more dominant role and are portrayed, more often, in a fair and sympathetic fashion.

Although television and other mass media can be magnificent sources for entertainment and learning, there has developed a concern over media violence and its impact upon behaviour, especially of children. There is, as yet, no consensus about the existence of a cause and effect relationship.

SOCIALIZATION AND THE LIFE COURSE

While focus is given to childhood in terms of the significance of socialization, this process is lifelong. Social experience is structured during different stages of the life course.

Childhood

Nike and Michael Jordan are criticized for the employment of children in the production of sneakers since *childhood* in Canadian culture lasts roughly the first twelve years of life and it is a period characterized by freedom from responsibilities. While most suggest it is an expanding period in technologically advanced societies, some research, especially on affluent families, suggests it actually may be getting shorter. The "hurried child" pattern reflects this idea. Critics of the concept suggest lower-class children have always accepted adult responsibilities as children. In primitive societies, moreover, less differentiation is made between childhood and adulthood. **Global Map** 5-1 (p. 128) shows how commonplace work is for children in the poorer societies of the world.

Adolescence

This period emerged as a distinct life cycle stage in industrial societies. This period corresponds roughly to the teen years. The social turmoil often associated with this stage appears to be the result of inconsistencies in the socialization process as opposed to physical changes. Examples concerning the status of teens in relation to voting and drinking are discussed, along with Margaret Mead's cross-cultural research which demonstrates that the period owes much to cultural definition. Social class also plays a role since working class youth are often working at age 18 while middle class individuals may be in graduate school at 30.

Adulthood

Adulthood is a period when most of our life's accomplishments occur, and, especially toward the end of this stage, people reflect upon what they have accomplished.

➤Early Adulthood

This period lasts approximately from the early 20's to age 40. While personality is largely set by this time, certain dislocations, like unemployment, divorce, or a serious illness can result in significant changes to the self. This period is dominated by meeting day-to-day responsibilities and achieving goals set earlier in life. The juggling of conflicting priorities also characterizes this period especially for women who work but who are expected to maintain the functions of mother and housewife.

➤Middle Adulthood

This period lasts roughly between the ages of 40 to 60. A distinctive quality of this period is reflection on personal achievements in light of earlier expectations. While working men and women are often forced to recognize their failure to realize earlier expectations, women must also confront their physical decline in a society which is less generous, in this respect, to them as compared to men. There is some evidence, however, that as our society ages, we are less likely to suggest that vibrant life ends at forty.

Old Age

This period begins during the mid-60s. The status of the aged varies greatly cross-culturally. In rapidly changing modern societies the aged tend to be defined as marginal or even obsolete. This period is quite different from previous ones as it is characterized by the leaving of roles instead of entering new ones. As the proportion of elderly people increases, as it will rather dramatically over the next thirty years, the anti-elderly bias will surely decline.

Dying

As the proportion of people in old age increases we will likely be more comfortable with death and perhaps even permit people to end pain and suffering by their own decision. More people now make legal and financial preparations for a surviving spouse.

THE LIFE COURSE: AN OVERVIEW

The life course is largely a social construction and each stage contains characteristic problems which, however, are affected by the dynamics of class, race, ethnicity and gender.

Life experience also varies by when people were born. Age cohorts or generations are likely to have experienced cultural and economic trends that other cohorts have not. Those born at mid-century faced economic expansion while today's youth face economic uncertainty.

RESOCIALIZATION: TOTAL INSTITUTIONS

A *total institution* is defined as a setting in which individuals are isolated from the rest of society and manipulated by an administrative staff. Erving Goffman has identified three distinct qualities of such institutions: (1) they control all aspects of the daily lives of the residents, (2) they subject residents to standardized activities, and (3) they apply formal rules and rigid scheduling to all activities. This structure is designed to achieve the policy of *resocialization*, or deliberate control of an environment to radically alter an inmates personality. This is understood as a two part process—the destruction of the individual's self-conception, and the systematic building of another one. A process known as *institutionalization* often occurs whereby residents become dependent on the structure of the institution and are unable to function outside the institution. The **Controversy and Debate** Box (p. 132) describes how Ontario's first boot camp can be conceptualized as a total institution.

KEY CONCEPTS

Define each of the following concepts on separate paper. Check the accuracy of your answers by referring to the key concepts section in the text, as well as by referring to italicized definitions located throughout the chapter.

adolescence	hidden curriculum
adulthood	mass media
anticipatory socialization	old age
childhood	peer group
cohort	personality
concrete operational stage	preoperational stage
dying	resocialization
ego	self
formal operational stage	sensorimotor stage
generalized other	socialization
id	superego
looking-glass self	total institution

STUDY QUESTIONS

True-False

1. T F   John Watson was a 19th century psychologist who argued that human behaviour was largely determined by heredity.

2. T F   Social scientists agree, personality characteristics have some genetic component.

3. T F   The Harlows' research on rhesus monkeys concerning social isolation illustrates that while short-term isolation can be overcome, long-term isolation appears to cause irreversible emotional and behavioural damage to the monkeys.

4. T F   In the case of Isabelle, who experienced more than six years of virtual isolation, a special training program enabled her to approximate a normal life.

5. T F   Freud envisioned biological factors as having little or no influence on personality development.

6. T F   At the preoperational stage, according to Piaget, children can now imagine themselves from the point of view of another person.

7. T F   Carol Gilligan argues that girls make moral judgements from a justice perspective.

8. T F   Mead's concept of the generalized other refers to widespread cultural norms and values used as a reference in evaluating ourselves.

9. T F   The concept "hidden curriculum" relates to the important informal cultural values being transmitted to children in school.

10. T F   Adolescence can be associated with the stage of life when young people establish some independence and learn specialized skills.

11. T F   A rigidly controlled total institution usually instils in its inmates the desire and capacity to adjust to the outside world.

✎ Multiple-Choice

1. The story of Anna illustrates the significance of _____ in personality development.

    (a) heredity   (d) ecological forces
    (b) social experience   (e) historical processes
    (c) physical conditions

2. Freud identified two basic needs or drives. One was the death instinct which he referred to as

_____.

    (a) eros   (d) id
    (b) thanatos   (e) ego
    (c) superego

3. Culture existing within the individual Freud called:

   (a) thanatos
   (b) eros
   (c) the ego
   (d) the id
   (e) the superego

4. According to Piaget, which of the following best describes the formal operational stage of cognitive development:

   (a) the level of human development in which the world is experienced only through sensory contact
   (b) the level of human development characterized by the use of logic to understand objects and events
   (c) the level of human development in which language and other symbols are first used
   (d) the level of human development characterized by highly abstract thought
   (e) none of the above

5. In Kohlberg's final stage of moral development, the postconventional level, individuals

   (a) conceptualize rightness as what feels good to them
   (b) define right and wrong in terms of what is consistent with cultural norms
   (c) are capable of arguing that what is conventional may not be right
   (d) all of the above
   (e) none of the above

6. Carol Gilligan defines the moral development of males and females differently. Males, she contends, have a _____.

   (a) perspective which relies on concrete principles to define right and wrong
   (b) perspective which relies on informal rules
   (c) care and responsibility perspective
   (d) responsibility perspective
   (e) care and responsibility perspective

7. The concept of the looking-glass self refers to:

   (a) Freud's argument that through psychoanalysis we can uncover our unconscious
   (b) Piaget's view that through biological maturation and social experience individuals become able to logically hypothesize about thoughts without relying on concrete reality
   (c) Watson's behaviourist notion that one can see through to a person's mind only by observing their behaviour
   (d) Cooley's idea that a person's self-conception is based on responses of others

8. In which of Erikson's eight stages of development do we find the challenge of intimacy versus isolation?

(a) Toddler
(b) Pre-adolescent
(c) Young adulthood
(d) Middle Adulthood
(e) None of the above

9. The process of social learning directed toward assuming a desired status and role in the future is called:

(a) resocialization
(b) looking-glass self
(c) socialization
(d) anticipatory socialization

10 Recent studies in Canada on television violence have concluded that

(a) television violence increases aggressive behaviour in children.
(b) the link between television violence and children's behaviour is inconclusive and contradictory.
(c) there is a link between violence on television and violence in society.
(d) all of the above
(e) a and c above

11. In industrial societies the stage of life often associated with emotional and social turmoil is called:

(a) childhood
(b) adolescence
(c) middle-adulthood
(d) old age
(e) none of the above

✎ Fill-In The Blank

1. In the absence of social experience _____ does not emerge at all.

2. The approach called _____ developed by John Watson in the early 20th century provided a perspective which stressed learning rather than instincts as the key to personality development.

3. According to Freud, the _____ represents the human beings basic drives which are unconscious and demand immediate satisfaction.

4. Piaget's work centred on human _____.

5. Carol Gilligan's research finds that girls _____ starts to slip away as they pass through adolescence.

6. The objective element of self was called by Mead the _____ .

7. _____ give young people the opportunity to discuss interests that may not be shared by adults.

8. Research finds that television viewing by children renders them more _____ .

9. A prison or mental hospital is an example of a _____ .

10. The deliberate manipulation of the environment in a prison, for example, has the ultimate goal of _____ .

Definition and Short-Answer

1. Briefly review the history of the nature-nurture debate concerning human development.

2. Review the cases of social isolation described in the text. What are the effects of social isolation on nonhuman primates? What are the effects of social isolation on children?

3. According to Freud, what are the basic components of personality? What stages of human development does Freud identify?

4. According to Piaget, what are the stages of cognitive development? What are the characteristics of each stage?

5. What do Kohlberg and Gilligan have to say about moral development.

6. What is Mead's theory of personality development? What are the stages identified in his model? What is the "self" and how does it develop?

7. How do men and women differ with respect to violent behaviour?

8. How does Erikson broaden our understanding of socialization?

9. What are the major agents of socialization? Briefly describe how each influences human development.

10. How is our conception of death likely to change over the next quarter century?

11. What is a total institution? Provide an example.

12. How are women and men differentially affected by the life process of socialization?

Answers to Study Questions

True-False

1. F (p. 112)	7. F (p. 118)
2. T (p. 113)	8. T (p. 120)
3. T (p. 113)	9. T (p. 122)
4. T (p. 114)	10. T (p. 127)
5. F (p. 115)	11. F (p. 133)
6. F (p. 116)	

Multiple-Choice

1. b (p. 111)	7. d (p. 119)
2. b (p. 115)	8. c (p. 121)
3. e (p. 115)	9. d (p. 123)
4. d (p. 117)	10. d (pp. 124-125)
5. c (p. 117)	11. b (p. 127)
6. a (p. 118)	

Fill-In

1. personality (p. 111)	6. me (pp. 119-120)
2. behaviourism (p. 112)	7. peer groups (p. 123)
3. id (p. 115)	8. passive (p. 124)
4. cognition (p. 116)	9. total institution (p. 131)
5. self-esteem (p. 118)	10. re-socialization (p. 131)

ANALYSIS AND COMMENT

Go back through the chapter and write down in the spaces below key points from each of the following boxes.

APPLYING SOCIOLOGY

"Gentle, Nurturing Women: Aggressive, Violent Men."
Key Points

_____

_____

_____

_____

_____

SOCIAL DIVERSITY

"How Do the Media Portray Minorities?"
Key Points:

_____

_____

_____

_____

_____

CONTROVERSY AND DEBATE

"Ontario's First Boot Camp as a Total Institution."
Key Points:

_____

_____

_____

_____

_____

SUGGESTED READINGS

Classic Sources

George Herbert Mead. 1962; orig. 1934. *Mind, Self, and Society From the Standpoint of a Social Behaviorist.* Charles W. Morris, ed. Chicago: University of Chicago Press.
Compiled after Mead's death by his students, this paperback presents Mead's analysis of the development of self.

Margaret Mead. 1961; orig. 1928. *Coming of Age in Samoa.* New York: Dell.
While still in her early twenties, Margaret Mead completed what is probably the best-known book in anthropology, in which she argues that the problems of adolescence are socially created rather than rooted in biology.

Contemporary Sources

Grace Craig. 1995. *Human Development.* 7th. Ed. Englewood Cliffs, N.J.: Prentice Hall.
This book is a good general reference for understanding socialization across the life course.

George H. Hill, Lorraine Raglin, and Charles Floyd Johnson. 1990. *Black Women and Television.* New York: Garland.
Mary Ellen Brown, ed. 1990. *Television and Women's Culture: The Politics of the Popular.* 1990. Newbury Park, Calif.: Sage Publications.
The first of these two books about television highlights African-American women and cites interesting "firsts." The second, a collection of thirteen essays, delves into the subject of television

and women, as actors and as audience.

John R. Seeley (et al.). 1963 *Crestwood Heights: A Study of the Culture of Suburban Life.* **New York: Wiley.**
A classic book on socialization amongst an elite community in Canada.

Margrit Eichler. 1988. *Families in Canada Today: Recent Changes and Their Policy Consequences.* **2ⁿᵈ. Ed. Toronto: Gage.**
The impact of Canadian public policy on family life is the focus of Eichler's book.

Craig McKie and Keith Thompson. 1990. *Canadian Social Trends.* **Toronto: Thompson Educational Publishing.**
A brief summary of a variety of analyses of timely data collected via the Canadian census.

Jean-Yves Soucy with Annette, Cecile, and
an ongoing study of more than five thousand men and women living throughout Britain, all born in 1946 and interviewed periodically since then.

Yvonne Dionne. 1996. *Family Secrets.* **Toronto: Stoddart.**

Global Sources

Alba N. Ambert and Marie D. Alvarez, eds. 1992. *Puerto Rican Children on the Mainland:* *Interdisciplinary Perspectives.* **New York: Garland.**
This collection of essays sketches a statistical portrait of Puerto Ricans on the U.S. mainland and investigates distinctive dimensions of socialization among young people.

M. E. J. Wadsworth. 1991. *The Imprint of Time: Childhood, History, and Adult Life.* **New York: Clarendon Press.**
Long-term studies of cohorts are difficult and, therefore, rare in social science. This book reports on

This is the most recent book on the Dionne family.
Meg Luxton. 1980. *More Than a Labour of Love.* **Toronto: Women's Press.**
A detailed examination of the lives of three generations of women in Flin Flon, Manitoba.

CHAPTER 6

Social Interaction in Everyday Life

- To identify the characteristics of social structure.

- To distinguish between the different types of statuses and roles and the interconnection between them.

- To describe the importance of role in social interaction.

- To explain the social construction of reality.

- To understand the theoretical approach within the symbolic-interaction paradigm known as ethnomethodology.

- To know the importance of performance, nonverbal communication, idealization, and embarrassment to the "presentation of self."

- To describe dramaturgical analysis.

- To be able to use gender and humour as illustrations of how people construct meaning in everyday life.

III CHAPTER REVIEW

The chapter begins with a description of how men and women deal differently with being lost. Women will ask for directions, often men will not. Such a vignette can be subjected to sociological analysis through the examination of *social interaction*, the process by which people act and react in relation to others.

SOCIAL STRUCTURE: A GUIDE TO EVERYDAY LIVING

The social structural aspects of a society provide a guide for behaviour. Once the signposts are learned the overall nature of the interaction process is clarified.

Status

One of the basic elements of social structure is **status**, a recognized social position that an individual occupies. Each position has duties and responsibilities, usually in relation to complementary status positions.

Status Set

No person holds only one status position, he or she holds many. All the statuses that a person holds at a given time are called a status set. One can be a female, a student, a daughter and a wife among others.

Ascribed Status and Achieved Status

Sociologists distinguish two ways in which statuses are obtained. An *ascribed status* is a social position that is received at birth or involuntarily assumed later in the life course. In contrast, an *achieved status* refers to a social position that is assumed voluntarily and that reflects a significant measure of personal ability and effort. Most often there is a combination of ascribed and achieved factors in each of our statuses.

Master Status

A *master status* is defined as a status that has an exceptional importance for social identity, often shaping a person's entire life. In our society, one's occupation often comprises this position. The **Social Diversity** box (p. 140) points out that physical disability becomes the master status for many people. Ascribed statuses such as race and sex are other examples of positions which can act as a person's master status.

ROLE

The concept *role* refers to patterns of expected behaviour attached to a particular status. Role performance can differ somewhat from the expectations society attaches to a role.

Role Set

Generally, a person has many more roles than statuses, as each status typically has multiple roles attached. Robert Merton defines a *role set* as a number of roles attached to a single status. Figure 6-1 (p. 141) provides an illustration of a status set and role set.

Role Conflict and Role Strain

The concept *role conflict* refers to incompatibility among the roles corresponding to two or more statuses. Even the roles attached to a single status can create problems for an individual. *Role strain* is the incompatibility among roles corresponding to a single status.

Role Exit

Role exit is the process by which people disengage from social roles that have been central to their lives. "Exes" often retain self-images from an earlier role which may interfere with the development of a new sense of self.

THE SOCIAL CONSTRUCTION OF REALITY

While statuses and roles structure our lives, we as individuals have considerable ability to shape patterns of interaction with others. The phrase *social construction of reality* refers to the process by which individuals creatively shape reality through social interaction. Social interaction is understood as a process of negotiation which generates a changing reality.

The Thomas Theorem

One observation made by sociologists is that situations that are defined as real are real in their consequences. This has become known as the *Thomas theorem* as constructed by W. I. Thomas.

Ethnomethodology

One approach to understanding the ways humans shape reality is called *ethnomethodology* which is based on the symbolic-interaction paradigm. Harold Garfinkel coined the term, which is defined as the study of the way that people make sense of their everyday lives. Garfinkel did research in which he had students deliberately "break the rules" of ordinary social interaction. This approach highlights awareness of many unspoken agreements that underlie various interaction situations.

Reality-Building: Some Broader Considerations

People build reality from the surrounding culture. These cultures vary widely globally and even vary substantially within a given society. The **Global Sociology** box (p. 146) indicates that human emotions are rooted in both biology and culture and the **Global Snapshot** (p. 144) finds that happiness is differentially distributed worldwide. The **Controversy and Debate** box (p. 155) suggests that the new information technology is changing how people work, how they see themselves and how they interact with others, including in cyberspace where face to face contact becomes unnecessary. (**Exploring Cyber Society**, p. 151)

DRAMATURGICAL ANALYSIS: "THE PRESENTATION OF SELF"

Another approach to understanding the social interaction of everyday life is *dramaturgical analysis* developed by Erving Goffman. This approach is defined as the analysis of social interaction in terms of theatrical performances. Goffman theorized that statuses and roles are used to create impressions. Central to this analysis is the process called the *presentation of self*, meaning the ways in which individuals, in various settings, attempt to create specific impressions in the minds of others. This process is also referred to as *impression management*.

Performances

Goffman referred to the conscious and unconscious efforts of people in conveying information about themselves as *performances*. These would include dress, tone of voice, objects being carried, etc.

➤An Illustration: The Doctor's Office

An interesting analysis of physicians and their offices and conversation with patients is discussed to illustrate the notion that the doctor is in charge.

Nonverbal Communication

Novelist William Sansom's description of a fictional character named Mr. Preedy walking across a beach in Spain is used to illustrate the process of *nonverbal communication*. This concept refers to communication using body movements, gestures, and facial expressions rather than spoken words. Types of smiles, eye contact and hand movements can convey particular meanings and when Aboriginals in Canada confront a court room their reluctance to establish eye contact makes them appear to look guilty to those unfamiliar with Native nonverbal communication norms.

➤Body Language and Deception

A discussion of Paul Ekman's research in the **Applying Sociology** Box (p. 148) reveals examples of nonverbal clues which can be identified to suggest if a person is telling a lie. Words, voice patterns, body language and facial expressions can be analyzed to see if the informal cues are consistent with the formal messages. Several photographs demonstrating emotional expression ask the reader to determine whether these are universal or culturally constrained.

Gender and Personal Performances

Gender is a central element in personal performances.
➤Demeanor

Demeanor refers to general conduct or deportment. It tends to vary by an individual's power. Given that men are more likely than women to be in positions of dominance it is suggested that women must craft their performances more formally and display appropriate deference.

➤Use of Space

Power is a key here as well. Masculinity has been traditionally associated with greater amounts of *personal space*, or the surrounding area over which a person makes some claim to privacy. Also, men tend to intrude on a woman's space more often than women intrude on a man's space.

➢Staring, Smiling, and Touching

While women tend to maintain interactions through sustaining eye contact longer than men do, men tend to stare more. Meanings associated with smiling also seem to vary with gender as do touching patterns, with men tending to touch women more than women touch men. Various rituals are created in which men tend to express their dominance over women.

Idealization

Goffman suggests that we attempt to idealize our intentions when it comes to our performances. The context of a hospital involving physicians making their rounds with patients is used to illustrate how people, in this case doctors, try to convince people they are abiding by ideal cultural standards, when, in fact, less noble reasons are often involved.

Embarrassment and Tact

As hard as we may try to craft perfect performances, slip-ups do occur and may cause embarrassment, or the recognition that we have failed through our performance to convince our audience. Often times audiences will ignore flaws in performances, using tact to enable the performance to continue. This is because embarrassment causes discomfort for all present.

While life is not a scripted play, to some extent, Shakespeare's "All the world's a stage" idea does portray our relationships within social structure.

INTERACTION IN EVERYDAY LIFE: TWO ILLUSTRATIONS

Language: The Gender Issue

Language conveys both obvious and not so obvious meanings. Gender is a trigger for differential definition in at least three ways.

➢Language and Control

One example of this is that males tend to attach female pronouns to valued objects, consistent with the concept of possession. Another illustration is women changing their name when they marry. When they fail to do so, the husband is seen by some as lacking in control.

➢Language and Value

Language conveys different levels of status in many subtle ways. Typically, the masculine terms carry higher status.

➢Language and Attention

The English language seems to almost ignore what is feminine. This is reflected in our pronoun usage and, indeed, in our National Anthem. Table 6-1 (p. 153) provides examples of bias and bias-free words.

Humour: Playing With Reality

Another example of the sociological importance of everyday interaction is in the analysis of humour. The issue of why something is funny is seldom analyzed critically by people.

➤The Foundation of Humour

Humour emerges out of ambiguity and double meanings involving two differing definitions of the situation, a contrasting of the *conventional* and the *unconventional*. The key to a good joke seems to lie in the opposition of realities. The **Sociology of Everyday Life** Box (p. 155) demonstrates the impact of mixed meanings in newspaper headlines.

➤The Dynamics of Humour: "Getting It"

To get the joke the listener must understand the two realities, the conventional and the unconventional. People derive satisfaction and even "insider status" by being able to "piece together" the realities to "get the joke", and even if they don't get it they make out as if they do.

➤The Topics of Humour

While humour is universal, what is viewed as funny is not. Yet, humour is everywhere closely tied to what is controversial. There is however a fine line between what is funny and what is "sick."

➤The Functions of Humour

The universality of humour reflects its function as a safety valve. Sentiments can be expressed that might be dangerous to relationships if taken seriously and explorations of alternative realities can take place.

➤Humour and Conflict

While humour can liberate it can also oppress as jokes about gays and "ethnics" attest. Often, however, minorities will joke about themselves as well as the powerful. Humour offers all some freedom from reality.

KEY CONCEPTS

Define each of the following concepts on separate paper. Check the accuracy of your answers by referring to the text as well as by referring to italicized definitions located throughout the chapter.

achieved status
ascribed status
dramaturgical analysis
ethnomethodology
master status
nonverbal communication
personal space
presentation of self
role
role conflict

role exit
role set
role strain
social construction of reality
social interaction
status
status set
Thomas theorem

STUDY QUESTIONS

✎ **True-False**

1. T F   A status refers to a pattern of expected behaviour for individual members of society.

2. T F   A status set refers to all the roles a person plays during his or her lifetime.

3. T F   Illness can operate as a master status.

4. T F   Statuses vary by culture but roles do not.

5. T F   The process by which people disengage from important social roles is called role exit.

6. T F   Ethnomethodology views society as a broad, abstract system.

7. T F   What triggers an emotion varies from one society to another.

8. T F   Women typically use more space than men do.

9. T F   Men often attach a male pronoun to things that they own.

10. T F   The essence of humour lies in the contrast between two incongruous realities, the conventional and the unconventional.

 **Multiple-Choice**

1. A social position that someone receives involuntarily is called a (n)

   (a) ascribed status
   (b) achieved status
   (c) master status
   (d) status set
   (e) role set

2. Which of the following is not a structural component of social interaction:

   (a) master status
   (b) role
   (c) value
   (d) role set
   (e) ascribed status

3. The behaviour expected of someone who holds a particular status is called a

   (a) master status
   (b) role
   (c) performance
   (d) dramaturgy
   (e) nonverbal communication

4. The incompatibility among the roles corresponding to two or more statuses refers to:

   (a) role conflict
   (b) role strain
   (c) status overload
   (d) status inconsistency
   (e) role set

5. When a mother is experiencing difficulty in disciplining her child because it conflicts with her deeply felt love for that child, she is experiencing

   (a) status diffusion
   (b) role conflict
   (c) role strain
   (d) role exit
   (e) none of the above

6. The Thomas theorem states:

   (a) roles are only as important as the statuses to which they are attached
   (b) statuses are only as important as the roles to which they are attached
   (c) the basis of humanity is built upon the dual existence of creativity and conformity
   (d) common sense is only as good as the social structure within which it is embedded
   (e) situations defined as real are real in their consequences

7. The methodology used by ethnomethodologists to study everyday interaction involves:

   (a) conducting surveys   (d) breaking the rules
   (b) unobtrusive observation   (e) experimentation
   (c) secondary analysis

8. The physicians private office and examination rooms were referred to by Goffman as the

   (a) front region   (c) back region
   (b) formal performance area   (d) informal performance area

9. Paul Ekman suggests scrutinizing four elements of a performance, for clues to deception. Which of the following is *not* one of Ekman's elements?

   (a) words   (d) facial expression
   (b) voice   (e) touch
   (c) body language

10. Which of the following is not an example provided in the text to illustrate how language functions to define the sexes:

    (a) attention   (d) control
    (b) value   (e) none were used
    (c) effectivity

11. What is quickly eroding our traditional economy and is likely to reshape university classes and textual materials?

    (a) "sick" jokes   (d) information technology
    (b) idealization   (e) lack of government spending
    (d) gender dislocation

✎ **Fill-In The Blank**

1. The process by which people act and react in relation to others is termed
   _____.

2. A _____ is a recognized social position that an individual occupies within society.

3. An _____ status is one that someone assumes voluntarily and that reflects ability and effort.

4. The phrase _____ _____ __ _____ refers to the process by which individuals creatively shape reality through social interaction.

5. The _____ theorem states that situations that are defined as real are real in their consequences.

94

6. _____ is the study of the way people make sense of their everyday lives.

7. _____ analysis is defined as the analysis of social interaction in terms of theatrical performance.

8. _____ _____ refers to the area around a person over which some claim to privacy is made.

9. Goffman describes embarrassment simply as ____ ___.

10. Disembodied and unconstrained by time or place, students and workers can engage in productive activity through _____ .

Definition and Short-Answer

1. Suggest how you, in interaction with people who have a physical disability as a master status, might make them feel comfortable.

2. What are the four types of information provided by a "performer" in terms of nonverbal communication which can be used to determine whether or not the person is telling the truth?

3. Refer to Figure 6-1 (p. 141) and using it as a model diagram your own status and role sets. Identify points of role conflict and role strain.

4. What are the three ways in which language functions to define the sexes differently? Provide an illustration for each.

5. What is ethnomethodology? Provide an illustration of how a researcher using this approach would study social interaction.

6. Define the concept idealization.

7. Discuss the issue of gender and personal performances as reviewed in the text. Provide illustrations from your own experience to demonstrate the points being made about the respective patterns of male and female social interaction.

8. What are the basic characteristics of humour? Write a joke and analyse how it manifests the characteristics discussed in the textbook.

9. Refer to Table 6-1 (p. 153) and identify additional gender biased words and their non-biased equivalents.

10. Take the role of disadvantaged people in your society and construct some jokes that you think they would see as humourous with respect to those who are powerful.

Answers to Study Questions

True-False

1. F (p. 138)	6. F (p. 142)
2. F (p. 138)	7. T (p. 146)
3. T (p. 139)	8. F (p. 148)
4. F (p. 139)	9. F (p. 152)
5. T (p. 141)	10. T (p. 153)

Multiple-Choice

1. a (p. 138)	7. d (p. 142)
2. c (pp. 138-141)	8. c (p. 145)
3. b (pp. 139)	9. e (p. 148)
4. a (p. 140)	10. c (pp. 152-153)
5. c (pp. 140-141)	11. d (p. 157)
6. e (p. 142)	

Fill-In

1. social interaction (p. 137)	6. ethnomethodology (p. 142)
2. status (p. 138)	7. dramaturgical (p. 144)
3. achieved (p. 138)	8. personal space (p. 149)
4. social construction of reality (p. 141)	9. losing face (p. 150)
5. Thomas (p. 142)	10. cyberspace (p. 151)

ANALYSIS AND COMMENT

Go back through the chapter and write down in the spaces below key points from each of the following boxes.

SOCIAL DIVERSITY

"Physical Disability as Master Status"
Key Points:

_____

_____

_____

_____

_____

GLOBAL SOCIOLOGY

"Emotions in Global Perspective: Do We All Feel the Same?"
Key Points:

_____

_____
_____
_____
_____

APPLYING SOCIOLOGY

"Hide Those Lyin' Eyes: Can You Do It?"
Key Points:

_____

_____
_____
_____
_____

EXPLORING CYBER-SOCIETY

"Social Interaction: Reaching Across Cyberspace"
Key Points:

_____

_____
_____
_____
_____

SOCIAL DIVERSITY

"Double Take: Real Headlines That Make People Laugh".
Key Points:

_____
_____
_____
_____

CONTROVERSY AND DEBATE

"Is Technology Changing Our Reality?"
Key Points:

_____
_____
_____
_____
_____

SUGGESTED READINGS

Classic Sources

Erving Goffman. 1959. *The Presentation of Self in Everyday Life.* **Garden City, N.Y.: Doubleday Anchor Books.**
Erving Goffman's first book is his best-known work.

Peter L. Berger and Thomas Luckmann. 1967. *The Social Construction of Reality: A Treatise in the Sociology of Knowledge.* **Garden City, NY: Doubleday Anchor Books.**
This book elaborates on the argument that individuals generate meaning through their social interaction.

Contemporary Sources

Adam Phillips. 1994. *On Flirtation.* **Cambridge: Harvard University Press.**
Flirtation allows us to experiment, and shows that life lacks an overall rigid plan.

William Rathje and Cullan Murphy. 1991. *Rubbish: The Archeology of Garbage.* **New York: HarperCollins.**
Researchers at the University of Arizona learned a great deal about people by studying their garbage.

Robert Prus and C.R.D. Sharper. 1977. *Road Hustler: Career Contingencies of Professional Card and Dice Hustlers. Lexington, MA.: Lexington Books.*
The Authors observed and participated in hustling in order to write this rich and detailed description of the life of professional hustlers.

Peter W. Archibald. 1978. *Social Psychology as Political Economy.* **Toronto: McGraw-Hill Ryerson.**
This book examines the political economy in social psychology interactions.

Elliott Leyton. 1986. *Hunting Humans: The Rise of the Modern Multiple Murderer.* **Toronto: McClelland & Stewart.**
This book is a fascinating inside account of the multiple murderer.

Global Sources

Catherine A. Lutz. 1988. *Unnatural Emotions: Everyday Sentiments on a Micronesian Atoll and Their Challenge to Western Theory.* **Chicago: University of Chicago Press.**
This report of research on a Pacific island points up

Michele Fine and Adrian Ash. 1990. *Women With Disabilities*. Philadelphia: Temple University Press.
How do people define others with physical disabilities? How do these individuals construct their own identity? This book provides some insights.

Jack Haas and William Shaffir. 1977. "The Professionalization of Medical Students: Developing Competence and a Cloak of Competence." *Symbolic Interaction*, 1:71-88.
Haas and Shaffir studied medical students at McMaster University in Hamilton. The article above describes some processes through which they become "professional."

how emotions, and the way people think about them, are culturally variable.

Christie Davies. 1990. *Ethnic Humor Around the World: A Comparative Analysis*. Bloomington: Indiana University Press.
Relatively little attention has been paid to the sociological analysis of humour. This book applies a global perspective to the issue.

References

**Daniel Albas and Cheryl Albas. 1993. "Disclaimer Mannerisms of Students: How to Avoid Being Labeled as Cheaters." *Canadian Review of Sociology and Anthropology, Vol 30, No. 4: 451-67.*

CHAPTER 7

I CHAPTER OUTLINE

I. **Social Groups**
    A. Groups, Categories, and Crowds
        1. Category   2. Crowd
    B. Primary and Secondary Groups
    C. Group Leadership
        1. Two Leadership Roles   2. Three Leadership Styles
    D. Group Conformity
        1. Asch's Research   3. Janis' Research
        2. Milgram's Research
    E. Reference Groups
        1. Stouffer's Research   2. Ingroups and Outgroups
    F. Group Size
        1. The Dyad   2. The Triad
    G. Social Diversity
    H. Networks

II. **Formal Organizations**
    A. Types of Formal Organizations
        1. Utilitarian Organizations   3. Coercive Organizations
        2. Normative Organizations
    B. Origins of Bureaucracy
    C. Characteristics of Bureaucracy
    D. Organizational Size
    E. The Informal Side of Bureaucracy
    F. Problems of Bureaucracy
        1. Bureaucratic Alienation   2. Bureaucratic Inefficiency and Ritualism
        3. Bureaucratic Inertia   4. Oligarchy
        5. Parkinson's Law and the Peter Principle
    G. Gender and Race in Organizations
    H. Beyond Bureaucracy: Humanizing Organizations
    I. Self-Managed Work Teams
    J. Organizational Environment
    K. The McDonaldization of Society
        1. McDonaldization: Four Principles   2. Can Rationality Be Irrational
    L. Formal Organizations in Japan

III. **Groups and Organizations in Global Perspective**
IV. **Summary**
V. **Critical Thinking Questions**
VI. **Applications And Exercises**
VII **Sites To See**

II LEARNING OBJECTIVES

- To explain the differences among primary groups, secondary groups, categories and crowds.

- To identify the various types of leaders associated with social groups.

- To compare and contrast the research of Asch, Milgram and Janis on group conformity.

- To explain the importance of reference groups to group dynamics by understanding Stouffer's research on soldiers.

- To distinguish between ingroups and outgroups.

- To explain the relevance of group size to the dynamics of social groups.

- To discover what characteristics predict which people will join particular groups or network with each other.

- To identify the types of formal organizations.

- To identify the primary characteristics of bureaucracy

- To compare and contrast the small group and the formal organization on the basis of their respective activities, hierarchies, norms, criteria for membership, relationships, communications, and focuses.

- To identify the outcomes of the informal side of bureaucracy.

- To explain the limitations of bureaucracy.

- To understand the effects of power and opportunity on employees and the effects of "humanizing" bureaucracy.

- To compare and contrast formal organizations in the U.S. and Japan and to understand formal organizations in a more global perspective.

- To understand what is meant by the McDonaldization of society.

III CHAPTER REVIEW

The introduction to this chapter illustrates how the principles of "fast food" preparation, started by McDonalds, are linked to the changing nature of social groups and formal organizational structures of society. This chapter provides insight into the extent to which social groups, from families to large-scale bureaucratic structures, have meaning in our lives.

SOCIAL GROUPS

A *social group* is defined as two or more people who identify and interact with one another. While we each have our own individuality, the "we" feeling that can only be achieved in social groups is central to our existence as human beings.

Groups, Categories and Crowds

➤ Category

Not all collections of individuals are social groups. People who share a status in common are defined as a *category*, but the vast majority never interact with one another.

➤Crowd

A crowd is a temporary cluster of individuals who may or may not interact. Ordinarily they are too transitory to qualify as a social group.

Primary and Secondary Groups

Charles Horton Cooley studied the extent to which people have personal concern for each other in social interaction settings. He distinguished between primary and secondary groups. *Primary groups* are defined as a typically small social group in which relationships are both personal and enduring. They are characterized as ends in and of themselves, they are critical in the socialization process, and members are considered unique and not interchangeable.

Secondary groups are defined as large and impersonal social groups usually based on a specific interest or activity. They are typically short-term with narrowly-defined relationships and are seen as a means to an end. The distinction in real life is not always as clear as these definitions might suggest. Table 7-1 (p. 164) provides a summary of the key differences between primary and secondary groups.

Group Leadership

Leadership plays a critical role in group dynamics. Secondary groups are more likely to identify formal leaders.

➤Two Leadership Roles

Research reveals that there are usually two types of leaders in social groups. *Instrumental leadership* refers to group leadership that emphasizes the completion of tasks. *Expressive leadership* emphasizes collective well-being. This differentiation is also linked to gender, with men typically taking the instrumental role and women taking the expressive role in leadership positions especially in the family.

➤Three Leadership Styles

Three decision-making styles are identified. One is ***authoritarian*** leadership which focuses on instrumental concerns. This type of leader makes decisions on his/her own, demanding strict compliance from subordinates. Another type is the ***democratic*** leader who takes a more expressive approach, seeking to include all members in the decision-making process. A third type is labelled ***laissez-faire***. Leaders using this approach tend to downplay their power, allowing the group to function on its own.

Group Conformity

Group conformity is a dimension of group dynamics where members seek the satisfaction of being like other members. The Reena Virk murder is used to illustrate that members of groups will exhibit extreme violence in order to fit in with group expectations. Three research projects illustrate the importance of group conformity to the sociological understanding of group processes.

➤Asch's Research

Solomon Asch conducted an experiment in which "naive" subjects were asked to answer questions concerning the length of lines. Accomplices of the experimenter comprised the rest of the group, who purposely gave incorrect answers. Often the naive subject would give a "wrong" answer in order to conform. Figure 7-1 (p. 165) illustrates an example of the cards used in this experiment. The experiment found that 1/3 of the subjects would compromise their judgement to agree with the group.

➤Milgram's Research

Stanley Milgram conducted an experiment which naive subjects believed was about learning and memory. The naive subject played the role of a "teacher" and the accomplice played the role of a "learner." If learners failed to correctly remember word pairs given by the teacher, the teacher was instructed by Milgram (a legitimate authority figure) to electrically shock the learner. His research suggests that people comply with almost blind obedience to authority figures. Further, if encouraged by others in a group situation, subjects were likely to administer even higher voltage shocks, indicating that even "ordinary" individuals can elicit conformity behaviour.

➤Janis' Research

Irving Janis researched the actions of high government officials by examining historical documents. He theorized that even experts in groups can be led to engage in behaviour that violates common sense. Janis discusses three factors which affect decision-making processes and create ***groupthink***, an adoption of a narrow consensus view caused by group conformity. The decision of the "yes" side to use slick advertising to sell the Charlottetown Accord and the lack of acceptance that Québec might vote to secede in the 1995 referendum are recent Canadian

examples of "groupthink".

Reference Groups

The term *reference group* signifies a social group that serves as a point of reference for people making evaluations and decisions. These groups can be primary or secondary. They are a major factor involved in anticipatory socialization processes.

➤Stouffer's Research

Stouffer conducted research on the morale and attitudes of soldiers in World War II in order to investigate the dynamics of reference groups. Stouffer found what appeared to be a paradox: soldiers in branches with higher promotion rates were more pessimistic about their own chances of being promoted than soldiers in branches with lower rates of promotion. This is explained however by the identification of the groups against which the soldiers measured their progress. In relative terms, those soldiers in branches with higher rates felt deprived.

➤Ingroups and Outgroups

Two other kinds of groups provide us with standards against which we evaluate ourselves. An *ingroup* is an esteemed social group commanding a member's loyalty. This group exists in relation to *outgroups*, or social groups toward which one feels competition or opposition. This dichotomy allows us to sharpen boundaries between groups and to highlight their distinctive qualities. The operation of the group dynamics created by these distinctions affects broader social patterns in society, such as social inequality between whites and people of colour.

Group Size

Group size significantly influences how members socially interact. As a group's membership is added to arithmetically, the number of possible relationships increases in a geometric progression. Figure 7-2 (p. 168) provides an illustration.

➤The Dyad

The dyad has two members and is characterized by intensity and instability. Marriages in Canada are a good example.

➤The Triad

The triad is composed of three members and often has more stability although the "third wheel" phenomenon is always a possibility.

As groups grow larger they become more stable because the loss of a member does not threaten the group. Larger groups, however, have less emotional intensity and greater formality.

Social Diversity

This section focuses on the research by Peter Blau who identifies four ways in which the structure of social groups regulates intergroup association. The four factors include group size, heterogeneity of group members, social parity within the group, and physical space.

Networks

The term *network* refers to a web of social ties that links people who identify and interact little with one another. Little sense of membership is felt by individuals in the network and only occasionally do they come into contact. Some can be operating at a primary level, but most are secondary in nature. Demographic characteristics, such as age, education, and residence patterns influence the likelihood of a person's involvement in networks. New information technology has generated a global network of immense size. **Global Map** 7-1 (p. 172) shows the extent of the internet and the **Exploring Cyber Society** Box (p. 173) examines the origins and possible future of Cyberspace which offers immense networking capabilities unencumbered by formal usage rules. There is even some evidence, as suggested in the **Applying Sociology** Box (p. 171), that meaningful relationships and a sense of community can be established in cyberspace.

FORMAL ORGANIZATIONS

Today our lives seem focussed around *formal organizations*, large, secondary groups that are organized to achieve their goals efficiently.

Types of Formal Organizations

Amitai Etzioni uses the variable of how members relate to the organization as a criterion for distinguishing three types of formal organizations.

➤**Utilitarian Organizations**

Utilitarian organizations provide material benefits for members in exchange for labour. Most people must join at least one organization in order to "make a living."

➤**Normative Organizations**

People join *normative organizations* to pursue some goal they consider morally worthwhile. Voluntary associations like the PTA and the Lions Club would be examples. Traditionally, because women had been excluded from the labour force they have had higher participation rates in such organizations than men. Figure 7-3 (p. 174) indicates that Canadians have high participation rates.

➤**Coercive Organizations**

Coercive organizations serve as a form of punishment (prisons) or treatment (mental hospitals). People are separated from the rest of society within distinct physical boundaries and are labelled as inmates or patients.

Origins of Bureaucracy

Formal organizations date back thousands of years. The type of formal organization called **bureaucracy** however, emerged as a result of changes occurring in societies in Europe and North America during the industrial revolution.

Characteristics of Bureaucracies

A bureaucracy is an organizational model rationally designed to perform complex tasks efficiently. Our telephone system is an example of the scope and capacity of bureaucratic organizations.

Max Weber identified six basic characteristics or elements of the ideal bureaucracy. These include: specialization, hierarchy of offices, rules and regulations, technical competence, impersonality, and formal, written communications.

In contrast to small groups, like families, which have a personal character, the organizational model of bureaucracy limits unpredictability and promotes efficiency. Table 7-2 (p. 175) differentiates between the qualities of bureaucracies and small groups.

Organizational Size

Large formal organizations typically have higher financial and promotion awards while smaller organizations provide more autonomy.

The Informal Side of Bureaucracy

While in principle bureaucracy has a highly formal structure, in reality not all behaviour in bureaucracies fits precisely the organizational rules. While it is the position or office which is supposed to carry the power, the personalities of the occupants are also important factors. In addition employees often establish informal networks, aided by the use of e-mail.

Problems of Bureaucracy

Although bureaucratic structures are widespread in today's society there are concerns about dehumanization, alienation and threats to democracy and personal freedom. The **Controversy and Debate** box (pp. 186-187) outlines the concerns for privacy as large organizations make use of electronic files to sell products or perhaps "snoop" on people's private lives.

➤Bureaucratic Alienation

The efficiency goals of the organization reduce human beings to small pieces of a large machine, leaving both worker and client feeling alienated.

➤Bureaucratic Inefficiency and Ritualism

The image of red tape is closely tied to bureaucracies. *Bureaucratic ritualism* signifies a preoccupation with rules and regulations as ends in themselves rather than as means to organizational goals. This process tends to reduce performance and stifle creativity of members.

➤Bureaucratic Inertia

Bureaucracies seem to have lives of their own. *Bureaucratic inertia* refers to the tendency of bureaucratic organizations to persist over time whether there is any reason for their existence beyond the jobs of its members.

➤Oligarchy

Robert Michels observed the fact that *oligarchy*, or the rule of the many by the few, was a typical outgrowth of bureaucracy. He suggested that individuals in high levels within a bureaucratic hierarchy tend to accumulate power and use it to promote their own objectives thereby endangering democratic principles. Canada Map 7-1 (p. 178) illustrates the size of government bureaucracy in Canada.

➤Parkinson's Law and the Peter Principle

The first suggests that no matter how little time a job takes, it will take all the time available while the second suggests that people will eventually get promoted to a position for which they are not competent. Large scale organizations are rife with examples.

Gender and Race in Organizations

Rosabeth Moss Kanter suggests that the ascribed statuses of gender and race predict the power structure of large organizations. Figure 7-4 (p. 180) shows that white males are over-represented.

Organizations with little opportunity for minority advancement create morale and loyalty problems while those with widespread opportunity produce employees with higher self esteem and stronger commitment to the organization. Other research finds that female managers are more open and communicative, leading to more democratic and flexible workplaces.

Beyond Bureaucracy: Humanizing Organizations

Humanizing organizations means fostering an organizational environment that recognizes and encourages the contributions of everyone. This seems to produce happier employees and better profits. Humanized organizational environments have certain basic characteristics which fall into three broad categories. These include: social inclusiveness, a sharing of responsibilities, and expanding opportunities for advancement.

Not all research supports the conclusion that diversity is automatically useful to organizational efficiency. Work groups require some similarity in outlook to operate well.

Self-Managed Work Teams

Recently bureaucratic organizations have become more decentralized, less top down in terms of decisions. Worker involvement in autonomous teams seems to lead to greater productivity and less of the alienation referred to earlier.

Organizational Environment

Organizational environment refers to a range of factors outside an organization that affect its operation. These include technology, politics, the economy, demographics, and other organizations.

The McDonaldization of Society

McDonalds is becoming pervasive with over 20,000 restaurants worldwide and its organizational principles are beginning to dominate our society.

➤**McDonaldization: Four Principles**

What is McDonald's? It is fast therefore *efficient.* It is consistent therefore it has *calculability.* It is uniform everywhere in the world, therefore it has *predictability* and it is rigidly controlled through *automation.* Automatic teller machines, automatic hatcheries and laser scanners in grocery stores are the latest examples of these principles applied elsewhere.

➤**Can Rationality Be Irrational?**

Does such rationality lead to dehumanization and loss of creativity and ultimately to a system that controls people rather than the reverse?

Formal Organizations in Japan

Japan's economic success during the past few decades has raised great interest among North Americans. Their formal organizations reflect their culture's collective identity and social solidarity. Americans and Canadians, on the other hand, have stressed individuality. Japan's approach to constructing organizations makes bureaucracies remarkably personal. Five distinctions between Japanese and Western formal organizations are highlighted by William Ouchi; these include: hiring and advancement, lifetime security, holistic involvement, broad-based training, and collective decision-making. The **Global Sociology** box (pp. 184-185) asks whether the Japanese model will work in North America.

GROUPS AND ORGANIZATIONS IN GLOBAL PERSPECTIVE

In recent years there has been a shift in focus from organizations themselves to organizational environments in which they operate. The Japanese success with more humanized and personal organizational environments has illustrated that organizations need not be impersonal. Collective identity and responsibility seem to be compatible with high organizational productivity. Perhaps also such organizational changes will increase social cohesion in the larger society.

KEY CONCEPTS

Define each of the following concepts on a separate paper. Check the accuracy of your answers by referring to the key concepts section at the end of the chapter in the text as well as by referring to italicized definitions located throughout the chapter.

Bureaucracy

Bureaucratic inertia

Bureaucratic ritualism

Category

Coercive organization

Crowd

Dyad

Expressive leadership

Formal organizations

Groupthink

Humanizing organizations

Ingroup

Instrumental leadership

network

normative organization

oligarchy

organizational environment

outgroup

Parkinson's law

Peter principle

primary group

reference group

secondary group

social group

triad

utilitarian organization

STUDY QUESTIONS
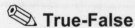 **True-False**

1. T F   While people who know each other well such as family members or neighbours are often identifiable as groups a crowd can never be considered a group.

2. T F   Instrumental leadership tends to focus upon the completion of tasks.

3. T F   Janis called the tendency of group members to conform by adopting a narrow view of some issue, "dumbing down."

4. T F   Stouffer's research on soldier's attitudes toward their own promotions during World War II demonstrates the significance of reference groups in making judgments about ourselves.

5. T F   According to research by Georg Simmel, larger groups tend to be more stable than small groups, such as dyads.

6. T F   The more internally heterogeneous a group is, the more likely its members are to interact with members of other groups.

7. T F   Most people join normative organizations for material rewards.

8. T F   The majority of the world's people now have access to the Internet.

9. T F   Studies of corporations document that the qualities and quirks of individuals have a tremendous impact on organizational outcomes.

10. T F   The tedious preoccupation with organizational routines and procedures is called "red tape."

11. T F   Parkinson's Law and the Peter Principle relate to processes of bureaucratic waste and incompetency.

12. T F   Helgesen finds that women are more flexible leaders who typically allow subordinates greater autonomy.

13. T F   McDonaldization appears to be on the decline in North America.

14. T F   A rigidly bureaucratic form of organization tends to unravel the social fabric.

✎ Multiple-Choice

1. A social group characterized by long-term personal relationships usually involving many activities is a _____.

    (a) primary group   (d) aggregate
    (b) secondary group   (e) normative organization
    (c) category

2. Which of the following is not true of primary groups:

   (a) they provide security for their members
   (b) they are focussed around specific activities
   (c) they are valued in and of themselves
   (d) they are viewed as ends in themselves

3. Which of the following theorists differentiated between primary and secondary groups:

   (a) Max Weber   (d) Charles Horton Cooley
   (b) Amitai Etzioni   (e) George Herbert Mead
   (c) Emile Durkheim

4. The type of leadership which allows the group to function more or less on its own is called

   (a) authoritarian   (d) laisez-faire
   (b) democratic   (e) normative
   (c) utilitarian

5. What researcher found that approximately 1/3 of subjects will conform and answer incorrectly a perceptually obvious question?

   (a) Solomon Asch   (d) Irving Janis
   (b) Charles Horton Cooley   (e) Rosabeth Moss Kanter
   (c) Stanley Milgram

6. A group toward which one feels competition or opposition is called a(n)

   (a) reference group   (d) secondary group
   (b) outgroup   (e) none of the above
   (c) ingroup

7. A "fuzzy" group which brings people into occasional contact but without a sense of belonging is called a(n):

   (a) triad   (d) cybergroup
   (b) homogeneous group   (e) coercive group
   (c) network

8. The structure of our society now turns on the operation of vast corporations and other bureaucracies that sociologists describe as _____.

    (a) rigid organizations   (d) informal organizations
    (b) conventional organizations   (e) formal organizations
    (c) customary organizations

9. Which of the following is *not* typical of a bureaucratic organization?

    (a) membership is based upon technical competence   (d) the focus is task oriented
    (b) relationships are typically primary in nature   (e) the hierarchy is clearly defined
    (c) communications are formal

10. Bureaucratic ritualism is:

    (a) the process of promoting people to their level of incompetence
    (b) the tendency of bureaucratic organizations to persist over time
    (c) the rule of the many by the few
    (d) a preoccupation with rules and regulations as ends in themselves rather than as means toward organizational goals

11. Robert Michels examination of bureaucratic tendency to oligarchy has found that:

    (a) technical competence cannot be maintained
    (b) hierarchical structure discourages democracy
    (c) bureaucrats get caught up in rule-making
    (d) specialization gives way to generalist orientations

12. As bureaucracies change from rigid hierarchical structures in order to improve productivity they are adopting

    (a) higher remuneration patterns for all   (c) self-managed work teams
    (b) a concealed vertical hierarchy   (d) ritualistic goals

13. Formal organizations in Japan

    (a) pay all age cohorts approximately the same   (d) a and b above
    (b) tend to offer life security   (e) b and c above
    (c) try to keep home and work environments separate

14. The tremendous number of files and data bases maintained in an information based society creates a threat to
    (a) the credit card industry   (c) large accumulations of wealth
    (b) privacy   (d) nepotism

✎ Fill-In The Blank

1. A _____ is defined as two or more people who identify and interact with one another.

2. Political organizations are examples of _____ groups.

3. _____ leadership makes a point of including everyone in the decision-making process.

4. _____ research shows that people will follow the directions of ordinary people as well as authority figures.

5. Irving Janis studied the group process he called _____ that reduces a group's capacity for critical reflection.

6. A _____ is a more stable social group than a dyad.

7. _____ is the country with the highest level of per capita Internet use.

8. Bureaucratic communication is typically formal and _____.

9. _____ is the term used to describe the tendency for bureaucratic organizations to perpetuate themselves.

10. The cultural emphasis on individual achievement in our society finds its parallel in Japanese _____.

Definition and Short-Answer

1. Differentiate between the qualities of bureaucracies and small groups. In what ways are they similar?

2. Critically analyze the research on group conformity.

3. What are the three factors in decision-making processes in groups that lead to "groupthink?"

4. What are the major limitations of bureaucracy? Provide an example for each.

5. In what ways do bureaucratic organizations in Japan differ from those in North America? What are the consequences of these differences?

6. Provide two examples of a normative organization.

7. What impact do gender and race have on formal organizational structure?

8. If bureaucracies are "humanized" what will be the result for productivity?

9. What impact has McDonaldization had on Canadian society?

10. Review Peter Blau's research concerning how the structure of social groups regulates intergroup association.

11. How do you think the Internet will impact upon organizational structure?

12. What are factors relating to the "organizational environment?" Provide an example for each.

Answers to Study Questions

True-False

1. F (p. 162)	8. F (p. 172)
2. T (p. 164)	9. T (p. 175)
3. F (p. 166)	10. T (p. 177)
4. T (p. 167)	11. T (p. 179)
5. T (p. 168)	12. T (p. 180)
6. T (p. 169)	13. F (p. 182)
7. F (p. 171)	14. T (p. 187)

Multiple-Choice

1. a (p. 162)	8. e (p. 170)
2. b (pp. 162-163)	9. b (pp. 174-175)
3. d (p. 162)	10. d (p. 177)
4. d (p. 164)	11. b (p. 177)
5. a (p. 165)	12. c (p. 181)
6. b (p. 167)	13. d (pp. 184-185)
7. c (p. 169)	14. b (P. 186)

Fill-In

1. social group (p. 161)	6. triad (p. 168)
2. secondary (p. 163)	7. Finland (p. 173)
3. democratic (p. 164)	8. written (p. 175)
4. Stanley Milgrams' (p. 166)	9. bureaucratic inertia (p. 177)
5. groupthink (p. 166)	10. groupism (p. 185)

ANALYSIS AND COMMENT

Go back through the chapter and write down in the spaces below key points from each of the following boxes.

APPLYING SOCIOLOGY

"Virtual Community: Reaching Out Through Cyberspace."
Key Points:

_____

_____

_____

_____

_____

CONTROVERSY AND DEBATE

"Are Large Organizations a Threat to Personal Privacy?"
Key Points:

_____

_____

_____

_____

_____

EXPLORING CYBER-SOCIETY

"The Internet: Welcome to Cyberspace."
Key Points:

_____

_____

_____

_____

GLOBAL SOCIOLOGY

"The Japanese Model: Will it Work in North America?"
Key Points:

_____

_____

_____

_____

_____

SUGGESTED READINGS

Contemporary Sources

Richard H. Hall. 1991. *Organizations: Structures, Processes, and Outcomes.* **Englewood Cliffs, N.J.: Prentice Hall.**
Cecilia L. Ridgeway. 1983. *The Dynamics of Small Groups.* **New York: St. Martin's Press.**
These two books delve into many of the issues addressed in this chapter.

Arthur G. Miller. 1986. *The Obedience Experiments: A Case Study of Controversy in Social Science.* **New York: Praeger.**
Controversy has dogged the obedience experiments of Stanley Milgram for more than thirty years. This book reviews Milgram's work and related studies, and tackles the broad ethical questions such research raises.
This brief book spells out strategies for effectively organizing people into task groups.

Michael Herzfeld. 1991. *The Social Production of Indifference: Exploring the Roots of Western Bureaucracy.* **New York: Berg.**
James Q. Wilson. 1989. *Bureaucracy: What Government Agencies Do and Why They Do It.* **New York: Basic Books.**
The first of these books challenges the conventional belief that traditional social patterns run counter to bureaucracy, revealing how both are shaped by the same cultural forces. The second, by a renowned organizational researcher, brings together essays showing that government bureaucracies are far more varied than Weber's model suggests.

Rosabeth Moss Kanter. 1989. *When Giants Learn*

Irving L. Janis. 1989. *Crucial Decisions: Leadership in Policymaking and Crisis Management.* **New York: The Free Press.**
This book, by the originator of the term "groupthink," examines organizational leadership.

Sally Helgesen. 1990. *The Female Advantage: Women's Ways of Leadership.* **New York: Doubleday.**
This intriguing book argues that women in managerial positions typically adopt a more humanized leadership style that works to the advantage of corporations.

Carl E. Larson and Frank M. J. LaFasto. 1989. *Teamwork: What Must Go Right/What Can Go Wrong.* **Newbury Park, CA: Sage.**

to Dance; Mastering the Challenges of Strategy, Management, and Careers in the 1990s. **New York: Simon and Schuster.**
Alvin Toffler. 1985. *The Adaptive Corporation.* **New York: McGraw-Hill.**
These two books exemplify the growing trend of applying sociological analysis to problems of corporate management. The first, by one of the best-known sociologists in the field of formal organizations, examines the future of corporate organization. The second, by a noted futurist, argues that simply "doing more of the same" in a changing society will surely lead to declining business.

Nicole Woolsey Biggart. 1989. *Charismatic Capitalism: Direct Selling Organizations in America.* **Chicago: The University of Chicago Press.**

Challenging the notion that formal organizations are based on cool-headed, rational behaviour, some organizations deliberately foster emotional intensity among their members. This study highlights companies such as Mary Kay cosmetics and Amway products that have used emotional, motivational techniques successfully.

Canadian Sources

Barry Wellman. 1979. "The Community Question: the Intimate Networks of East Yorkers." *American Journal of Sociology* **Vol. 84, No. 5: 1201-31.**
This article deals with the"intimate networks" in a Toronto borough, revealing that these close ties extend throughout the metropolitan area and beyond.

Isabel Bassett. 1985. *The Bassett Report: Career Success and Canadian Women.* **Toronto: Collins.**

This analysis of factors affecting the careers of Canadian women is based on in-depth interviews and a Goldfarb poll commissioned by Bassett (a television journalist).

Diane Francis. 1986. *Controlling Interest: Who Owns Canada?* **Toronto: McMillan.** According to Diane Francis, corporate concentration is particularly alarming in Canada. Here she tells the story of the small number of families and corporations that effectively run our country.

John Anderson and M. Gunderson. 1982. *Union Management Relations in Canada.* **Don Mills, ON: Addison-Wesley.**
This collection of articles dealing with Canadian industrial relations includes Canada-U.S.-Europe comparisons.

Dianne Collier. 1994. *Hurry Up and Wait: An Inside Look at Life as a Canadian Military Wife.* **Carp, ON: Creative Bound.**
Canada's military complex very effectively controls the lives of its military men, but it also makes tremendous demands upon military wives and children. This very readable book tells their story.

Global Sources

Boye De Mente. 1987. *Japanese Etiquette and Ethics in Business.* **5th ed. Lincolnwod, IL: NTC Business Books.**
This is one of the better books contrasting formal organizations in the United States with those in Japan.

CHAPTER 8

Sexuality

1. The Social Construction of Sexuality
2. Global Comparisons

    C. Social Conflict Analysis
1. Sexuality: Reflecting Social Inequality
2. Sexuality: Creating Social Inequality
3. Queer Theory

VI.   **Summary**
VII.   **Critical Thinking Questions**
VIII.   **Applications And Exercises**
IX.   **Sites To See**

II LEARNING OBJECTIVES

- To gain a sociological understanding of human sexuality focusing on both biological and cultural factors.

- To become more aware of the sexual attitudes found in North America.

- To be able to describe both the sexual revolution and sexual counter-revolution that occurred during the last half century in North America.

- To be able to discuss human sexuality as it is experienced across different stages of the human life course.

- To be able to discuss issues relating to the biological and social causes of sexual orientation.

- To be able to describe the demographics of sexual orientation in our society, including the research methods used to obtain such information about our population.

- To gain a sociological perspective on several sexual controversies, including teen pregnancy, pornography, prostitution and sexual violence and abuse.

- To be able to discuss issues relating to human sexuality from the viewpoints offered by structural-functional, symbolic-interactionist, and social-conflict analyses.

III CHAPTER REVIEW

UNDERSTANDING SEXUALITY

Sexuality is a common theme in our society, sometimes dominating everyday conversations and certainly producing huge profits for the sex industry. To some extent, however, sex has been a cultural taboo historically, thereby producing anxiety and a distinct lack of scientific understanding. That changed in the middle of the twentieth century, so much so that the transsexual relationship discussed in the opening scenario is readily accepted in the Canadian military.

Sex—A Biological Issue

Sex refers to the biological distinction between females and males. It is the means by which humans reproduce, resulting in the birth of 105 males for every 100 females.

Sex and the Body

At birth, males and females are distinguished by *primary sex characteristics*, the genitals used for reproduction. At puberty additional sex differentiation produces *secondary sex characteristics*, bodily differences, other than genitals, which distinguish males and females.

➤Hermaphrodites

Occasionally hormone imbalances before birth produce a *hermaphrodite*, a human being with some combination of male and female genitalia.

➤Transsexuals

These are people who feel they are one sex when biologically they are the other. Some have surgery to alter their genitals since they feel "trapped" in the wrong body. The **Social Diversity** Box (p. 193) deals with a similar issue. A twin boy had his penis severed during circumcision and the decision was made to alter him surgically and raise him as a girl. He was given a female *gender identity* through socialization but he was never satisfied and ultimately received a gender reassignment and now lies as a married man.

Sex: A Cultural Issue

While sexuality has a biological foundation, its expression is widely variant.

➤Cultural Variation

Norms of types of intercourse and with whom one can have sex varies by culture.

The Incest Taboo

One cultural universal with respect to sex is the *incest taboo*, a norm forbidding sexual relations or marriage between certain relatives. The relatives are not the same in all societies but the taboo operates everywhere to protect the social organization of the family.

SEXUAL ATTITUDES

North American attitudes about sexuality have been inconsistent, a mixture of European rigidity that suggested sex existed inside marriage for reproductive purposes and a commitment to individuality which suggested people should be able to do what they wish, as long as others are not harmed. The balance in this mixture shifted over time.

The Sexual Revolution

Migration to towns and cities helped to create the "Roaring Twenties" with its relaxed sexual standards. Kinsey's studies of sexuality in the United States opened up the topic to scientific analysis and the findings suggested people were less conventional than previously thought. In the 1960s youth culture dominated as the boomers came of age. Figure 8-1 (p. 198) shows how much change took place among female boomers compared to previous generations with respect to premarital partners. The pill gave women the opportunity to engage in sex without elaborate preparation.

The Sexual Counterrevolution

Not everyone thought the sexual revolution was productive for society. A counterrevolution set in, calling for a return to family values. The movement to sexual responsibility meant that some were abstaining from sex before marriage or limiting their sexual partners. The fear of STDs, especially AIDS was probably another precipitating factor.

Premarital Sex

The sexual revolution and counterrevolution have resulted in more favourable attitudes about premarital sexuality in Canadians than Americans as indicated in Table 8-1 (p. 198) Women have certainly increased their participation in premarital sexuality (almost as high as the male rates), but they are much more likely than men to adhere to a "love"standard rather than a "fun"standard than are men.

Sex Among Adults

Canadians are active sexually but age is a determining factor. Sexual activity peaks in the 30s and declines thereafter.

Extramarital Sex

Eight-five to ninety percent of Americans and Canadians say extramarital sexuality is wrong but behavioural studies indicate 25% of men and 10% of women have engaged in extramarital sexuality.

SEXUAL ORIENTATION

Sexual orientation refers to an individuals preference in terms of sexual partners: same sex, other sex, either sex, neither sex. Although the norm is *heterosexuality* (other), *homosexuality* (same sex) is not uncommon, and *bisexuality* (either sex) and *asexuality* (neither sex) are also known. In some societies, homosexual relations have not only been tolerated, but preferred.

What Gives Us A Sexual Orientation?

➤**Sexual Orientation: A Product of Society.**

There are some historical and cultural examples which suggest that homosexuality is a social construction.

➤**Sexual Orientation: A Product of Biology**

Some genetic research and brain structure research suggests a biological origin to sexual orientation.

If the biological explanation is correct, gay and lesbian people should expect legal protection from discrimination like other minorities.

How Many Gay People?

Given that sexuality doesn't always fit into neat categories and that not all individuals are willing to reveal their sexual orientation, it is difficult to estimate the extent of homosexuality. At one time a one in ten estimate was made but recent surveys indicate that the numbers of people who consider themselves exclusively homosexual is much less than that. What is problematic is the number of people who may be shifting between behaviours and are difficult to classify as having a particular sexual orientation.

The Gay Rights Movement

Homophobia, the dread of close personal interaction with people thought to be gay, lesbian, or bisexual is certainly on the decline in Canada and the United States, to a large extent because of the success of the gay rights movement. In 1969 Canada removed homosexual activity that took place in private between consenting adults from the Criminal Code, benefits have been extended to partners in same-sex relationships and Toronto's Metropolitan Community Church in the year 2001 has successfully married homosexuals by publishing the banns for three Sundays prior to marriage.

SEXUAL CONTROVERSIES

Teen Pregnancy

Sexuality without social maturity often leads to pregnancy. These mothers are at high risk of not finishing school which often leads to them and their children living in poverty.

Pornography

In Canada the issue of pornography is linked to the illegality of *obscenity*, which involves undue exploitation of sex and violation of community standards. Traditionally pornography was judged on moral grounds but increasingly it is seen as a *power issue* because women are depicted as sexual objects.

Canada attempts to balance free expression with objectionable sexual materials.

Prostitution

Prostitution is the selling of sexual services. It is illegal in most American states but not in Canada where it is soliciting or communicating for the purpose of prostitution in a public place. In Thailand, (**Global Sociology** Box p. 204) 10 percent of the female population is in the sex industry and the abuse of girls as young as twelve or thirteen is rampant.

➤**Types of Prostitution.**
   Call girls control their own dates but brothel workers or street walkers are under the control of madams or pimps.

➤**A Victimless Crime.**
   Many consider prostitution a victimless crime but many women become trapped and victimized.

Sexual Violence And Abuse

➤**Rape.**
   In Canada, rape is called sexual assault and the reported cases are only a fraction of the total.

➤**Date Rape.**
   Most rapes are not committed by strangers but by people who know the victim. The **Applying Sociology** Box (pp. 206-207) describes the mythology and the reality of rape in North America.

THEORETICAL ANALYSIS OF SEXUALITY

Structural Functional Analysis

This analysis highlights the contribution any social pattern makes to the overall operation of the society.

➤**The Need to Regulate Sexuality**
   The need to regulate reproduction for the maintenance of the family unit is clear. Free sexual expression and "illegimate" reproduction would not provide appropriate protection for children.

➤**Latent Functions: The Case of Prostitution**
   While prostitution spreads disease and exploits women, it does serve to meet the sexual needs of some who might not otherwise be successful.

Symbolic-Interaction Analysis

➤The Social Construction of Sexuality

While structural functional approaches to understanding sexuality focus on continuity rather than change, symbolic-interactionists demonstrate how social construction leads to changes in definition .

Prior to the separation of sex and reproduction, a pre-marital virginity norm was in place. Today, three-quarters of university students are sexually experienced.

➤Global Comparisons

A normative behaviour in Melanesia such as sexual experimentation in children, would be frowned upon in Canada.

Social-Conflict Analysis

Sexuality can both reflect and contribute to patterns of inequality.

➤Sexuality: Reflecting Social Inequality.

If women had equal economic opportunities to men, how many would be involved in prostitution? Prostitution is a transaction involving two people, but the prostitute is arrested more often than the "john".

➤Sexuality: Creating Social Inequality.

To some extent pornography leads to women being perceived as sexual objects and playthings of men.

➤Queer Theory.

This theory callenges an allegedly heterosexual bias in sociology and asserts that our society is characterized by *heterosexism*, a view stigmatizing anyone who is not heterosexual as queer.

Structural-functionalism tends to ignore change, symbolic-interaction over-emphasizes differences and change, and social conflict analysis underestimates the reduction in inequality that has occurred and forgets that sexuality is not a power issue for everybody.

The **Controversy and Debate** Box (p. 210) discusses the most divisive sexuality issue, *abortion*, the deliberate termination of a pregnancy. The passion of the "pro-choice" and "pro-life" arguments is described.

KEY CONCEPTS

Define each of the following concepts on separate paper. Check the accuracy of your answers by referring to the key concepts in the text as well as by referring to italicized definitions located throughout the chapter.

abortion
asexuality
bisexuality
gender identity
hermaphrodite
heterosexuality
heterosexism
homophobia
homosexuality

incest taboo
pornography
primary sex characteristics
prostitution
queer theory
secondary sex characteristics
sex
sexual orientation
transsexuals

STUDY QUESTIONS

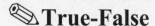 ## True-False

1. T F   Social scientists long considered sex off limits for research. It was not until the middle of the twentieth century that researchers turned attention to this pervasive dimension of social life.

2. T F   Primary sex characteristics are those that develop during puberty.

3. T F   The traits that females and males, guided by their culture, incorporate into their personalities, are called gender identity.

4. T F   Hermaphrodites are people who feel they are one sex even though biologically they are of the other.

5. T F   Almost any sexual practice shows considerable variation from one society to another.

6. T F   Every known culture has some form of *incest taboo*—it is a cultural universal.

7. T F   According to the authors the sexual counterrevolution occurred in our society during the 1960s.

8. T F   Among Canadian university students, males are more likely than females to endorse the recreational aspect of premarital sex.

9. T F   Sexual orientation refers to the biological distinction of being female or male.

10. T F   Pornography refers to sexually explicit material that causes sexual arousal.

11. T F   Among the types of prostitutes, call girls have the lowest status.

12. T F   A common myth is that most victims of rapes are raped by strangers.

13. T F   According to survey research, over forty percent of adults in the U.S. and Canada think that a woman should be able to obtain a legal abortion for any reason if she wants to.

14. T F   The gay rights movement in Canada has had no success in advancing social acceptance for gay people.

✎ Multiple-Choice

1. _____refers to the biological distinction between females and males.
   (a) gender
   (b) sex
   (c) sexual orientation
   (d) human sexuality
   (e) sex characteristics

2. _____are people who feel they are one sex even though biologically they are of the other sex.

   (a) Hermaphrodites
   (b) Transvestites
   (c) Homophobics
   (d) Transsexuals

3. During the last century, people witnessed profound changes in sexual attitudes and practices. The first indications of this change occurred in the

   (a) 1920s
   (b) 1940s
   (c) 1960s
   (d) 1970s
   (e) 1980s

4. 39% of Canadians in 1975 felt that premarital sex was "not wrong at all." By 1995 the figure was

   (a) 26%
   (b) 39%
   (c) 47%
   (d) 57%
   (e) 83%

5. _____refers to a person's preference in terms of sexual partner: same sex, other sex, either sex, neither sex.

   (a) sexual orientation
   (b) sex
   (c) gender
   (e) sexual response

6. Attitudes towards homosexuality are changing. Which of the following statements are correct with respect to that change?

(a) By 1995 only 52% of Canadians strongly disapproved of homosexuality.
(b) In 1969, Canada removed homosexual activity that took place in private between consenting adults from the Criminal Code.
(c) By 1978 Canada had extended benefits to same-sex couples in committed relationships.
(d) (a) and (b) above
(e) (b) and (c) above

7. Strictly speaking, pornography is legal in Canada. It is _____ that is illegal.

(a) Smut
(b) Snuff
(c) Obscenity
(d) Erotica
(e) X-rated videos

8. Which of the following is *inaccurate* about prostitution?

(a) Most prostitutes are women
(b) Most prostitutes offer heterosexual services
(c) Call girls are the lowest prestige type of prostitution
(d) Prostitution is greatest in poor countries where patriarchy is strong and traditional cultural norms limit women's ability to earn a living.

9. Which of the following is/are evidence of a societal need to regulate sex?

(a) Most societies condemn married people for having sex with someone other than their spouse.
(b) Every society has some form of incest taboo.
(c) Historically, the social control of sexuality was strong, mostly because sex commonly led to childbirth
(d) All of the above
(e) (a) and (b) above

10. Which of the following is inaccurate concerning the perspective offered by the structural-functionalist paradigm?

   (a) It helps us to appreciate how sexuality plays an important part in how society is organized.
   (b) It focuses attention on how societies, through the incest taboo and other cultural norms have always paid attention to who has sex with who, especially who reproduces with who.
   (c) This approach pays considerable attention to the great diversity of sexual ideas and practices found around the world.
   (d) All of the above are accurate.

11. Which of the following is a criticism of the symbolic-interactionist paradigm?

   (a) It fails to take into account how social patterns regarding sexuality are socially constructed.
   (b) It fails to help us appreciate the variety of sexual practices found over the course of history and around the world.
   (c) It fails to identify the broader social structures that establish certain patterns of sexual behaviours cross-culturally.
   (d) None of the above are criticism of symbolic-interactionism

12. _____refers to a view stigmatizing anyone who is not heterosexual as "queer".

   (a) Asexuality
   (b) Heterosexism
   (c) Bisexuality
   (d) Homophobia
   (e) Heterophobia

✎ Fill-In The Blank

1. _____refers to the biological distinction between females and males.

2. _____ sex characteristics refer to bodily differences, apart from the genitals, that distinguish biologically mature females and males.

3. Human beings with some combination of female and male genitalia are referred to as ___.

4. One cultural universal—an element found in every society the world over—is the __, a norm forbidding sexual relations or marriage between certain relatives.

5. The most recent studies in the U.S. targeting men and women born in the 1970s show that
   __percent of men and _____percent of women had premarital sexual intercourse by their
   senior year in high school.

6. Some research suggests that sexual orientation is rooted in biology. Simon LeVay links
   sexual orientation to the structure of the _____ _____.

7. On January 14, 2001, Toronto made history, witnessing the world's first legal
   _____ marriages since the Middle Ages.

8. _____describes the dread of close personal interaction with people thought to be
   gay, lesbian or bisexual.

9. Traditionally, people have criticized pornography on _____grounds. Today, however,
   pornography is seen as a _____ issue because it depicts women as the sexual
   playthings of men.

10. At the bottom of the sex-worker hierarchy are _____ _____ .

11. Communicating for the purposes of prostitution is against the law in Canada, but many
    people consider it a _____ crime.

12. Only _____ of Canadians would prohibit abortion under any circumstances.

Definition and Short-Answer

1. What are the important anatomical differences between males and females? In what ways are
   these differences important in terms of the relative statuses and roles of women and men in
   social institutions such as the family and the economy?

2. What evidence was used by Alfred Kinsey to suggest considerable cultural variation exists in
   terms of sexual practices?

3. What are the functions served by the incest taboo for both individuals and society as a
   whole?

4. When was the sexual revolution? What social and cultural factors influenced this revolution?
   What was the sexual counterrevolution? What social and cultural factors helped bring it
   about?

5. How would you summarize our society's attitudes concerning premarital sex?

6. What is the evidence that sexual orientation is a product of society? What is the evidence that it is a product of biology?

7. How has the gay rights movement influenced Canadian attitudes towards gay people?

8. To what extent would you agree that pornography today is less a moral issue than it is an issue concerning power? Why?

9. Is prostitution really a victimless crime? Why?

10. Why is it important for society to regulate sexuality?

11. What evidence do symbolic-interactionists use to suggest sexuality is socially constructed?

12. Social-conflict theorists argue that sexuality is at the root of inequality between women and men. How is this so?

Answers To Study Questions

True-False
1. T (p. 192)	8. T (p. 198)
2. F (pp. 192-193)	9. F (p. 199)
3. T (p. 193)	10. T (p. 202)
4. F (pp. 193-194)	11. F (p. 204)
5. T (p. 194)	12. T (p. 206)
6. T (p. 195)	13. T (p. 210)
7. F (p. 197	14. F (p. 211)

Multiple-Choice

1. b (p. 192)	7. c (p. 202)
2. d (p. 194)	8. c (pp 203-204)
3. a (p. 196)	9. d (pp. 205-206)
4. d (p. 198)	10. c (p. 208)
5. a (p. 199)	11. c (p. 208-209)
6. d (p. 201)	12. b (p. 209)

Fill-In

1. Sex (p. 192)	7. homosexual. (p. 201)
2. Secondary (p. 193)	8. Homophobia (p. 201)
3. Hermaphrodite (pp. 193-194)	9. moral, power (p. 202)
4. incest taboo (p. 195)	10. street walker (p. 204)
5. 76, 66 (p. 198)	11. Victimless (p. 205)
6. human brain (p. 199)	12. 5% (p. 210)

ANALYSIS AND COMMENT

Go back through the chapter and write down in the spaces below key points from each of the following boxes.

SOCIAL DIVERSITY

"The Boy Who Was Raised as a Girl
Key Points

_____
_____
_____
_____
_____

APPLYING SOCIOLOGY

"Date Rape: Exposing Dangerous Myths."
Key Points:

_____
_____
_____
_____
_____

GLOBAL SOCIOLOGY

"Sexual Slavery: A Report from Thailand"
Key Points:

_____
_____
_____
_____
_____

CONTROVERSY AND DEBATE

"The Abortion Controversy?"
Key Points:

_____

_____

_____

_____

_____

_____

SUGGESTED READINGS

Classic Sources

Edgar Gregersen. 1983 *Sexual Practices. The Story of Human Sexuality.* New York: Franklin Watts.
This book contains a vast amount of material on cross cultural sexual practices along with fascinating illustrations.

Vern L. Bullough. 1994. *Science in the Bedroom: A History of Sex Research.* New York: Basic Books.
Details about sex research from the Ancient Greeks to Hirschfield, Ellis and Freud.

Richard von Kraft-Ebing. 1886. *Psychopathia Sexualis.* New York: Putnam (Reprint).

Contemporary Sources

Robert Michael, John Gagnon, Edward O. Laumann and Gina Kolata. 1994. Sex in America: A Definitive Survey. Boston: Little Brown.
Contains the results of the National Health and Social Life Survey, conducted by the National Opinion Research Center.

Bernie Zilbergeld. 1999. *The New Male Sexuality.* New York: Bantam Books.
Insightful observations from the author's experiences as a sex therapist.

Glen Wilson. 1987. *Varient Sexuality: Research and Theory.* Baltimore: Johns Hopkins University Press.
Theoretical explanations for sexual variations.

Canadian Sources

Canadian Journal of Human Sexuality.
A quarterly journal which publishes recent research on human sexuality.

Alan King, Richard P. Beazley, Wendy K. Warren, Catherine A. Harkins, Alan S. Robertson, and Joyce L. Radford. 1988. The Canada Youth and AIDS Study. Kingston Ont. Social program Evaluation Group, Queens University.
This study examined whether a number of risk factors were associated with engaging in sexual intercourse.

Eleanor Maticka-Tyndale and Edward S. Herold. 1999. Condom Use on Spring Break Vacation: The Influence of Intentions, Prior Use and Context. Journal of Applied Psychology, 29, 1010-1027.
This article identifies recent research by these authors and others which deal with the relationship between sexual scripts and risk-taking sexual behaviours.

David Cruise and Alison Grifiths. 1997. On South Mountain: The Dark Secrets of the Golen Clan. Toronto: Viking.
A chilling tale of child sexual abuse within the Golen family of Nova Scotia.

Julian Roberts and Renate M Mohr. 1995. Confronting Sexual Assault: A Decade of Legal Change. Toronto: University of Toronto Press.
Discusses the issues leading up to changes in the offences relating to sexual assault and child sexual abuse.

Global Sources

Neil Miller. 1992. Out in the World: Gay and Lesbian Life from Buenos Aires to Bangkok. New York: Random House.
Fascinating accounts of gay and lesbian communities around the world.

Roberta Perkins and Gerry Bennett. 1985. Being a Prostitute. London: Allen and Unwin.
The story of a prostitue in Australia.

CHAPTER 9

Deviance

- To use the sociological perspective to explain deviance as a product of society.

- To understand the biological and psychological explanations for deviance.

- To understand the structural-functional, symbolic-interactional and social-conflict explanations of deviant behaviour.

- Within the structural-functional framework to understand the works of Durkheim, Merton and Cloward and Ohlin.

- Within the symbolic-interactional framework to understand labeling theory, differential-association theory and control theory.

- From within the social conflict perspective to understand how power affects deviant definitions.

- To explain how gender and race impact upon deviant definitions.

- To know how crime is defined and how age, gender, social class, race and ethnicity are related to differential distributions of crime.

- To know the limitations of criminal statistics.

- To identify and explain the elements of our criminal justice system.

III CHAPTER REVIEW

This chapter addresses questions concerning deviance. For example, why do societies create laws: Why are some people more likely than others to be accused of violations?

WHAT IS DEVIANCE?

Deviance is the recognized violation of cultural norms. It is a very broad concept and many characteristics are used by members of society in identifying deviance. One familiar type of deviance is *crime*, or the violation of norms formally enacted into criminal law. A special category of crime is *juvenile delinquency*, or the violation of legal standards by the young.

It is pointed out that deviance can be negative or positive, but in that it stems from *difference* it causes us to react to another person as an "outsider."

Social Control

Social control is defined as attempts by society to regulate the behaviour of individuals. Much of its effort is an informal effort by significant others but a very formal response comes from the *criminal justice system*, or a societal reaction to alleged violations of the law through using police, courts, and prison officials.

The Biological Context

A century ago most human behaviour was explained by biological instincts. Understandably early attempts to understand deviance emphasized biological causes.

Early work by Lombroso and later, William Sheldon suggested that criminals possessed distinctive physical traits or body types. Today there continues to be genetic research with attempts to isolate predisposition to criminality. While it may be true that biology affects some behaviour, the majority of current research focuses upon social influences.

Personality Factors

Psychological explanations of deviance concentrate on personality abnormalities, and like biological theories are focused on "individualistic" characteristics.

Containment theory suggests that non-delinquents have personalities that intervene in any social impulses towards deviance. Longitudinal research by Reckless and Dinitz in the 1960s supported this notion.

Since, however, most serious crime is committed by people who are psychologically normal, the limitations of this theoretical approach are obvious. What is also ignored is the different likelihoods of being labelled as deviant, depending upon people's location within the power structure of society.

The Social Foundations of Deviance

Deviance is not simply a matter of free choice or personal failings. Both conformity and deviance are shaped by society and this is evident in three ways. Deviance exists only in relation to cultural norms; people become deviant as others define them that way, and both rule-making and rule-breaking involve social power.

STRUCTURAL-FUNCTIONAL ANALYSIS

Emile Durkheim: The Functions of Deviance

While on the surface deviance may appear to be only harmful for society, Emile Durkheim asserted that deviance is an integral part of all societies and serves four major functions. These include affirming cultural values and norms, clarifying moral boundaries, promoting social unity, and encouraging social change.

➤An Illustration: The Puritans of Massachusetts Bay

Kai Erikson's historical research on this highly religious society supports Durkheim's theory concerning the functions of deviance. For these people deviance helped clarify various moral boundaries. Over time, he noted, what was defined as deviant changed as social and environmental conditions changed. However, what remained constant was the proportion of people viewed as deviant.

Robert Merton: Strain Theory

Merton uses strain theory to point out imbalances between socially endorsed "means" available to different groups of people and the widely held goals and values in society. As a result of this structured inequality of opportunity, some people are prone to deviant responses. Four adaptive strategies are identified by Merton: innovation, ritualism, retreatism, and rebellion. Figure 9-1 (p. 220) outlines the components of this theory. Conformity, or the acceptance of both cultural goals and means is seen as the result of successful socialization and the opportunity to pursue these goals through socially approved means. The text discusses Rocco Perri's life as an example of Merton's "innovation" mode of adaptation for those experiencing social marginality.

Merton finds that many people respond to the strain by abandoning success goals through ritualistic maintenance of rules. Others reject the goals of success and the means and retreat, perhaps into drugs or alcohol. The final group rejects both goals and means but replaces them with others through rebellion.

As insightful as Merton is in identifying structural sources of deviance, strain theory does not explain all kinds of deviance equally well nor does every individual necessarily seek wealth for personal success.

Deviant Subcultures

Researchers Richard Cloward and Lloyd Ohlin have attempted to extend the work of Merton utilizing the concept of relative opportunity structure. They argue criminal deviance occurs when there is limited opportunity to achieve success accompanied by accessible illegitimate opportunities. They further suggest that criminal subcultures emerge to organize and expand systems of deviance. Again, Rocco Perri's life is an example. In poor and highly transient neighbourhoods "conflict subcultures" (i.e., violent gangs) are more often the form this process takes. Those who fail to achieve success even through criminal means are likely to fall into "retreatist subcultures" (i.e., alcoholics).

Albert Cohen found that deviant subcultures occur more often in the lower classes and are based on values that oppose the dominant culture. Walter Miller, while agreeing that deviant subcultures are more likely to develop in the lower classes, suggests that the values which emerge are not a reaction against the middle-class way of life. Rather, he suggests that their values emerge out of daily experiences within contexts of limited opportunities. He described six focal concerns of these delinquent subcultures, trouble, toughness, smartness, excitement, fate, and autonomy. What structural-functional theories primarily ignore is that becoming a deviant is a complex process. The section on symbolic-interaction attempts to elucidate that process.

SYMBOLIC-INTERACTION ANALYSIS

The symbolic-interaction paradigm focuses upon deviance as a social process.

138

Labeling Theory

Labeling theory, the assertion that deviance and conformity result from the response of others, stresses the relativity of deviance. Of critical significance to proponents of this perspective is the process by which people label others as deviant.

➤Primary and Secondary Deviance

Edwin Lemert has distinguished between the concepts of *primary deviance*, initial acts of deviance that may provoke little action and *secondary deviance*, repeated norm violations that lead the individual to accept the deviant definition.

➤Stigma

Erving Goffman suggested secondary deviance is the beginning of a "deviant career." This is typically a consequence of acquiring a *stigma*, or a powerful negative social label that radically changes a person's social identity and self-concept. Some people may go through a "*degradation ceremony*," like a criminal prosecution, where a community formally condemns the person for deviance allegedly committed.

➤Labeling: Past and Future

Retrospective labeling is the interpretation of someone's past consistent with present deviance. In this case, other people selectively rethink the "deviant's" past, arguing all the evidence was there that would predict the person's problem.

Projective labeling is the projection of a deviant identity into the future such that escape from stigma is difficult.

➤Labeling and Mental Illness

Thomas Szaz argues that the concept "mental illness" should not be applied to people. He says that only the "body" can become ill, and mental illness is therefore a myth. Szaz suggests the label mental illness is attached to people who are different and who disturb the status quo of society. It acts as a justification for forcing people to comply with cultural norms.

The Medicalization of Deviance

Over the last fifty years the field of medicine has had a tremendous influence on how deviance has been understood and explained. The *medicalization of deviance* relates to the transformation of moral and legal issues into medical matters. Instead of seeing conformity and deviance as matters of "bad" and "good," we conceive the dichotomy as one of "well" versus "sick." The general view of alcoholism in our society in recent years is a good illustration of this process.

If a medical definition is used there are profound consequences. Rather than the police, clinical specialists will respond and the response will be in a treatment rather than punishment mode. Finally, while a moral response would make the perpetrator responsible, a medical response suggests that the person is incompetent, leaving others to make treatment decisions.

Sutherland's Differential Association Theory

Edwin Sutherland suggests that deviance is learned through association with others. Accordingly, a person's likelihood of violating norms is dependent upon the frequency of association with those who encourage norm violation.

Hirschi's Control Theory

Hirschi's point is that what really requires explanation is conformity. He suggests conformity results from four types of social controls: attachment, opportunity, involvement, and belief. Once again, a person's position in the social structural system is important in determining one's likelihood of being involved in subcultural deviance. Those with little to lose become rule-breakers.

The symbolic-interactional approach ignores why society defines certain activities as deviant in the first place. It also glosses over the fact that certain behaviours are defined as deviant almost everywhere, suggesting that cultural relativity is not appropriate to all behavioural acts. As well not all, even well-orchestrated, labels are accepted by the individuals named and in some instances the label is not avoided but eagerly sought.

SOCIAL-CONFLICT ANALYSIS

Deviance and Power

Social inequality serves as the basis of social-conflict theory as it relates to deviance. Certainly less powerful people in society are more likely to be defined as deviant. This pattern is explained in three ways. First, the norms of society generally reflect the interests of the status quo. Second, even if the behaviour of the powerful is questioned they have the resources to resist deviant labels. And third, laws and norms are usually never questioned, being viewed as "natural", even if inherently unfair.

Deviance and Capitalism

Steven Spitzer has suggested that deviant labels are attached to people who interfere with capitalism. Four qualities of capitalism are critical to recognize in order to understand who is labeled as deviant. These are: private ownership, production labour, respect for authority, and acceptance of the status quo. He differentiates between two types of problem populations. One is represented by nonproductive, but nonthreatening members of society. Another is characterized by people perceived as directly threatening to the capitalist system. Spitzer says that capitalism itself creates these groups, though the individuals themselves are blamed for their own problems.

➢**White-Collar Crime**

The concept *white-collar crime*, or crimes committed by persons of high social position in the course of their occupations, was defined by Edwin Sutherland in the 1940s. This type of crime involves powerful people taking illegal advantage of their occupational position. While it is estimated that the harm done to society by white-collar crime is greater than street crime, most people are not particularly concerned about this form of deviance. This is in part illustrated by the fact that violators who are caught are typically dealt with in civil court rather than criminal court.

Social-conflict theory focuses our attention on the significance of power and inequality in understanding how deviance is defined and controlled. However, some weaknesses of this approach have been identified. The assumption that the rich and powerful directly create and control cultural norms is questionable given the nature of our political process. Secondly, the approach suggests that only when inequality exists is there deviance, yet even economically egalitarian societies exhibit types of deviance, and as Durkheim has pointed out deviance can be functional.

Table 9-1 (p. 226) summarizes the major contributions of each of the sociological explanations of deviance.

DEVIANCE AND SOCIAL DIVERSITY

Power strongly predicts the shape of deviance in society. The **Applying Sociology** Box (p. 227) discusses the high rates of suicide among Aboriginal peoples in Canada within the context of lack of power over life conditions.

Deviance and Gender

The inclusion of gender in the study of deviant behaviour has been insignificant especially in the structural-functional and conflict perspectives. Only in the labeling approach has the gender issue been examined carefully and it is found that the behaviour of males and females are evaluated by different standards. Further, because of their position within the power structure men often escape responsibility when they victimize women.

CRIME

Crime is the violation of criminal law statutes. In Canada it is enacted by the federal government.

The Components of Crime

Crime is composed of the act itself and criminal intent or "mens rea." Degree of intent is important with respect to determining the seriousness of a crime.

➤Types of Crimes

In Canada information on crime is obtained from the Uniform Crime Reporting System in a Statistics Canada publication, *Canadian Crime Statistics*. *Violent crimes*, crimes against people that involve violence or the threat of violence, include murder, manslaughter, sexual assault and robbery among others and *property crimes*, crimes that involve theft of property belonging to others, including theft over $1,000.00, fraud and possession of stolen goods among others, are the two major crime categories. A third is *victimless crimes*, violation of laws in which there is no readily apparent victims, such as prostitution and gambling. This category is often a misnomer since the young runaway lured into prostitution could readily be seen as a victim of circumstance.

➤Criminal Statistics

Canada's crime statistics indicate a steady increase in violent and property crimes from 1962 to 1992, followed by a clear decline. Figure 9.2 (p. 228) indicates these changes. Our homicide rates are less than one quarter the American rates but there is a substantial differential between the provinces as indicated on the **Canada Map** 9-1 (p. 229).

It should be noted that official crime statistics are far from accurate and seriously under-estimate the real levels. Homicides are almost always brought to the attention of police but sexual assault and property crime are often not. Victimization reports indicate that real rates of crime are much higher than official statistics indicate.

The "Street" Criminal: A Profile

The likelihood of engaging in crime increases sharply during adolescence and declines thereafter. While only 20% of the population is between the ages of 12-24, this age group accounts for over 60% of all charges for property crimes and 35% of those charged for violent crimes.

Statistics indicate crime to be predominantly a male activity. In Canada 85-90% of arrests involve males and 97% of prison inmates are male. While recent evidence suggests the disparity is shrinking, women are still involved primarily in victimless crimes and shoplifting. There is also, of course, the reluctance to define women as criminal (note Karla Homolka).

While most people believe that poor people simply commit more crime, the situation is actually more complex. Research suggests crime exists across all social strata; it is the types of crimes committed which vary. Those who are victimized are also disproportionately at the lower economic levels of society.

The relationship between race and crime is a complex one but certainly blacks and aboriginals are grossly over represented with respect to arrests and incarceration. Prejudice would appear to play a role as these categories of race are more likely to be reported by citizens and arrested by police. As well race is related to social class which itself leads to over-criminalization. Finally, white collar crimes, committed primarily by middle-class whites are under-reported and often not counted in official crime statistics. The recent report of the Commission on Systemic Racism in the Ontario Criminal Justice System reports that blacks are treated more harshly at every stage in the justice system.

➤Crime in Global Perspective

Relative to European societies, the United States has a very high crime rate and Canada is also relatively high by world standards. The U.S. rates are affected by an emphasis on individual economic success, the weakening of family support systems and high levels of unemployment which create categories of chronically poor people along with a high proportion of privately owned guns. All these factors but guns are in place in Canada, suggesting that we can expect an increase in our crime rates unless social change reduces the impact of these factors. The recent diminution of Canada's social safety net may accelerate this change.

The Canadian government's recent gun control legislation is a recognition of the danger associated with widespread availability of guns. Figure 9-3 (p. 233) shows the death rates by handguns for six countries, and Figure 9-4 (p. 233) shows Canadian firearm homicides by type of firearm.

Less economically developed societies tend to have low rates of crime but all societies have surging rates of rape and increasing amounts of prostitution, probably because of restricted economic opportunity for women. . Drug related crime is also on the increase because of the increased demand in North America and the dependency in some low income countries on the currency earned through the production of illicit drugs. **Global Map** 9.1 (p. 234) indicates that countries have different strategies for dealing with crime; capital punishment is used in some although the trend is towards abolition.

THE CRIMINAL JUSTICE SYSTEM

The criminal justice system is comprised of three component parts. These are:

The Police

The police represent the point of contact between the public and the criminal justice system. They are responsible for maintaining public order by uniformly enforcing the law. However, particularly because of the relatively small number of police in our population, they must exercise much discretion about which situations receive their attention. In Ontario police are less likely to make an arrest when their actions are not observed or if they feel an individual is trustworthy. Perhaps that is why blacks and aboriginals are disproportionately arrested and why greater numbers of police are found in areas of large income disparities and large numbers of minorities. The sheer presence of the officers may lead to higher rates of arrest.

The Courts

It is within this component of the system where guilt or innocence is determined. In practice a large number of cases are dealt with through *plea bargaining* where the prosecution reduces the charge in exchange for a guilty plea. This saves the court time and expense but it abuses protection for defendants and perhaps for the public as well; note the public response to Karla Homolka's successful plea bargaining.

Punishment

Clearly approaches to punishment have changed over time. Children and juveniles are treated differently in the justice system in Canada and there has been a shift towards changing the behaviour patterns of offenders, and away from elimination of behaviour through incarceration. Even spanking, although permissable by law, is questioned by social scientists. (**Applying Sociology** Box, p. 237)

The four justifications for using punishment include: *retribution*, subjecting an offender to suffering comparable to that caused by the offense; *deterrence*, the attempt to discourage criminality through punishment; *rehabilitation*, reforming the offender to preclude subsequent offenses; and *social protection*, rendering an offender incapable of further offenses either temporarily during a period of incarceration or permanently by execution. These justifications of punishment are summarized in Table 9-2 (p. 238) and Figure 9-5 (p. 239) shows incarceration rates for selected countries.

While these justifications are widely recognized, demonstrating their consequences is very problematic. Their relative effectiveness is questioned given the high *criminal recidivism* rates, or subsequent offenses by people previously convicted of crimes. Likewise, specific deterrence expectations associated with capital punishment are shown to have no effect. The **Controversy and Debate** Box (p. 236) discusses various ways of intervening prior to crime commission since the usual modes of punishment work so poorly.

KEY CONCEPTS

Define each of the following concepts on separate paper. Check the accuracy of your answers by referring to the key concepts in the text as well as by referring to italicized definitions located throughout the chapter.

Crime	projective labeling
Criminal justice system	property crimes
Criminal recidivism	rehabilitation
Deterrence	retribution
Deviance	retrospective labeling
Differential association	secondary deviance
Juvenile delinquency	social protection
Labeling theory	stigma
Medicalization of deviance	victimless crimes
plea bargaining	violent crimes
primary deviance	white-collar crime

STUDY QUESTIONS

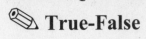 **True-False**

1. T F   The vast majority of conformity behaviour takes place simply because people think its the right and natural thing to do.

2. T F   William Sheldon posited that body structure might predict criminality.

3. T F   The vast majority of serious crimes are committed by people whose psychological profiles are not normal.

4. T F   In Merton's adaptive category called "innovation" there is seen to be a balance between cultural goals and means to attain those goals.

5. T F   According to Cloward and Ohlin deviance or conformity grows out of the relative opportunity structure that frames young people's lives.

6. T F   Primary deviance is the type where an individual engages in repeated norm violations and begins to take on a deviant identity.

7. T F   Thomas Szaz argues that mental illness is a myth and is a label used by the powerful in society to force people to follow dominant cultural norms.

8. T F   Our authors suggest that during the last fifty years there as been a trend away from what is known as the "medicalization of deviance."

9. T F   Hirschi suggests that people who have little to lose from deviance are most likely to become rule breakers.

10. T F   The social-conflict perspective suggests that even the powerful do not have the resources to resist deviant labels.

11. T F   Rates of suicide among Aboriginal youth are five to six times higher than among their non-Aboriginal peers.

✎ Multiple-Choice

1. This researcher worked in prisons and discerned that criminals had distinctive physical features:

   (a) Sheldon Glueck
   (b) Walter Miller
   (d) Cesare Lombroso

   (d) Charles Goring
   (e) Emile Durkheim

2. Which of the following is not a social foundation of deviance according to our authors:

   (a) deviance exists in relation to cultural norms
   (b) people become deviant in that others define them that way
   (c) both norms and the way people define social situations
       involve social power
   (d) all are identified as foundations of deviance
   (e) none are identified as foundations of deviance

3. Which of the following is *not* one of the functions which Durkheim suggested deviance serves?

   (a) deviance affirms cultural values
   (b) responses to deviance clarifies moral boundaries
   (c) responses to deviance attacks social unity
   (d) deviance encourages social change

4. Kai Erikson's historical research on the Puritans of Massachusetts Bay supports:

   (a) Durkheim's structural-functional perspective concerning the functions of deviance
   (b) the psychological theory of containment
   (c) the genetic inbreeding theory of deviance
   (d) the body structure theory of deviance
   (e) the social conflict theory of deviance

5. Merton's strain theory has been criticized for:

   (a) explaining only some forms of deviance.
   (b) ignoring the dislocation between goals and means in society
   (c) limiting the definition of success to wealth
   (d) a and b above
   (e) a and c above

6. What is the term for the behaviour of an individual who engages in repeated norm violation and begins to take on a deviant identity?

(a) retreatist deviance
(b) ritualistic deviance
(e) rebellious deviance
(d) secondary deviance
(e) primary deviance

7. When, after stigmatizing a person, people begin interpreting someone's past consistent with present deviance they are engaging in

(a) primary deviance
(b) secondary deviance
(c) labeling
(d) retrospective labeling
(e) opportunity

8. Crimes committed by persons of high social position in the course of their occupations is called

(a) white-collar crimes
(b) capitalist deviance
(c) power crime
(d) harmless burden
(e) victimless crime

9. Which of the following are categories included in the Canadian Uniform Crime Reporting System?

(a) white-collar crime and property crime
(b) victimless crime and statutory crime
(c) index crime and property crime
(d) violent crimes and property crimes
(e) statutory crime and summary crime

10. Crime rates in Canada are highest for

(a) individuals between the ages 25 and 44
(b) males
(c) blacks and native people
(d) a and b above
(e) b and c above

11. A legal negotiation in which the prosecution reduces a defendant's charge in exchange for a guilty plea is called

(a) retribution
(b) reduced levy
(c) neutral deterrence
(d) plea bargaining
(e) reassessment

12. Which of the following is *not* one of the usual justifications for punishment

(a) retribution
(b) sanctification
(c) deterrence

(d) rehabilitation
(e) social protection

✎ Fill-In The Blank

1. The _____ _____ _____ is a societal reaction to alleged violations of the law through the use of police, courts, and punishment.

2. A psychological explanation of deviance which posits the view that if boys have developed strong moral values and a positive self-image they will not become delinquents is called _____ theory.

3. In Merton's _____ response, people resolve the strain of limited success by compulsive efforts to live "respectably."

4. Sometimes an entire community formally stigmatizes individuals through what Harold Garfinkel calls a _____ _____.

5. In _____ _____ Hirschi claims that the essence of social control lies in people's anticipation of the consequences of their behaviour.

6. Stephen Spitzer argues that deviant labels are applied to people who impede the operation of _____.

7. _____ surveys show that the actual level of crime is three times as great as that indicated by official reports.

8. The Canadian criminal justice system consists of three elements: _____, _____, _____.

9. In Canada young people under the age of eighteen years of age are seen to have a _____for crime.

10. After 1976, when capital punishment was abolished in Canada, the murder rate went _____.

Definition and Short-Answer
1. According to Hirschi's control theory there are four types of social controls. What are these? Provide an example of each.

148

2. According to Merton's strain theory, what are the four deviant responses by individuals to dominant cultural patterns?

3. What are the functions of deviance according to Durkheim?

4. What characteristics are likely to have people labelled as being a member of a "problem population" according to Spitzer?

5. How do researchers using the differential association theory explain deviance?

6. What is meant by the term "medicalization of deviance"?

7. According to Elliot Currie, what factors are responsible for the relatively high crime rates in the U.S.?

8. What are the four justifications for the use of punishment against criminals?

9. What are the social foundations of deviance? Illustrate each.

10. Summarize the basic explanations of deviance using each of the following perspectives: social-conflict, symbolic-interactionism, and structural-functionalism.

Answers to Study Questions

True-False

1. T (p. 215)   7. T (p. 222)
2. T (p. 216)   8. F (p. 222)
3. F (p. 217)   9. T (p. 223)
4. F (p. 219)   10. F (p. 224)
5. T (p. 220)   11. T (p. 227)
6. F (pp. 221-222)

Multiple-Choice

1. c (p. 216)   7. d (p. 222)
2. d (pp. 217-218)   8. a (p. 226)
3. c (p. 218)   9. d (pp. 228)
4. a (pp. 218-219)   10. e (pp. 230-232)
5. e (p. 221)   11. d (p. 235)
6. d (pp. 221-222   12. b (pp. 237-238)

Fill-In

1. criminal justice system (p. 216)
2. containment (p. 217)
3. ritualism (p. 220)
4. degradation ceremony (p. 222)
5. control theory (p. 223)

6. capitalism (p. 224)
7. victimization (p. 230)
8. the police, the courts, punishment (pp. 235-239)
9. lower capacity (p. 237)
10. down (p. 237)

ANALYSIS AND COMMENT

Go back through the chapter and write down in the spaces below key points from each of the following boxes.

APPLYING SOCIOLOGY

"Suicide Among Aboriginal People"
Key Points:

"Is Spanking Allowed in Canada? "
Key Points:

CONTROVERSY AND DEBATE

"What Can Be Done About Crime? "
Key Points:

CYBER.SCOPE

This section of the text is concluded by asking how the Information Revolution is changing our culture and society. Does our culture shift away from success as measured by the accumulation of things toward gaining new ideas? Will Cyber-socialization reduce regional diversity in Canada and will parents lose even more capacity to meet the emotional and moral needs of their children? Will the self develop differently since, on the Internet, nobody really has the same access to signs of your identity? Since no technological shift is neutral, it changes the world; how will our human needs be met in the new cyber-society?

SUGGESTED READINGS
Contemporary Sources

Eileen B. Leonard. 1982. *Women, Crime and Society: A Critique of Theoretical Criminology*. New York: Longman.

Thompson Educational Publishing.
These three books are valuable efforts to incorporate gender into the study of deviance. The first explains how women have virtually been ignored up to the present in studies of crime; the second applies labeling theory to gender issues; the third looks at women as victims.

Charles W. Thomas. 1987. *Corrections in America: Problems of the Past and the Present*. Newbury Park, CA: Sage.
D. Owen Carrigan. 1991. *Crime and Punishment in Canada: A History*. Toronto: McClelland and Stewart.
These two books present the history and many contemporary controversies surrounding crime and punishment in Canada and the United States.

Robert M. Bohm. 1991. *The Death Penalty in America: Current Research*. Cincinnati, OH: Anderson Publishing.
This book offers eight essays dealing with the death penalty.

Bernard J. Gallagher III. 1991. *The Sociology of Mental Illness*. 3rd ed. Englewood Cliffs, NJ: Prentice Hall.
This sociological account of mental illness delves into who in the United States is affected by such conditions and the social role of the mental patient.

Anne Campbell. 1991. *The Girls in the Gang*. 2nd ed. Cambridge, MA: Basil Blackwell.
Most research about youth gangs is by and about men. Anne Campbell provides a rare and insightful account of young women in New York street gangs.

Edwin M. Schur. 1983. *Labeling Women Deviant: Gender, Stigma, and Social Control*. Philadelphia: Temple University Press.
Walter S. DeKeseredy and Ronald Hinch. 1991. *Woman Abuse: Sociological Perspectives*. Toronto Toronto: University of Toronto Press.

Robert B. Edgerton. 1976. *Deviance: A Cross-Cultural Perspective*. Menlo Park, CA: Cummings.
This book shows the relativity of deviance, illustrating the extent to which the definition of deviant behaviour varies with time and across cultures.

Daniel Wolf. 1991. The Rebels: A Brotherhood of Outlaw Bikers. Toronto: University of Toronto Press.
A professor of anthropology reports on field work which involved riding for three years with a biker gang.

Canadian Sources

David Suzuki and Peter Knudtson. 1989. *Genetics: The Clash Between the New Genetics and Human Values*. Cambridge, MA: Harvard University Press.

Global Sources

Ikuyo Sato. *Kamikaze Biker: Parody and Anomy in Affluent Japan*. Chicago: University of Chicago Press, 1991.
In the tradition of Emile Durkheim, this account of juvenile delinquency in Japan highlights the breakdown of traditional social controls that often accompanies material affluence.

CHAPTER 10

Social Stratification

I CHAPTER OUTLINE

I.   **What is Social Stratification?**

II.   **Caste and Class Systems**

        A. The Caste System

           1. Two Illustrations: India and South Africa

           2. Caste and Agrarian Life

        B. The Class System

           1. Status Consistency

        C. Caste and Class Together: The United Kingdom

           1. The Estate System

           2. The United Kingdom Today

        D. Another Example: Japan

           1. Feudal Japan   2. Japan Today

        E. The Former Soviet Union

           1. A Classless Society?   2. The Second Russian Revolution

        F. Ideology: The "Staying Power" of Stratification

           1. Plato and Marx on Ideology

           2. Historical Patterns of Ideology

III.   **The Functions of Social Stratification**

        A. The Davis-Moore Thesis

        B. Meritocracy

IV.   **Stratification and Conflict**

        A. Karl Marx: Class and Conflict

        B. Why No Marxist Revolution?

        C. A Counterpoint

        D. Max Weber: Class, Status and Power

           1. The Socioeconomic Status Hierarchy

           2. Inequality in History

V.   **Stratification and Technology in Global Perspective**

        A. Hunting and Gathering Societies

        B. Horticultural, Pastoral and Agrarian Societies

        C. Industrial Societies

        D. The Kuznets Curve

VI.   **Social Stratification: Facts and Values**

VII.   **Summary**

VIII.   **Critical-Thinking Questions**

IX.   **Applications and Exercises**

X.   **Sites To See**

- To understand the four basic principles of social stratification.

- To differentiate between two systems of stratification: caste and class, and to be able to provide historical and cross-cultural examples of each.

- To know the relationship between culture, ideology and stratification.

- To differentiate between the structural-functional and social-conflict perspectives of stratification.

- To understand the views of Max Weber concerning the various dimensions of social class.

- To know the synthesis approach to understanding social stratification put forward by the Lenskis.

- To understand the limitations of the relationship between intelligence and social class.

WHAT IS SOCIAL STRATIFICATION?

Social inequality, characterized by the unequal distribution of valued resources, is found in every society. Some of the inequality is the result of individual differences in ability and effort, but much of it also relates to societal structures. *Social stratification* refers to a system by which categories of people in society are ranked in a hierarchy. This chapter opens with an illustration of the sinking of the *Titanic* to show the consequences of social inequality in terms of who survived the disaster and who did not. Four principles are identified which help explain why social stratification exists. First, social stratification is a characteristic of society and not merely of individuals. Second, social stratification is universal but variable. Third, it persists over generations. And, fourth, it is supported by patterns of belief.

CASTE AND CLASS SYSTEMS

Sociologists distinguish between two general systems of social stratification based on the degree of social mobility representative of the system.

The Caste System

A *caste system* is a system of social stratification based on ascription. Pure caste systems are "closed" with no social mobility.

➤Two Illustrations: India and South Africa

The Hindu social system of rural India and racial apartheid in South Africa are used to illustrate caste systems. In such systems three factors underlie the fact that ascription determines virtually everything about a person's life. First, birth determines one's occupation. Second, marriage unites people of the same social standing through the rule of endogamy. And, third, powerful cultural beliefs underlie such systems. The **Global Sociology** box (pp. 248) discusses the changing situation in South Africa where apartheid has created a caste type system based on race but is now challenged by democratic reforms. Nonetheless, race-based stratification is still in place.

➤Caste and Agrarian Life

Caste systems are much more typical of agrarian societies where lifelong agricultural routines depend upon a rigid sense of duty and discipline.

The Class System

Representative of industrial societies, *class systems* are defined as systems of social stratification based on individual achievement. Social categories are not as rigidly defined as in the caste system. Individual ability, promoted by open social mobility, is critical to this system. Other factors characteristic of industrial economies which are central to such a system are high levels of migration to cities, democratic principles, and high immigration rates.

➤Status Consistency

Status consistency refers to the degree of consistency of a person's social standing across various dimensions of social inequality. Class systems have lower levels of status consistency.

Caste and Class Together: The United Kingdom

The United Kingdom represents a society where caste qualities of its agrarian past still are interwoven within the modern day industrial class system.

➤The Estate System

The United Kingdom's agrarian past, with deep historical roots, was based on a caste-like estate system. Three estates, the first (nobles), the second (primarily clergy), and the third (commoners) comprised this system. The law of *primogeniture* by which property of parents could only be inherited by the eldest son helped maintain this system. The Industrial Revolution allowed some commoners in the cities to amass wealth sufficient to rival the power of the nobility and led to the blurring of social rankings.

➤The United Kingdom Today

Aspects of their feudal past persist today. For example, a monarch still stands as Britain's head of state, and descendants of traditional nobility still maintain inherited wealth and property. However, power in government resides in the House of Commons, which is primarily comprised of people who have achieved their positions. Today, about 25% of the United Kingdom's population falls into the middle-class, and 50% into the working-class. Almost 25% are "poor." Although their stratification system is based primarily on class, social mobility is less likely than in the United States or Canada. The greater rigidity of this class system is reflected in very distinct linguistic patterns.

Another Example: Japan

Like Great Britain, Japan mixes both the traditional and contemporary in their social stratification system.

➤Feudal Japan

For many centuries of agrarian feudalism, Japan was one of the most rigidly stratified cultures in the world. An imperial family maintained a network of regional nobility called *shoguns*. A warrior caste, called *samurai*, fell just below the nobility. The majority of people were commoners, like serfs in feudal Europe. However, there was an additional ranking, called *burakumin*, or outcasts, who were below the commoners.

➤Japan Today

Industrialization, urbanization, and intercultural contact have dramatically changed Japan over the last century. The nobility lost its legal standing after World War II. For many though, tradition is still revered and family background continues to remain important in determining social status. Traditional male dominance, for example, remains well embedded.

The Former Soviet Union

The USSR. was born of revolution in 1917 and the hereditary nobility who governed a feudal estate system was at an end. Most private ownership shifted to state control.

➤A Classless Society?

The Soviet Union, guided by the ideas of Karl Marx, after 1917 claimed itself to be a classless society because of the elimination of private ownership of the productive components of society. Yet, it remained socially stratified as occupations generally fell into four major categories: high government officials, the intelligentsia, manual labourers, and rural peasantry. Even so, it had less economic inequality than capitalist societies.

➤The Second Russian Revolution

The reforms spurred by Mikhail Gorbachev's economic program of restructuring, known as *perestroika*, were significant. The efforts to elevate living standards through economic reform ultimately led to the overthrow of the ruling class, the Communist party.

While there has been greater social mobility in the last century in the old Soviet Union than in the capitalist societies, the last decade has brought economic turbulence and a significant downward mobility. This kind of mobility is what sociologists call *structural social mobility*, where the shift is due to changes in the society and economy rather than to individual effort.

Ideology: The "Staying Power" of Stratification

Despite the maldistribution of resources in systems characterized by social inequality they are remarkably persistent, at least partly because of *ideology*, cultural beliefs that serve to justify stratification.

➤Plato and Marx on Ideology

Plato and Marx both recognize that ideologies exist in all societies to justify whatever stratification scheme is in place. Marx was critical, however, of inequality that channelled wealth and power into the hands of a few.

➤Historical Patterns of Ideology

The ideas that support stratification change with technology and the economy. Agrarian societies propped up nobility with slaves and serfs who took their place in a "natural order." Industrial capitalism rewards individualism and achievement suggesting that social stratification is based upon unequal effort and ability. Nowhere is this notion more clearly identified than in the work of Herbert Spencer whose dictum on the social Darwinist concept "the survival of the fittest" is described in the **Social Diversity** box (p. 254). While sociologists argue that social standing is not simply a matter of personal effort the view that people get more or less what they deserve is not unknown in Canada today. Eventually, however, traditions are challenged and "truths" questioned. Women, for example, have questioned the historical notions of "woman's place" and, although some inequality persists, the trend to equality of treatment for men and women is unmistakable. The **Applying Sociology** Box (p. 255) identifies the movement of women into medicine, academia and business, some of whom control immense wealth.

THE FUNCTIONS OF SOCIAL STRATIFICATION

The Davis-Moore Thesis

The Davis-Moore thesis asserts that some degree of social stratification is even a social necessity. They theorize that certain tasks in society are of more value than others, and in order to ensure the most qualified people fill these positions they must be rewarded better than others.

156

Meritocracy

Meritocracy, a system of social stratification based on personal merit, would, theoretically, be a very productive system. Melvin Tumin argues that functional importance of tasks is difficult to measure, other structures block equal access to jobs and that social conflict is promoted by stratification. The **Controversy and Debate** box (pp. 256-57) suggests that the market forces which reward athletes, entertainers and chief executive officers of large corporations are obviously not operating according to the principles of functional importance.

STRATIFICATION AND CONFLICT

Karl Marx: Class and Conflict

Marx's view of social stratification is based on his observations of industrialization in Europe during the second half of the 19th century. He saw a class division between the *capitalists* (owners of the means of production) and the *workers* (proletariat). This resulted in separation and inevitable conflict. As influential as Marx's thinking has been for sociological understanding of social stratification, it does overlook its motivating value. The insight provided by the Davis-Moore thesis perhaps explains, in part, the low productivity characteristic of former socialist economies. Supporters of Marx still contend, however, that people are not inherently selfish and could be motivated to perform social roles for more intrinsic rewards.

Why No Marxist Revolution?

The overthrow of the capitalist system has not occurred for at least four central reasons as identified by Dahrendorf. First, the capitalist class has become fragmented over the last century, with numerous stockholders assuming ownership. Second, the proletariat has been significantly changed by the "white-collar revolution." A century ago the vast majority of workers in North America had *blue-collar occupations*, or work involving mostly manual labour. Today, most members of the labour force hold *white-collar occupations*, or work that involves mostly mental activity.   Most of this change has occurred through structural social mobility. A third factor involves the fact that the workers' conditions have improved through labour organizations. Finally, legal protection has been widely expanded for workers.

➤**A Counterpoint**

The value of Marx's perspective is still significant. There continues to be exploitation of workers, and a small percentage of people control the vast majority of wealth in our society. Table 10-1 (p. 260) compares and contrasts the structural-functional and social-conflict explanations of social stratification.

Max Weber: Class, Status, and Power

Max Weber viewed Marx's ideas of social class as being too simplistic. Weber theorized that there were three dimensions of social inequality, class, status, and power.

➤The Socioeconomic Status Hierarchy

Weber theorized that a single individual's rankings on the three dimensions might be quite different, thus, a multi-dimensional aspect of social inequality was important to him. The term used today to reflect this idea is *socioeconomic status* referring to a composite social ranking based on various dimensions of social inequality.

➤Inequality in History

Weber noted that each of the three dimensions of social inequality predominates at different points in history. In agrarian societies status or social prestige stand out while industrialization and capitalism place more focus on class and finally with increasing bureaucratization, power becomes centered in the hands of bureaucrats whether the society be capitalist or socialist.

Although Weber's multidimensional approach remains influential the enormous wealth of privileged Canadians contrasts sharply with the grinding poverty of the poor.

STRATIFICATION AND TECHNOLOGY IN GLOBAL PERSPECTIVE

The Lenskis model of sociocultural evolution (outlined in Chapter 4) can help us to understand the varying degrees of inequality found in the world.

Hunting and Gathering Societies

In technologically simple societies no categories of people have more than others.

Horticultural, Pastoral and Agrarian Societies

As technology advances and surpluses in resources occur fairly rigid social strata emerge where the elite wield enormous power.

Industrial Societies

As technology continues to advance in industrial societies inequality tends to diminish as the workforce becomes better educated and participates in decision making.

The Kuznet's Curve
(Figure 10-1, p. 262)

This curve suggests that technological progress first sharply increases but then moderates the intensity of stratification.

Global Map 10.1 (p. 263) generally supports the notion expressed in Kuznet's Curve where less income inequality is found in the highly industrialized countries. It may well be, however, that the Information Revolution will increase the economic polarization in Canada.

SOCIAL STRATIFICATION: FACTS AND VALUES

A quote from a Kurt Vonnegut novel describes a fictional America in the later 21st century represented by absolutely no social inequality. It highlights the significant social meaning social inequality actually has for us in our everyday lives.

Theoretical explanations contain both fact and value position, as comparison between the structural-functional and social-conflict paradigms illustrates. The same facts can be perceived and understood differently. The **Controversy and Debate** box (pp. 264-265) discusses the link between intelligence and social class where, indeed, value positions influence how apparent facts can be perceived differently.

KEY CONCEPTS

Define each of the following concepts on separate paper. Check the accuracy of your answers by referring to the key concepts in the text as well as by referring to italicized definitions located throughout the chapter.

blue-collar occupations	social mobility
caste system	social stratification
class system	socioeconomic status
Davis-Moore thesis	status consistency
ideology	structural social mobility
Kuznets curve	white-collar occupations
meritocracy	

STUDY QUESTIONS

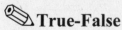True-False

1. T F   Age and class were found to be important predictive characteristics with respect to who died when the Titanic sunk.

2. T F   Ascription is fundamental to social stratification systems based on castes.

3. T F   Caste systems today are more typical of industrial societies.

4. T F   Class systems tend to eliminate inequality.

5. T F   In the United Kingdom today social mobility occurs as often as it does in Canada and the United States.

6. T F   Social hierarchies are supported by ideologies.

7. T F   In Germany, 60% of all businesses are owned by women.

8. T F   The Davis-Moore thesis is a component of the social-conflict perspective of social stratification

9. T F   The revolutionary developments that Marx considered inevitable have materialized.

10. T F   Max Weber developed a unidimensional model of social stratification which was very dominant in the early part of this century.

11. T F   The Lenskis argue that hunting and gathering societies have greater social inequality than agrarian or horticultural societies.

12. T F   The Kuznets curve projects greater social inequality as industrial societies advance through technological change.

13. T F   Kurt Vonnegut warns that social equality can be dangerous in practice.

14. T F   The authors of The Bell Curve: Intelligence and Class Structure in American Life suggest that only 30 percent of human intelligence is transmitted genetically.

✎ Multiple-Choice

1. Industrialization has the effect of _____ social mobility and of _____ at least some kinds of social inequality.

   (a) decreasing; increasing   (d) decreasing; maintaining
   (b) decreasing; reducing   (e) increasing; reducing
   (c) increasing; maintaining

2. Which of the following principles is not a basic factor in explaining the existence of social stratification?

(a) Social stratification is universal and variable.
(b) Social stratification persists over generations.
(c) Social stratification is supported by patterns of belief.
(d) Social stratification is a characteristic of society, not simply of individuals.
(e) All are basic factors in explaining social stratification.

3. In England during the Middle Ages the clergy were often referred to as the

(a) first estate   (c) third estate
(b) second estate   (d) fourth estate

4. In Feudal Japan the caste who were comprised of soldiers was called

(a) shoguns   (d) lords
(b) samurai   (e) suffei
(c) burakumin

5. A shift in the social position of large numbers of people due primarily to changes in the society itself rather than individual effort is called

(a) apparatchik   (d) structural social mobility
(b) gateway behaviour   (e) meritocratic stratification
(c) perestroika

6. The thesis that social stratification has beneficial consequences for the operation of a society was posited by

(a) Marx and Engels   (d) Mantle and Maris
(b) Goethe   (e) Plato and Socrates
(c) Davis and Moore

7. Tumin criticizes "functional importance" theories of stratification because

(a) it is difficult to measure functional importance
(b) stratification does not necessarily guarantee the development of individual talent
(c) social inequality promotes conflict
(d) all of the above
(e) a and b above

8. The Marxist revolution has not occurred because of

(a) the development of white-collar work   (d) a and b above
(b) more extensive worker organizations   (e) a and c above
(c) less extensive legal protections for workers

9. A composite ranking based on various dimensions of social inequality is called

    (a) social prestige   (d) Weberian multidimension
    (b) socioeconomic status   (e) none of the above
    (c) social stratification

10. According to Gerhard and Jean Lenski, social stratification is at its peak in:

    (a) hunting and gathering societies   (c) horticultural, pastoral, and agrarian societies
    (b) post-industrial societies   (d) industrial societies

✎ Fill-In The Blank

1. _____ is a change in a person's position in a social hierarchy.

2. A _____ is a system of social stratification based on ascription.

3. When people marry others of the same rank the marriage is called _____.

4. In feudal Great Britain, the law of _____ mandated that only the eldest son inherit property of parents.

5. Below the commoners in feudal Japan were the lowest social strata called

    _____.

6. Among the 10 wealthiest women in the world, _____ inherited their wealth from fathers and husbands.

7. Although caste systems waste human potential they are quite _____.
    _____.

8. According to Marx _____ society reproduces the class structure in each new generation.

9. The three dimensions of Weber's model of social stratification are termed _____, _____, and _____.

10. The Lenskis argue that the level of _____ representative of a society is a very significant factor in determining the nature of social stratification in that society.

Definition and Short-Answer

1. What are the four basic principles which help explain the existence of social stratification?

2. Briefly describe the social stratification system of Great Britain today.

3. According to information provided in the text, why hasn't the Marxist revolution occurred?

4. What are the basic qualities of a caste system?

5. What is meant by the concept "structural social mobility?"

6. What are the components of Weber's multidimensional model of social stratification?

7. What are the three criteria of the Davis-Moore thesis?

8. How do structural-functionalists and social-conflict theorists differ in terms of helping us understand social stratification?

9. Discuss the Lenskis' sociocultural evolution perspective and how it relates to a global and historical understanding of social stratification.

Answers to Study Questions

True-False

1. T (p. 245)   8. F (pp. 255-256)
2. T (p. 247)   9. F (p. 258)
3. F (p. 248)   10. F (p. 260)
4. F (p. 249)   11. F (p. 261)
5. F (p. 250)   12. F (p. 262)
6. T (p. 253)   13. T (p. 264)
7. T (p. 255)   14. F (p. 264)

Multiple-Choice

1. e (p. 246)   6. c (p. 256)
2. e (p. 246)   7. d (pp. 257-258)
3. b (p. 249)   8. d (p. 259)
4. b (p. 250)   9. b (p. 260)
5. d (p. 253)   10. c (p. 261)

Fill-In

1. social mobility (p. 246)
2. caste (p. 247)
3. endogamous (p. 247)
4. primogeniture (p. 249)
5. burakumin (p. 250)

6. nine (p. 255)
7. orderly (p. 257)
8. capitalist (p. 258)
9. class, status, power (p. 260)
10. technology (p. 261)

ANALYSIS AND COMMENT

Go back through the chapter and write down in the spaces below key points from each of the following boxes.

GLOBAL SOCIOLOGY

"Race As Caste: A Report from South Africa"
Key Points:

_____

_____

_____

_____

_____

SOCIAL DIVERSITY

"Is Getting Rich 'the Survival of the Fittest'?"
Key Points:

_____

_____

_____

_____

_____

APPLYING SOCIOLOGY

"How Wealthy Are the World's Richest Women?"
Key Points:

_____

_____

_____

_____

_____

CONTROVERSY AND DEBATE

"Salaries: Are the Rich Worth What They Earn?"
Key Points:

_____

_____

_____

_____

_____

"The Bell Curve Debate: Are Rich People Really Smarter?"
Key Points:

_____

_____

_____

_____

_____

SUGGESTED READINGS

Classic Sources

Lilian Breslow Rubin. 1976. *Worlds of Pain: Life in the Working-Class Family.* New York: Basic Books.

Based on interviews with fifty working-class families, Rubin skilfully explores the effects of social stratification on everyday life.

C. Wright Mills. 1956. *The Power Elite.* **New York: Oxford University Press.**
In this treatise, written in the Marxist tradition, Mills argues that U.S. society is dominated by a small, well-integrated group that controls the economy, the government, and the military.

Contemporary Sources

Charles E. Hurst. 1992. *Social Inequality: Forms, Causes, and Consequences.* **Needham Heights, MA: Allyn and Bacon**
Michael D. Grimes. 1991. *Class in Twentieth-Century American Sociology: An Analysis of Theories and Measurement Strategies.* **New York: Praeger.**
The first of these two books explores a number of issues raised in this chapter. The second, a historical account, traces how sociology has grappled with the study of social stratification.

David B. Grusky, ed. 1992. *Social Stratification: Class, Race, and Gender in Sociological Perspective.* **Boulder, CO: Westview.**
This collection of essays brings together a number of influential points of view concerning social diversity and hierarchy.
Margaret S. Clark, ed. 1991. *Prosocial Behaviour.* **Newbury Park, CA: Sage.**
Discussions about social hierarchy often revolve around the thorny question of whether, by nature,
Lorne Tepperman. 1976. "A Simulation of Social Mobility in Industrial Societies." *Canadian Review of Sociology and Anthropology,* Vol. 13:26-42.
The rate of mobility in a society is largely a function of the shape or structure of its stratification system. Tepperman develops a model that deals with shifts int he shape of both stratification systems and social mobility with industrialization.

Global Sources

Sven E. Olsson. 1990. *Social Policy and Welfare State in Sweden.* **Lund, Sweden: Arkiv.**
This analysis of social stratification in Sweden points up the role of culture and national politics in the creation of this nation's extensive welfare system.

individuals are selfish or altruistic. This collection of a dozen essays presents comparative evidence of the existence of altruism in every culture.

Russell Jacoby and Naomi Glauberman, eds. 1995. *The Bell Curve Debate: History Documents, Opinions.* **New York: Times Books.**
Presenting the ideas of dozens of scholars and journalists, this is an excellent collection of commentary and analysis of the Bell Curve thesis--the alleged link between intelligence and social class.

Canadian Sources

James Curtis, Edward Grabb, Neil Guppy, and Sid Gilbert, eds. 1993. *Social Inequality in Canada.* **Toronto: Prentice Hall Canada.**
This collection of reprinted articles approaches social inequality from a number of perspectives.

Monica Boyd, John Goyder, Frank E. Jones, Hugh A. McRoberts, Peter Pineo, and John Porter. 1981. "Status Attainment in Canada: Findings of the Canadian Mobility Study." *Canadian Review of Sociology and Anthropology,* Vol. 18:657-73.
John Porter and a number of colleagues set out to replicate and expand upon work by Blau and Duncan on American status attainment. This paper shows that Canada's social mobility rate is almost identical to that of the United States.

Sidney Verba with Steven Kelman, Gary R. Orren, Ichiro Miyake, Joji Watanuki, Ikuo Kabashima, and G. Donald Ferree, Jr. 1987. *Elites and the Idea of Equality: A Comparison of Japan, Sweden, and the United States.* **Cambridge, MA: Harvard University Press.**
This book compares social equality in three distinctive societies.

James Curtis and Lorne Tepperman, eds. 1994. *Haves and Have Nots: An International Reader on Social Inequality.* **Englewood Cliffs, N.J.: Prentice Hall.**
This collection of essays by Canadian authors presents a global survey of social stratification.

CHAPTER 11

I CHAPTER OUTLINE

I. **Dimensions of Social Inequality**
- A. Income
- B. Wealth
- C. Power
- D. Occupational Prestige
- E. Schooling

II. **Ascription and Social Stratification**
- A. Ancestry
- B. Gender
- C. Race and Ethnicity

III. **Social Classes in Canada**
- A. The Upper Class
  - 1. Upper-uppers
  - 2. Lower-uppers
- B. The Middle Class
  - 1. Upper-Middles
  - 2. Average-Middles
- C. The Working Class
- D. The Lower Class
- E. Class, Family and Gender

IV. **Social Mobility**
- A. Myth Versus Reality
- B. The Global Economy and Canadian Class Structure

V. **Poverty in Canada**
- A. The Extent of Canadian Poverty
- B. Who are the Poor
  - 1. Age
  - 2. Education
  - 3. Race and Ethnicity
  - 4. Gender and Family Patterns
- C. Explaining Poverty
  - 1. One View: Blame the Poor
  - 2. Counterpoint: Blame Society
  - 3. The Working Poor
- D. Homelessness
- E. Class and Welfare: Politics and Values

VI. **Summary**

VII. **Critical Thinking Questions**

VIII. **Applications And Exercises**

IX. **Sites To See**

II LEARNING OBJECTIVES

- To understand the extent of social inequality in Canada.

- To understand the concept of socioeconomic status and its dimensions.

- To explain the role of income, wealth, power, occupational prestige, gender and education in the Canadian class system.

- To identify and trace the significance of various ascribed statuses for the construction and maintenance of social stratification in Canada.

- To describe the general characteristics of the upper, middle, working, and lower classes in Canadian society.

- To understand that Native People run the gamet of the Canadian class system.

- To understand the nature of intragenerational and intergenerational social mobility.

- To distinguish between relative and absolute poverty.

- To explain the causes of poverty.

- To describe the demographics of poverty in Canada.

- To understand the debate over who has responsibility for poverty.

- To explain the reasons for the existence of homelessness.

- To understand how class in Canada is affected by politics and values.

- To understand the impact of welfare on those who receive it and the society that supplies it.

III CHAPTER REVIEW

The chapter begins with a description of a young, single-parent mother moving residences for the third time in seven months. Her welfare has been cut by the Ontario government and she has lost her funding for a college program she hoped would raise her out of poverty.

Hers is a common story which demonstrates the power of stratification to positively or negatively imprint people's lives regardless of their personal talents or ambitions.

DIMENSIONS OF SOCIAL INEQUALITY

Canadians tend to underestimate the amount of social inequality in our society; there is a general belief that equality of opportunity allows individual initiative to decide who gets ahead. Certainly, compared to most other societies Canadians perceive themselves to be well-off. In reality, however, we tend to interact with those who are close to us in the class system, insulating us from the true dimensions of social inequality. Although money is an important component of inequality *socioeconomic status* encompasses, as well, power, occupational prestige and schooling.

Income

An important dimension of social inequality is *income*. The average family income in 1998 was $62,146, a partial recovery from the dip in 1993 (Figure 11-1, p. 270). Essentially, family income has levelled off since about 1980 and most of the earlier increases were a result of an increasing number of dual income families. Table 11-1 (p. 271) shows that the top 20% of families receive 40.6% of the income, while the bottom 20% receive only 6.1% of the income. This level of inequality has been maintained for 45 years. Clearly, Canada has less income disparity than the United States but, as indicated in Figure 11-2, more than Sweden, but less than Great Britain. **Canada Map** 11-1 (p. 272) indicates, as well, that income is not distributed equally across Canada.

Wealth

Wealth, which includes the total amount of money and valuable goods that a person or family controls, is even more unequally distributed than income.

Power

Wealth is an important source of power in our society. Do the wealthy, in part through the social links dominate political and economic decisions?

Occupational Prestige

Occupation, as well as being a major determinant of income, wealth and power is an important source of social prestige. Table 11-2 (p. 273) shows the ranking of various occupational categories in Canada in 1986 using income and education to assess socio-economic status. These rankings are very similar to those surveys which measure occupational prestige. We see that white collar workers tend to receive higher incomes and are accorded more prestige than blue-collar workers. As well, women are paid less in almost all categories than are men, especially in *pink ghetto* jobs which are concentrated in the service and clerical areas.

Schooling

Education is an important determinant of labour force participation, occupation and income and is highly valued in Canada and other industrial societies. Although education is generally conceived to be a right there has not always been equal participation by women. Lately, however, as indicated in Table 11-2 (p. 273) women have completed more schooling than men.

ASCRIPTION AND SOCIAL STRATIFICATION

Who we are at birth greatly influences what we later become.

Ancestry

Our point of entry into the system of social inequality is determined, in large part, by our *ancestry*. Being born to privilege or poverty sets the stage for our future schooling, occupation and income.

Gender

Women earn less income, accumulate less wealth and enjoy less occupational prestige than men.

Race and Ethnicity

Race and ethnicity are important determinants of social position. Income levels for males in Canada are rank ordered as demonstrated in Table 11-3 (p. 274); British, French, Asian, black and Native, with Native incomes substantially below the others. Female incomes are lower in every category as they experience difficulty in translating their educational attainments into well paid occupations. Figure 11-4 (p. 274) demonstrates that 15.8% of British-origin males have substantial incomes while only 3.3% of Native males do.

SOCIAL CLASSES IN CANADA

Despite the difficulty in clearly defining class levels in Canadian society because of low levels of status consistency and the fluidity provided by social mobility it is possible to think of four general social classes in Canada.

The Upper Class

Perhaps 3 to 5% of Canadians fall into this class. Much of their wealth is inherited, their children go to private schools and they exercise great power in occupational positions. Although this group has historically been primarily of British origin, it is now more widely distributed.

➢Upper-uppers

One percent belong to an upper-upper level distinguished primarily by "old money".

➢Lower-uppers

The remaining 2-4% fall into the lower-upper level and depend more on earnings than inherited wealth.

The Middle Class

Roughly 40-50% of the Canadian population falls into this category. Because of its size it has tremendous influence on patterns of North American culture. There is considerable racial and ethnic diversity in this class and it is not characterized by exclusiveness and familiarity. The top half of this category is termed the "upper-middle" class with family incomes of $50,000 to $100,000 earned from upper managerial or professional fields. The rest of the middle class (average middles) typically work in less prestigious white-collar occupations or highly skilled blue-collar jobs. According to the **Social Diversity** Box (p. 280-81) the middle class dominate the Calgary Stampede.

The Working Class

This class comprises about one-third of the population and has lower incomes than the middle-class and virtually no accumulated wealth. Their jobs provide less personal satisfaction.

The Lower Class

The remaining 20% of our population is identified as the lower class. In 1996 roughly 18% of the Canadian population were labeled as poor. Many are supported entirely by welfare payments while others are among the "working poor" whose incomes are insufficient to cover necessities like food, shelter and clothing. They typically live in less desirable neighbourhoods— often racially or ethnically distinct—and their children are often resigned to living the same hopeless lives of their parents. Recent government cut-backs on welfare in some provinces may lead to even greater living constraints for this group of people.

Class, Family and Gender

Family life tends to reproduce the class structure in each generation. Parents define children's expectations and the middle-class clearly has higher educational and occupational expectations of their children than the working class. The box on **Exploring Cyber Society** (pp. 276-277) posits the possibility that exposure to home computers might give children an occupational advantage in the information society. The children of the affluent are more likely to receive that exposure. Spousal relationships also differ with more rigid role segregation in the working class as compared to more egalitarian relationships in the middle class which also contain more emotional intimacy.

SOCIAL MOBILITY

Canada is characterized by a significant measure of social mobility. Social mobility can result from personal achievement or structural change in the society itself. It can be upward or downward and intragenerational or intergenerational. *Intragenerational social mobility* refers to a change in social position occurring during a person's lifetime. *Intergenerational social mobility* refers to upward or downward social mobility of children in relation to their parents.

Myth Versus Reality

Canadians have generally expected that each new generation will do better than the last. Recent data suggest that while there is much upward and downward activity on balance not much shift takes place between generations. Men experience more occupational inheritance than women and education is the key to occupational mobility in Canada. Divorce is a good predictor of downward social mobility for women but not men.

The Global Economy and Canadian Class Structure

The rates of social mobility in Canada have been much the same as other industrial societies, not very extensive. The restructuring of the Canadian economy with manufacturing jobs moving elsewhere and service jobs replacing them, leads fewer Canadians to expect that their children will experience better standards of living than they experienced themselves. The late 1990s, however, saw a dramatic decrease in unemployment because of an expanding economy.

POVERTY IN CANADA

Social stratification creates "haves" and "have-nots." The "have-nots" can experience *relative poverty*, a deprivation in relation to those who have more, or *absolute poverty*, a deprivation of resources that is life threatening. Roughly one in seven of the world's population lives in conditions of absolute poverty while few Canadians do.

The Extent of Canadian Poverty

Approximately 4.5 million Canadians live below the "poverty line," that point below which people spend approximately 55% of pre-tax income on food, clothing and shelter. A recent United Nations report has criticized Canada for making no measurable progress in alleviating poverty. A "wealthy" society finds 2 million people regularly making use of food banks and soup kitchens.

172

Who are the Poor

➤Age

Children are more likely to be poor than any other age group. 21% of people under the age of eighteen are officially classified as poor. Figure 11-5 (p. 284) would suggest that conditions of poverty in the U.S., as reflected in infant mortality rates, are more extensive than those in Canada.

The poverty rate for the elderly has been declining but as the boomers retire, we will see a rise in the absolute number of elderly poor.

➤Education

People who have higher levels of education are considerably less likely to be unemployed and experience poverty conditions. Figure 11-6 (p. 284) clearly indicates the role of education.

➤Race and Ethnicity

While British and French-background Canadians are not at the top of the income categories as measured by average male income (Welsh, Scottish, Jewish and Japanese are higher) blacks, West Indians, Latin Americans, some Asian groups and Natives are clearly near the bottom. As the **Applying Sociology** Box (p. 279) makes clear, however, Native people, although in aggregate are at the bottom, they are represented in every class level in Canadian society.

➤Gender and Family Patterns

Women who head households bear the brunt of poverty. They are less likely to be employed and when they are, they earn less than men. Figure 11-7 (p. 285) shows that female-headed lone parent families have a low average income, in fact, Figure 11-8 (p. 285) demonstrates that 48% of them fall below the poverty line. This situation has been described as the *feminization_of poverty*.

Explaining Poverty

Sociologists generally agree that poverty is a product of social structure but two distinct views about who is responsible are debated in the society.

➤One View: Blame the Poor

On one side are those who suggest that the poor are responsible for their own poverty. Oscar Lewis speaks of a *culture of poverty* where diminished expectations are the rule and Edward Banfield identifies a "present-time" orientation which guarantees a perpetuation of poverty.

➤Counterpoint: Blame Society

On the other side are those who suggest that society is primarily responsible for poverty. William Ryan holds that unequal distribution of resources is the problem and that any lack of ambition on the part of the poor is a consequence rather than a cause of their lack of opportunity.

There are advocates for both sides of this argument. Clearly individual initiative plays a role in shaping a person's social position but many people work hard but at minimum wages and find themselves below the poverty line. As well, a comprehensive child care system would provide single parent females with a better opportunity to seek training and/or find a job.

➤The Working Poor

Not all poor people are jobless but many work at jobs, sometimes several jobs, that do not provide enough resources to move above the poverty line.

Homelessness

Although estimates of the level of homelessness are difficult to make, the familiar stereotypes of men sleeping in doorways and women carrying all their possessions in a shopping bag are no longer appropriate as whole families can no longer afford their housing because of job loss. All homeless people have one thing in common, poverty. While many of them are poverty stricken because of personal problems, there are an increasing number who find themselves homeless because of societal dislocation and government cut-backs on support.

Class and Welfare, Politics and Values

Our perception of the distribution of resources in Canadian society is affected by our political values. Conservative-minded individuals focus upon personal merit, effort and responsibility while the economically disadvantaged and those on the political left suggest that structural constraints maintain poverty. To some extent we all share a general North American belief in a meritocracy. Such a belief leads to the "hidden injury of class" where poverty lowers the self-image of disadvantaged people. The **Controversy and Debate** box (pp. 288-289) discusses this issue.

KEY CONCEPTS

Define each of the following concepts on separate paper. Check the accuracy of your answers by referring to the text as well as by referring to italicized definitions located throughout the chapter.

absolute poverty
culture of poverty
feminization of poverty
hidden injury of class
intergenerational mobility

intragenerational mobility
relative poverty
wealth
income

STUDY QUESTIONS

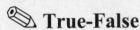 **True-False**

1. T F   The income gap between the rich and the poor was greater in 1996 than any other time since 1951.

2. T F   The poorest 20% of Canadians control approximately 6% of the total income distributed.

3. T F   1995 incomes in Canada were highest in Ontario, The Yukon and Northwest Territories.

4. T F   Defining social classes in Canada is difficult owing to relatively low level status consistency.

5. T F   Members of the lower-upper class are said to have earnings as their primary source of income.

6. T F   University training is a significant part of the experience of children of working-class parents.

7. T F   Native people are found in only one of the Marxist class categories, the proletariat.

8. T F   Working class parents encourage their children to express their individuality.

9. T F   Occupational inheritance is more common for men than women.

10. T F   In 1995 there were 4.5 million Canadians with incomes below the poverty line.

11. T F   48% of female-headed lone-parent families fall below the poverty line.

12. T F   Today the homeless are typically drug dependent men and women who sleep in doorways.

✎ Multiple-Choice

1. Canadians tend to underestimate the amount of inequality in society. Which of the following is *not* a reason for this underestimation.

   (a) the mass media project a middle-class picture of our social world.
   (b) because Canadians are insulated from those in different class categories
   (c) because Canadians emphasize status conferred from birth
   (d) our values suggest that we experience equality of opportunity.

2. Statistics show that the incomes of Canadian families vary considerably. Which of the following statistics is accurate?

   (a) the average family income in 1998 was $43,331
   (e) the top 20% of earners receive 60% of the total income distributed
   (f) wealth in Canada is more evenly distributed than income
   (g) the richest 20% of earners receive 40.6% of the total income distributed.

3. Which of the following categories of people had the lowest percentage in 1990 earning over $50,000 or more?

   (a) French women   (d) Black men
   (b) British men   (e) Native men
   (c) Asian women

4. The textbook suggests that the working class

   (a) comprises about one quarter of the total population
   (b) comprises about one half of the total population
   (c) tend to instill in their children the values of resistance to authority
   (d) typically have the power to shape events
   (e) typically have jobs that provide less satisfaction than is the case in other social classes

5. Working class families tend to instil in their children the values of:

   (a) obedience   (d) a and b above
   (b) disrespect for authority   (e) a and c above
   (c) conformity to conventional beliefs

6. In 1995 _____ % of the Canadian population were classified as poor.

   (a) 5.4   (b) 11.2   (c) 17.8   (d) 21.0   (e) 28.6

7. A change in the social position of children relative to that of their parents is called:

   (a) individual social mobility   (c) intragenerational mobility
   (b) structural social mobility   (d) intergenerational mobility

8. A person's first job in the labour market is principally affected by

   (a) gender   (d) occupational inheritance
   (b) education   (e) race
   (c) ancestry

9. The feminization of poverty in Canada is clearly related to:

   (a) female lone-parent families
   (b) sexual harassment in the workplace
   (c) the lower level of educational attainment of females
   (d) reduced female participation in the labour force

10. The fastest growing category of the homeless is now

    (a) male alcoholics   (d) the mentally ill
    (b) lone-parent females   (e) drug addicts
    (c) children

11. The tax write-offs to the affluent in Canadian society have been referred to by Canadian liberals as

    (a) corporate welfare   (d) snowbirditus
    (b) wealthfare   (e) none of the above
    (c) wealthy bums

✎ Fill-In The Blank

1. Socioeconomic status includes the dimensions of money, power, occupational prestige and

   _____.

2. While _____ is defined as occupational wages or salaries from investments, _____ refers to the total amount of money and goods that a person or family controls.

3. Women tend to be concentrated in _____ _____ jobs.

4. Women's salaries as compared to men's are most comparable in the category

   _____.

5. The lower-upper class make up less than _____% of the total population.

6. The _____ _____ participate more extensively in the Calgary Stampede than other classes.

7. _____ social mobility refers to a change in social position occurring during a person's lifetime.

8. _____ poverty refers to a deprivation of resources that is life threatening.

9. Slightly more than _____ in ten poor Canadians are under the age of 18 years.

10. Edward Banfield suggests that the poor have a _____ which focuses on living for the moment.

11. Sennet and Cobb referred to the lowering of self-image due to poverty as the of class.

Definition and Short-Answer

1. What are the reasons Canadians tend to underestimate the extent of social inequality in our society?

2. How is income distributed (by quintiles) in Canada? How has this distribution changed in the last 40 years?

3. How does gender affect occupational status?

4. To what extent do ascribed statuses affect a person's place in our stratification system?

5. How do the four classes differ in lifestyle?

6. What is the reality of social mobility in Canadian society?

7. Who are the poor in Canadian society?

8. What is the "culture of poverty?"

9. How can society be identified as responsible for poverty?

10. What is meant by the "feminization of poverty?" To what extent is it a sizeable problem in Canada?

Answers to Study Questions

True-False

1. F (p. 271)	7. F (p. 279)
2. T (p. 271)	8. T (p. 280)
3. T (p. 271)	9. T (p. 282)
4. T (p. 275)	10. T (p. 283)
5. T (p. 277)	11. F (p. 285)
6. F (p. 278)	12. F (p. 288)

Multiple-Choice

1. c (pp. 269-270)	7. d (p. 281)
2. d (pp. 270-271)	8. b (p. 282)
3. a (p. 274)	9. a (p. 285)
4. e (p. 278)	10. b (p. 288)
5. e (pp. 280-281)	11. c (p. 289)
6. c (p. 283)	

Fill-In

1. schooling (p. 270)
2. income / wealth (pp. 270-271)
3. pink ghetto (p. 273)
4. self-employed professional (p. 273)
5. 3-5% (p. 276)
6. middle-class (p. 280)
7. intragenerational (p. 281)
8. absolute (p. 283)
9. three (p. 284)
10. present time orientation (p. 286)
11. hidden injury (p. 288)

ANALYSIS AND COMMENT

Go back through the chapter and write down in the spaces below key points from each of the following boxes.

EXPLORING CYBER-SOCIETY
"Computers and Social Class."

Key Points:

_____

_____

_____

_____

_____

Fill-In

1. Second World (p. 296)
2. low-income (p. 296)
3. severe/extensive (p. 298)
4. Canada (p. 299)
5. neocolonialism (p. 304)

6. modernization theory (p. 305)
7. industrial (p. 305)
8. dependency theory (p. 308)
9. foreign debt (p. 310)
10. 90 million (p. 315)

ANALYSIS AND COMMENT

Go back through the chapter and write down in the spaces below key points from each of the following boxes.

GLOBAL SOCIOLOGY

"God Made Me to Be a Slave."
Key Points:

_____
_____
_____
_____

"Modernization and Women: A Report from Rural Bangladesh."
Key Points:

_____
_____
_____
_____

APPLYING SOCIOLOGY

"Seeking Livelihood Sustainability for Yucatan Farmers."
Key Points:

_____
_____
_____
_____

CONTROVERSY AND DEBATE

"Will the World Starve?"
Key Points:

_____

_____

_____

_____

SUGGESTED READINGS

Classic Sources

W. W. Rostow. 1960. *The Stages of Economic Growth: A Non-Communist Manifesto.* **Cambridge, U.K.: Cambridge University Press.**
Although this book draws on the thinking of several classic sociologists (including Emile Durkheim and Max Weber), it represents the first systematic statement of modernization theory.

Frantz Fanon. *The Wretched of the Earth.* **New York: Grove Press, 1963.**
This classic analysis highlights the role of colonization, nationalism, and violence in the Algerian struggle for independence.

Contemporary Sources

United Nations Development Programme. 1995. *Human Development Report, 1995.* **New York: Oxford University Press.**
The World Bank. 1995. *World Development Report 1995: Workers in an Integrating World.* **New York: Oxford University Press.**
These two annual publications provide a wide range of data on the comparative economic development of the world's nations.

Frances Moore Lappe and Joseph Collins. 1986. *World Hunger: Twelve Myths.* **New York: Grove Press/ Food First Books.**
Peter Berger. 1986. *The Capitalist Revolution: Fifty Propositions About Prosperity, Equality, and Liberty.* **New York: Basic Books.**
The first of these two books, by two long-time hunger

activists, is guided by dependency theory. The second, written by a well-known contemporary sociologist, argues the merits of modernization theory.

Global Sources

Nancy Scheper-Hughes. 1992. *Death Without Weeping: The Violence of Everyday Life in Brazil.* **Berkeley, CA: University of California Press.**
Offering a moving portrait of suffering in the shantytowns of Brazil, this researcher identifies strongly with her subjects and makes an outspoken call for change.

Catherin A. Lutz and Jane L. Collins. 1993. *Reading "National Geographic."* **Chicago: University of Chicago Press.**
Reviewing more than thirty years of popular *National Geographic* magazines, these researchers argue that this prominent publication presents a sugar-coated.

Canadian Sources

Canadian International Development Association (CIDA). 1987. *Sharing our Future: Canadian International Development Assistance.* **Ottawa: CIDA.**
This policy statement by CIDA makes an attempt to deal with supports for capitalism (economic structural adjustment) and more humanitarian aims, including the involvement of women in development.

Jamie Swift and Brian Tomlinson, eds. 1991. *Conflicts of Interest: Canada and the Third World.* **Toronto: Between the Lines Press.**

This collection of essays provides an overview of
Canada's perspective on Third-World issues as well
as the nature of its involvement. Among the topics
covered are the debt crisis, women in development,
environment, and mass media.
vision of life in poor countries

CHAPTER 13

I CHAPTER OUTLINE

I. **Gender and Inequality**
   - A. Male-Female Differences
   - B. Gender in Global Perspective
     1. The Israeli Kibbutzim
     2. Margaret Mead's Research
     3. George Murdock's Research
     4. In Sum: Gender and Culture
   - C. Patriarchy and Sexism
     1. The Cost of Sexism
     2. Is Patriarchy Inevitable?

II. **Gender Socialization**
   - A. Gender and the Family
   - B. Gender and the Peer Group
   - C. Gender and Schooling
   - D. Gender and the Mass Media

III. **Gender Stratification**
   - A. Working Men and Women
     1. Gender and Occupations
   - B. Housework: Women's "Second Shift"
   - C. Gender, Income, and Wealth
   - D. Gender and Education
   - E. Gender and Politics
   - F. Are Women a Minority?
   - G. Minority Women
   - H. Violence Against Women
     1. Sexual Harassment
     2. Pornography

IV. **Theoretical Analysis of Gender**
   - A. Structural-Functional Analysis
     1. Talcott Parsons: Gender and Complementarity
   - B. Social-Conflict Analysis
     1. Friedrich Engels: Gender and Class

V. **Feminism**
   - A. Basic Feminist Ideas
   - B. Variations Within Feminism
     1. Liberal Feminism
     2. Socialist Feminism
     3. Radical Feminism
     4. Opposition to Feminism

II LEARNING OBJECTIVES

- To understand the relationship between gender and inequality.

- To describe how culture defines gender relationships.

- To describe the link between patriarchy and sexism.

- To know the arguments in the debate over whether patriarchy is inevitable.

- To describe the role that gender plays in socialization in the family, the peer group, schooling and the mass media.

- To explain how gender stratification occurs in the work-world, housework, economics, education, and politics.

- To understand the gender gap in income.

- To identify the key arguments in the debate over whether women constitute a minority.

- To understand the sources of the expression of violence against women.

- To compare and contrast the two sociological analyses of gender: structural-functional analysis and social-conflict analysis.

- To define and explain the central ideas of feminism, variations of feminism, and opposition to feminism.

- To project the future of male and female roles in Canadian society.

III CHAPTER REVIEW

The chapter opens with a description of an important meeting in 1848 in Seneca Falls, New York where Elizabeth Cady Stanton and three hundred other women challenge the legitimacy of their second-class citizenship. While much has changed in a century and a half, women and men still lead different lives in Canada and elsewhere around the world. Like class position, gender is a major dimension of social stratification.

Gender and Equality

Gender refers to the personal traits and social position that members of a society attach to being male and female. Gender involves hierarchy, leading sociologists to talk of gender stratification, the unequal distribution of wealth, power and privilege between men and women.

200

Male-Female Differences

There are certainly physical differences between males and females but many of the social differences have nothing to do with biology and everything to do with cultural conventions. As Figure 13-1 (p. 320) indicates, even some of the physical differences attributed to the natural inferiority of females have begun to disappear.

Gender in Global Perspective

➢The Israeli Kibbutzim

The significance of culture is revealed using studies which focus on egalitarian gender role patterns in Israeli kibbutzim. Although social equality is not complete, the effort to share roles equally is noteworthy.

➢Margaret Mead's and George Murdock's Research and Conclusions to be Drawn

Research by Mead and Murdock indicates that what is defined as feminine or masculine varies widely across different cultures. Behaviour by males and females is clearly more a matter of social definition than biological imperative.

Patriarchy and Sexism

While conceptions of gender vary cross-culturally and historically, there is an apparent universal pattern of *patriarchy*, a form of social organization in which males dominant females. *Matriarchy*, defined as a form of social organization in which females dominate males has never been documented. The relative power of males over females does however vary significantly between societies. **Global Map** 13-1 (p. 323) shows that variation. Patriarchy is based upon *sexism*, the belief that one sex is innately superior to the other. *Institutionalized sexism*, or sexism built into the various institutions of our society, is evident in the lack of attention historically to violence against women and their concentration in low-paying jobs.

➢The Costs of Sexism

The costs to women who are denied opportunities and the cost to society of loss of talent are clear. There are also costs to men who die younger and experience less intimacy. The **Controversy and Debate** box (p. 340) also outlines the privilege of men to experience more violent crime, lose custody of their children and feel the affects of affirmative action policies.

➢Is Patriarchy Inevitable?

This discussion illustrates that patriarchy in societies with simple technology tends to reflect biological sex differences. In industrialized societies, technology minimizes the significance of any biological differences.

Generally, the opinion of sociologists is that gender is principally a social construction and therefore patriarchy is subject to change.

GENDER SOCIALIZATION

Males and females are encouraged through the socialization process to incorporate gender into their personal identities. Table 13-1 (p. 325) identifies the traditional gender identity characteristics along the dimensions of masculinity and femininity. Studies show, however, that most young Canadians do not develop consistently "feminine" or "masculine" characteristics.

Gender roles are attitudes and activities that a society links to each sex. Males are expected to be ambitious and competitive while women are expected to be deferential and emotional.

Gender and the Family

In many societies gender is at work before birth as the preference is to have a male child. At birth families usher girls and boys into different "pink" and "blue" worlds. These differences are accentuated over time as parents stress independence and action for their boys and passivity and emotion for their girls.

Gender and the Peer Group

Janet Lever's research on peer group influences on gender suggests that the cultural lessons being taught boys and girls are very different. Boys are more likely to play in team sports with complex rules and clear objectives. Girls are more likely to be engaging in activities in smaller groups involving fewer formal rules and more spontaneity, and rarely leading to a "victory."

Carol Gilligan has conducted research on moral reasoning and has demonstrated differences between boys and girls. Girls seem to understand morality in terms of responsibility and maintaining close relationships. Boys, on the other hand, reason according to rules and abstract principles.

Gender and Schooling

Historically school texts have shown males doing more interesting things than females. This has begun to change but sex-stereotyping persists.

At the high school and university levels females and males still tend to choose different majors and new areas of study are often sex-linked with males studying computer science and females taking gender studies.

Gender and the Mass Media

The mass media has placed males at centre stage. Women have been shown as less competent than men, and often as sex objects. Changes are occurring, but very slowly. This is particularly true in advertising which has clung to traditional cultural views of women and men.

Erving Goffman's research on how men and women are presented in photos for advertisements reveals many subtle examples of sexism such as men focussing on products while women focus on men. The "beauty myth" as presented in the **Social Diversity** Box (p. 326) remains a part of the culture of advertising.

The **Social Diversity** box (p. 334-335) indicates that women have begun to shed the image of "soft and beautiful" as the Canadian women's hockey team competes for gold in Nagano.

GENDER STRATIFICATION

Gender stratification refers to the unequal distribution of wealth, power, and privilege between the sexes.

Working Men and Women

Women working has become the norm in Canada. In 1996 while 72.7% of men over fifteen were in the labour force, 58.6% of women were as well. **Global Map** 13-2 (p. 327) indicates that this pattern is similar in the industrialized world but not in poorer societies.

Women who work are not typically single or childless. Indeed married women with children under sixteen at home have a higher employment rate than those without children living at home.

➢Gender and Occupations

While the movement of women into the workforce has been impressive, they are still positioned primarily in lower-paying, traditionally female occupations. Although the numbers are declining we still see 44% of working women in the "pink-collar" positions of clerical or service as indicated in Table 13-2 (p. 328). Men dominate in all other job categories except health, teaching and social science. They predominate in salary as well. Table 13-3 in the **Applying Sociology** Box (p. 329) shows that men receive more income than women in all occupational categories. Overall female income is 71% of male income.

Housework: Women's "Second Shift"

Despite women's rapid entry into the labour force they continue to do most of the shopping, cooking and cleaning, amounting to what sociologists call a "second shift", a shift which introduces considerable stress to their lives. **Global Map** 13-3 (p.330) outlines the proportions of housework performed by women globally.

Gender, Income, and Wealth

At all levels of completed education women earn less than men. Even female university graduates who work full time earn 3/4 of the income of their male counterparts. However, the differences have been declining in recent decades, due to increasing opportunities for working women.

Part of the disparity is accounted for in the different kind of jobs held by women and men as we have already seen. In some jurisdictions, including Ontario under a recent N.D.P.

government, pay equity legislation attempted to correct the imbalance by evaluating the "comparable worth" of various jobs. The second cause is related to family responsibilities which are accepted primarily by women, thereby affecting their time devoted to the job and perhaps their seniority. "Mommy tracks" have been proposed to allow women less intense periods in their occupations but critics suggest this may further label women as less reliable. Finally, discrimination accounts partly for the disparity as many women encounter the barrier of a "glass ceiling."

Gender and Education

Women were traditionally discouraged from participating in higher education. Recently, however, more than half of all BAs and slightly less than half of all MAs were earned by women. More of these have been in fine arts, education and the humanities but a growing number of women are entering the fields of medicine, engineering and science.

Gender and Politics

Before 1918 women could not vote in federal elections, but by 1940 all eligible women could vote in both federal and provincial elections. Table 13-4 (p. 333) cites the milestones in women's movement into Canadian political life.

Today women are involved in politics at all levels but primarily at the municipal level. Change is occurring however; currently 20% of M.P.s are women, the national leader of the N.D.P. is a woman and many women have taken dominant roles in both federal and provincial cabinets. A recent global survey finds that only in the Nordic nations does the share of parliamentary seats held by women even remotely match their share of the population.

Are Women a Minority?

As a category women can be viewed as a minority group because of being socially disadvantaged. However, subjectively, most white women in Canada do not perceive themselves as such.

Minority Women

Minority women, especially Aboriginals, face a double disadvantage of gender and race or ethnicity. Aboriginal women have the lowest labour force participation, the second highest unemployment rate and a 1990 income level that places 33 percent of them below the low income cutoff.

Violence Against Women

Because violence is commonplace in our society, and closely linked to gender, it is often found where men and women interact most intensively (i.e., dating and the family). Sexual violence, it is argued, is mostly about *power*.

➢Sexual Harassment

Sexual harassment is defined as comments, gestures, or physical contact of a sexual nature that is deliberate, repeated, and unwelcome. Most victims of sexual harassment are women probably because men are socialized to be sexually assertive and are more likely to be in positions of power. While some of it is blatant, other is subtle but seen as creating a *hostile environment*.

➢Pornography

The definition of pornography is very ambiguous as well. Current law requires different jurisdictions to decide for themselves what violates "community standards" of decency and lacks any redeeming social value. There seems to be a pattern in our society of now seeing pornography as a *political* issue as well as a *moral* one. Like sexual harassment, pornography raises complex and conflicting concerns including discrimination against women and the exercise of freedom of expression.

THEORETICAL ANALYSIS OF GENDER

Structural-Functional Analysis

Theorists using this perspective understand gender role patterns over history to be the result of the functional contributions these patterns make to social organization. Although industrial technology has allowed greater variation in gender roles, they still reflect long-standing social mores.

➢Talcott Parsons: Gender and Complementarity

Talcott Parsons theorized that gender plays a part in integrating society by providing men and women with a set of complementary roles (*instrumental* and *expressive*) which they learn through the socialization process. The primary societal responsibility of women, in this view, is child-rearing. Thus, they are socialized to display expressive qualities. Men are responsible for achievement in the labour force and therefore are socialized to exhibit instrumental traits.

Criticisms of this approach include the lack of recognition that many women have traditionally worked outside the home, the neglect of the personal strains associated with such a family orientation and the fact that what is reinforced is simply male domination.

Social-Conflict Analysis

Social-conflict analysis of gender stratification focuses on the inequality of men and women. This theoretical view holds that women are disadvantaged while men benefit by the distinction of gender.

➤Friedrich Engels: Gender and Class

Friedrich Engels saw technology leading to a productive surplus and a class system to dispose of the surplus wealth. With agricultural surplus gender inequality was created as monogamous marriage and progeny were necessary to maintain control of private property and women built their lives around husbands and children. Engels contended that capitalism intensified this male domination.

Criticisms of this approach suggest that cooperative, happy families are ignored and that gender stratification exists everywhere not just in capitalist societies.

FEMINISM

Feminism is defined as the advocacy of social equality for the sexes in opposition to patriarchy and sexism. Its first wave in this country occurred in the 19th century, culminating with the right to vote for women.

Basic Feminist Ideas

Feminists suggest that personal experiences are linked to gender. How we think of ourselves, how we act and how we are stratified in society relative to the opposite sex, are seen as products of how our society attaches meaning to gender. Five ideas considered central to feminism are:

1. The importance of change
2. Expanding human choice
3. Eliminating gender stratification
4. Ending sexual violence
5. Promoting sexual autonomy

Figure 13-2 (p. 338) provides a snapshot of the global use of contraception by married women of childbearing age.

Variations Within Feminism

Three distinct forms of feminism are identified. These include:

➤ Liberal Feminism

Liberal feminism accepts the basic organization of society, but seeks the same rights and opportunities for women and men.

➤ Socialist Feminism

Socialist feminism supports the reforms of liberal feminists but believes they can be gained only though the elimination of the capitalist economy and the success of a socialist revolution.

➤ Radical Feminism

Radical feminism advocates the elimination of patriarchy altogether by organizing a gender-free society.

➤Opposition to Feminism

Feminism has encountered resistance from both men and women. Some men do not wish to lose their privilege, others are concerned about the traditions of marriage and family life and still others see feminism as a threat to their masculinity. Women who centre their lives in their families see feminism as a threat to their values and others see women as losing rather than gaining identity. Some academics are also concerned that feminism ignores any evidence that men and women are innately different and ignores the contribution of women to child-rearing. Generally speaking, there is broad support in Canada for the ideals of liberal feminism but not for socialist and radical feminism.

LOOKING AHEAD: GENDER IN THE TWENTY-FIRST CENTURY

There has been a trend over the past century to greater gender equality. Industrialization has reduced the necessity for strength in most occupations and medical technology allows people to control reproduction. As well more men and women are deliberately pursuing equality. While opposition to this shift persists the trend to greater equality for women is likely to grow.

KEY CONCEPTS

Define each of the following concepts in the space provided or on separate paper. Check the accuracy of your answers by referring to the text as well as by referring to italicized definitions located throughout the chapter.

feminism
gender
gender roles
gender stratification
matriarchy

minority
patriarchy
sexism
sexual harassment

STUDY QUESTIONS

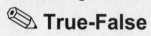 **True-False**

1. T F   Women met in 1848 at the Seneca Falls convention to demand an end to their second-class citizenship.

2. T F   Personal traits and social positions that members of society attach to being male and female is called sex.

3. T F   The performance gap between males and females in the marathon event have widened in the last 25 years.

4. T F   There is some evidence to indicate that Margaret Mead's "reversal hypothesis" about the Tchambuli was incorrect.

5. T F   In global perspective, the vast majority of activities are consistently defined as feminine or masculine.

6. T F   Masculinity is closely linked to suicide, violence and diseases related to stress.

7. T F   With respect to power, women generally fare better in rich countries than in poor ones.

8. T F   Carol Gilligan's research on moral reasoning finds that girls observe morality in terms of their responsibilities to others.

9. T F   The employment for women without children under 16 at home is higher than those with children under 16 at home.

10. T F   Female associate professors earn 95% of what male associate professors do.

11. T F   Felice Schwartz, in her research of women who seek both a career and a family, suggests that corporations allow women to continue their careers with greater intensity while caring for families.

12. T F   It is estimated that approximately 50% of women are subject to violence at the hands of an intimate partner.

✎ Multiple-Choice

1. Which of the following statements are correct with respect to gender?

   (a) It refers to social positions society attaches to being male and female.
   (b) It is a dimension of social organization
   (c) It involves hierarchy
   (d) All of the above
   (e) None of the above

2. Which of the following were limitations on women's lives in 1848 in the United States?

   (a) They could only keep their wages if they were married.
   (b) Only white women could own property.
   (c) Only married women could vote.
   (d) They could be beaten by their husbands with a stick provided it was no thicker than a thumb.
   (e) All of the above

3. Adolescent males exhibit greater

   (a) mathematical skills   (d) ability to deal with pain
   (b) verbal skills   (e) gender identity
   (c) long-term endurance

4. The social inequality of men and women has been shown to be culturally based rather than exclusively biological by which of the following studies?

   (a) George Murdock's research   (d) all of the above
   (b) Israeli kibbutzim   (e) none of the above
   (c) New Guinea studies by Margaret Mead

5. A form of social organization in which females are dominated by males is termed:

   (a) matriarchy   (c) patriarchy
   (b) oligarchy   (d) egalitarian

6. In which of the following societies is women's power promoted?

   (a) Scandinavian countries   (d) West African countries
   (b) The United States and Canada (e) South American countries
   (c) Southeast Asian countries

7. The sociologist who suggested that soon after birth family members usher infants into the "pink world" of girls or the "blue world" of boys is

   (a) Janet Lever   (d) Carol Gilligan
   (b) Dorothy Smith   (e) Joy Silverman
   (c) Jessie Bernard

8. Forty-four percent of working females are found within these two employment groups:

   (a) teaching and health   (c) clerical and services
   (b) self employed and manufacturing   (d) sales and social sciences

9. What percentage of Aboriginal women have incomes below Canada's low-income cutoff?

   (a) 8.3%   (d) 27.0%
   (b) 14.2%   (e) 33.0%
   (c) 19.8%

10. Pornography in Canada is defined as
    (a) erotic, lascivious material
    (b) material which violates community standards of decency and lacks any redeeming social value.
    (c) Any graphic presentation of male and female genitals in contact with each other.
    (d) Any material which has graphic presentations of homosexual sexuality.

11. Talcott Parsons argues that there exists two complementary role sets which link males and females together within social institutions. He calls these:

    (a) rational and irrational   (d) residual and basic
    (b) effective and affective   (e) instrumental and expressive
    (c) fundamental and secondary

12. The kind of feminism which suggests that gender equality can be realized only by eliminating the cultural notion of gender itself is

    (a) socialist feminism   (d) politically correct feminism
    (b) liberal feminism   (e) radical feminism
    (c) oppressive feminism

✎ Fill-In The Blank

1. The unequal distribution of wealth, power and privilege between men and women is called
   _____ _____ .

2. _____ refers to personal traits and social positions that members of a society attach to being male and female.

3. _____ is the belief that one sex is innately superior to the other.

4. _____ are attitudes and activities that a culture links to each sex.

5. When women return to the home after working in the occupational world and they begin the tasks of cooking, cleaning and childcare they are said to be performing a _____.

6. Before _____ women could not vote in federal elections.

7. Comments, gestures or physical contact of a sexual nature that are deliberate, repeated and unwelcome are referred to as _____.

8. In _____ analysis gender involves just not differences in behaviour but disparities in power.

9. _____ is defined as the advocacy for social equality of the sexes, in opposition to patriarchy and sexism.

10. By 1995 the idea in Canada of equal pay for equal work was supported by _____ % of a representative sample.

Definition and Short-Answer

1. Compare the research by Margaret Mead in New Guinea with the research done at the Israeli kibbutzim in terms of the cultural variability concerning gender.

3. What generalizations about the linkage between sex and gender can be made based on the cross-cultural research of George Murdock?

3. What is meant by the "beauty myth?"

4. Review table 13-2. How equal are men and women in the occupational world?

5. According to our authors, is patriarchy inevitable? Why? What roles have technological advances and industrialization played in terms of changing the relative status of women and men in our society.

6. In what ways do the family, peer group and educational institution affect how women and men come to perceive themselves?

7. Discuss the issue of sexual harassment against women in our society. What needs to be done help solve this problem?

8. In what ways is pornography an underlying factor for violence against women in our society? Explain.

9. Carol Gilligan suggests that moral reasoning is different for females and males. Briefly explain her points. How could a researcher measure such a difference in moral reasoning?

10. What is the meaning of the phrase "housework as a second shift for women"? What evidence exists of this in our society today?

11. Identify five important demographic facts about gender stratification within the occupational domain of our society.

12. What is meant by the policy of the "mommy-track"? What is your opinion about such a policy?

13. Are women a minority group? What are the arguments for and against this idea?

14. Compare and contrast the analyses of gender stratification as provided by structural-functionalists and social-conflict theorists.

15. What are the three types of feminism? Briefly differentiate between them in terms of the arguments being made about gender roles in our society.

Answers to Study Questions

True-False

1. T (p. 319)   7. T (p. 323)
2. F (p. 319)   8. T (p. 324)
3. F (p. 320)   9. F (p. 326)
4. T (p. 321)   10. T (p. 329)
5. F (p. 321)   11. F (p. 331)
6. T (p. 322)   12. F (p. 333)

Multiple-Choice

1. d (p. 319)   7. c (p. 324)
2. d (p. 319)   8. c (p. 328)
3. a (p. 320)   9. e (p. 333)
4. d (pp. 320-321) 10. b (p. 335)
5. c (p. 322)   11. e (p. 337)
6. a (p. 323)   12. e (p. 340)

Fill-In

1. gender stratification (p.319)
2. gender (p. 319)
3. sexism (p. 322)
4. gender roles (p. 324)
5. second shift (p. 328)

6. 1918 (p. 332)
7. sexual harassment (p.334)
8. social-conflict (p. 337)
9. feminism (p. 338)
10. 98 (p. 341)

ANALYSIS AND COMMENT

Go back through the chapter and write down in the spaces below key points from each of the following boxes.

SOCIAL DIVERSITY

"Pretty Is as Pretty Does: The Beauty Myth."
Key Points:

_____
_____
_____
_____

APPLYING SOCIOLOGY

"The Pink Ghetto and the Gender Gap in Income."
Key Points:

_____
_____
_____
_____

SOCIAL DIVERSITY

"Canadian Women In Hockey: Going for Gold."
Key Points:

_____
_____
_____
_____

CONTROVERSY AND DEBATE

"Men's Rights! Are Men Really So Privileged?"
Key Points:

_____

_____

_____

_____

_____

SUGGESTED READINGS

Classic Sources

Margaret Mead. 1963; orig. 1935. *Sex and Temperament in Three Primitive Societies.* New York: William Morrow.
This comparative study carried out in New Guinea was an early effort to advance the social equality of the sexes.

Jessie Bernard. 1981. *The Female World.* New York: The Free Press.
This more recent classic explores how females and males live in different, socially constructed worlds

Global Sources

Marnia Lazreg. 1994. *The Eloquence of Silence: Algerian Women in Question.* New York: Routledge.
This historical survey of the lives of women in a North African nation suggests that women everywhere--despite profound cultural differences--confront many of the same basic problems.

Cynthia Enloe. 1990. *Bananas, Beaches, and Bases: Making Feminist Sense of International Politics.* Berkeley, CA: University of California
Anita Fochs Heller. 1986. *Health and Home: Women as Health Guardians.* Ottawa: Canadian Advisory Council on the Status of Women.
M. Janine Brodie and Jill M. Vickers. 1982. *Canadian Women in Politics: An Overview.* Ottawa: Canadian Research Institute for the Advancement of Women.

Statistics Canada. 1990. *Women in Canada: A Statistical Report.* Ottawa: Statistics Canada.
Morley Gunderson, Leon Muszynski, and Jennifer Keck. 1990. *Women and Labour Market Poverty.* Ottawa: Canadian Advisory Council on the Status of Women.
L. MacLeod. 1980. *Wife Battering in Canada: The Vicious Circle.* Ottawa: Advisory Council on the Status of Women.
The above books are publications of the Canadian Research Institute for the Advancement of Women, Statistics Canada, or the Advisory Council on the Status of Women. The first documents the nature and extent of women's health work in the home. The second is a description of the political participation of Canadian women both today and in historical context. The third publication provides a review of the status and role of women in Canada today and in a historical context. The fourth describes women's labour force

This book pushes the issue of gender into the international arena, arguing that gender (along with race and class) are important dimensions of the geopolitical system.

Canadian Sources

Walter DeKeseredy and Ronald Hinch. 1991. *Woman Abuse: Sociological Perspective.* Toronto press.
Thompson Educational Pub. Inc.
This book describes the abuse of women in the home, in the streets, and in the corporate sector.

Susanna J. Wilson. 1986. *Women, the Family and the Economy*. Toronto: Prentice Hall Canada.
This is an overview of sociological data and interpretations of Canadian women in the family and in the economy.

Dawn H. Currie and Valerie Raoul. 1992. *Anatomy of Gender; Women's Struggle for the Body*. Ottawa: University of Ottawa Press.
This is a collection of various interpretations of women's bodies.

Dorothy Smith. 1987. *The Everyday World as Problematic: A Feminist Sociology*. Toronto: University of Toronto Press.
This is a description and analysis of Smith's methodology of and for women.

Meg Luxton. 1980. *More Than a Labour of Love: Three Generations of Women's Work in the Home*. Toronto: The Women's Press.
This is an examination of women's lives over three generations in the company town of Flin lon, Manitoba.

Hugh Armstrong and Pat Armstrong. 1978. *The Double Ghetto: Canadian Women and their Segregated Work*. Toronto: McClelland & Stewart.
This book provides an overview of the gendered basis of the labour force.

participation. The fifth and sixth document the extent of wife abuse and the various "prevention" policies and programs associated with wife abuse.

Contemporary Sources

Margrit Eichler. 1980. *The Double Standard: A Feminist Critique of Feminist Social Science*. New York: St. Martin's Press.
This is a critique of social science from the perspective of a feminist.

Mary O'Brien. 1981. *The Politics of Reproduction*. Boston: Routledge and Kegan Paul.
This book examines the thsis that gender inequity is based on the alienation of men from reproduction

CHAPTER 14

Race and Ethnicity

- To understand the biological basis for definitions of race.

- To distinguish between the biological concept of race and the cultural concept of ethnicity.

- To identify the two major characteristics of any minority group.

- To describe the two forms of prejudice: stereotyping and racism.

- To identify and explain the four theories of prejudice.

- To distinguish between prejudice and discrimination.

- To provide examples of institutional prejudice and discrimination.

- To explain how prejudice and discrimination combine to create a vicious cycle of persistent beliefs and practices.

- To compare and contrast the patterns of interaction between minorities and the majority identifying the four major models.

- To describe the history and relative status of each of the racial and ethnic groups in Canada.

- To understand the changes in immigration policy in Canada and the likely future of race and ethnic relations in this country.

III CHAPTER SUMMARY

Being black in Canada in the 1940s sometimes meant being treated less civilly than a German prisoner of war. While segregation has ended today and race relations in other portions of the world are far worse, racial discrimination is not unknown. The **Social Diversity** Box (p. 356) outlines a history of racism in this country.

Ethnicity and race can be sources of group unity but they are sources also of conflict and subjugation. This chapter investigates the meanings and consequences of race and ethnicity.

THE SOCIAL SIGNIFICANCE OF RACE AND ETHNICITY

Race

A *race* is a category composed of people who share biologically transmitted traits that are defined as socially significant. Common distinguishing characteristics include skin colour, hair texture, shape of facial features, and body type. Over thousands of generations, the physical environments that humans lived in created physical variability. In addition, migration and intermarriage spread genetic characteristics throughout the world.

Racial Typology

During the 19th century biologists developed a three-part scheme of racial classification, including *Caucasian*, *Negroid*, and *Mongoloid*. Although research confirms that no pure races exist cultural definitions still operate as if the differences are meaningful, especially if they support a system of social inequality. The **Social Diversity** box (p. 350) outlines how I.Q. tests have been used to justify systems of social inequality. Recently in Canada we have attempted to measure our racial composition but because of biological mixing the attempt is, at best, an approximation.

Ethnicity

Ethnicity is a cultural heritage shared by a category of people. Objective criteria are those of ancestry, cultural practices, language and dress while subjective criteria are those involving the internalization of a distinctive identity. Sometimes the objective components may be lost through assimilation but the subjective identification remains. While ethnicity is cultural, race is biological but the two often go hand in hand. Ethnicity is also sometimes lost; people simply lose touch with their ethnic origins.

Minorities

A racial or ethnic *minority* is a category of people, distinguished by physical or cultural traits, who are socially disadvantaged. Table 14-1 (p. 357) presents 1996 data on the approximate sizes of different racial and ethnic groups in Canada. Minority groups have two distinctive characteristics, they maintain a distinctive identity, and are subordinated through the social stratification system. While usually being a relatively small segment of a society, there are exceptions, for example blacks in South Africa and women in Canada.

PREJUDICE

Prejudice is a rigid and irrational generalization about an entire category of people which can be positive or negative in nature, and vary in intensity.

Stereotypes

Stereotypes are sets of prejudices concerning some category of people. They involve inaccurate descriptions of a category of people even when evidence would contradict the description. Because it involves strong, emotional attitudes, a stereotype is difficult to change.

Racism

A powerful form of prejudice is *racism*, or the belief that one racial category is innately superior or inferior to another. Racism has a long and terrifying history globally and in Canada which, for example, has treated Natives as if they are innately inferior. Overt racism appears to be declining in this country and Canadians exhibit more sensitivity toward visible minorities than do Americans.

Theories of Prejudice

➤Scapegoat Theory

Scapegoat theory suggests that frustration leads to prejudice especially on the part of people who themselves are disadvantaged. A *scapegoat* is a person or category of people unfairly blamed for the troubles of others.

➤Authoritarian Personality Theory

The *authoritarian personality* notion, first suggested by T. W. Adorno, holds that extreme prejudice is a personality trait linked to persons who conform rigidly to cultural norms and values. Such people typically have little education and were raised by cold and demanding parents.

➤Cultural Theory

This view suggests that some prejudice is embedded in cultural values. Emory Bogardus developed the concept of social distance to measure the attitudes of Americans toward different racial and ethnic groups. His findings conclude that prejudice is operative throughout American society.

Although Canadians may be more tolerant than Americans toward racial and ethnic minorities there is evidence still of a Eurocentric bias.

➤Conflict Theory

This approach argues that prejudice results from social conflict among categories of people. Prejudice is used as an ideology to legitimate the oppression of certain groups or categories of people. A different argument is also presented in this context which focuses on the climate of *race consciousness* being created by minorities themselves as a political strategy to gain power and privilege.

DISCRIMINATION

Discrimination involves treating various categories of people unequally. While prejudice concerns attitudes and beliefs, discrimination involves behaviour. The interrelationship between prejudice and discrimination is addressed by Robert Merton, whose analysis is reviewed in Figure 14-1 (p. 352). Four types of people are revealed: active bigots, timid bigots, all-weather liberals, and fair-weather liberals.

Institutional Prejudice and Discrimination

Institutional discrimination refers to discrimination that is an action inherent in the operation of the economy, the educational institution or some other social institution. Notions about a persons "place" are sometimes deeply entrenched as Natives have discovered who have sought employment at the Department of Indian Affairs.

Prejudice and Discrimination: The Vicious Cycle

It is argued that these characteristics in our society persist because they are mutually reinforcing. The Thomas Theorem, discussed in chapter 6, relates to this situation. The stages of the *vicious cycle* of prejudice and discrimination are outlined in Figure 14-2 (p. 353).

MAJORITY AND MINORITY: PATTERNS OF INTERACTION

Four models can be used to describe patterns of interaction between minorities and the majority.

Pluralism

Pluralism is a state in which racial and ethnic minorities are distinct but have social parity. Social diversity has been a source of pride in Canada and multiculturalism is officially adopted as government policy. To the extent that an ethnic community has "institutional completeness" the needs of its members might be met within the boundaries of the group. While various heritage programs support and celebrate the multicultural ideal some critics suggest that the policy is detrimental to the development of a shared and coherent Canadian identity and a strong social fabric. There is also evidence that Canada's "cultural mosaic" and the U.S. "melting pot" do not produce discernable differences in assimilation, economic integration and ethnic distinctiveness.

Assimilation

Assimilation is the process by which minorities gradually adopt patterns of the dominant culture. The notion of the "melting pot" is inappropriately linked to the process of assimilation. Instead of a new cultural pattern emerging, minorities in the U.S. more often adopt the traits of the dominant culture.

Some minority groups have maintained separate patterns despite the assimilation ideal in the U.S. and in Canada where we officially encourage distinctive patterns, assimilation, in fact, occurs.

The process of assimilation involves changes in ethnicity, but not race. However, racial traits may diminish over the generations through *miscegenation*, or the biological process of reproduction among racial categories.

Segregation

Segregation is the physical and social separation of categories of people. It is generally an involuntary separation of the minority groups, although voluntary segregation occurs occasionally, such as in the case of the Hutterites. Racial segregation has a long history in the U.S. *De jure* segregation, or "by law" has ended, however *de facto*, or "by fact" segregation continues. Residential segregation is a particularly crucial problem in American society, and has declined only slightly in recent decades. Canadians do not wish to view themselves as a society which practices segregation but the examples of Africville in Halifax, Buxton in Southern Ontario and Native reserves indicate otherwise.

Genocide

Genocide is the systematic annihilation of one category of people by another. While being contrary to virtually every moral standard, genocide has existed throughout history.

RACE AND ETHNICITY IN CANADA

Canada truly is a land of immigrants starting with the aboriginal peoples crossing the Bering Strait from Siberia to Alaska several thousand years ago. The French and English came in the 1600s and 1700s, ignored the Aboriginals and declared themselves the founding nations. They were followed mostly by Europeans and finally the newest of Canadians have come from Asia, Africa, the Caribbean and Latin America, and many other countries under stress, by way of refugee status.

While the largest categories used to be English and French, Table 14-1 (p. 357) tells us that almost a third of Canadians now claim "Canadian" ethnicity. After Canadian, the largest are English and French, but the rest of Canada is made up of a remarkable ethnic diversity. Table 14-2 (p. 358) indicates diversity of ethnicity by region of Canada and Figure 14-3 (p. 360), using 1996 census data, shows that visible minorities are highly represented in the Yukon and Northwest Territories (Aboriginal) and Ontario and British Columbia (recent immigrants).

Social Standing

There appears to be in Canada a system of social inequality based upon race. Recent immigrants and visible minorities are at the bottom of the income scale as indicated in Table 14-3 (p. 361). This occurs despite the fact that Asians and blacks have higher levels of post-secondary education and participation full-time in the labour force. Part of the explanation, however, may reside in their more recent entry into the Canadian labour force. Native peoples rank at the bottom in education, labour force participation and income.

SPECIAL STATUS SOCIETIES

Two categories of people have unique relationships in Canada with the federal government.

Native Peoples (First Nations)

There are fifty-five or more sovereign peoples who established themselves on the North American continent thousands of years before the Europeans arrived. Included are the major groupings, Indian, Inuit and Métis, a category of biracial descent, usually French and Indian.

The Indians can be registered under the Indian Act, treaty or non-treaty depending on whether their ancestors signed treaties and an undetermined group who may be biologically or culturally Indian but are not officially declared as such. There are perhaps 1.5 million people of Native ancestry, making up 6 percent of the Canadian population. Registered Indians who live on reserves are the special responsibility of the Department of Indian and Northern Affairs. The relationship with Ottawa has been paternalistic and has led to a severe erosion of their cultural fabric and community life. Residential schools for Native children were a devastating blow to their culture. Non-status Indians, the Métis and the Inuit were never confined to reservations but their cultural integrity is certainly diminished. There are many Native communities who are solving their problems but many others who are in a process of social disintegration. Contemporary leaders point the way to a brighter future of self-government which was punctuated in 1999 with the creation of Nunavut, a new territorial government carved out of the Northwest Territories and controlled by an Inuit majority.

The Québécois

The French presence in Canada goes back to 1608, the first permanent settlement being established at Québec City. New France at first grew slowly but two centuries later at confederation Canada's population was 31% French. The B.N.A. Act of 1867 recognized the province's civil law, language and Catholic schools. The French and English communities co-existed and eventually bilingualism was strengthened by the Official Languages Act of 1969.

Québec at the time of Confederation was a traditional society and was ineffectively governed. The church took responsibility for education, health care and social welfare but was more concerned with maintaining its position than helping people adjust to changing circumstances. The economic institution was controlled by the minority English in Montréal. Not until the Quiet Revolution of the 1960s was the power of the church diminished. The government of Jean Lesage focussed on education, attracting industry and integrating Québec into the North American economic structure. Québeckers eventually reached the conclusion that their language and culture needed protection in the sea of English North America. Their demand for institutional dominance led to a demand for sovereignty. Although they voted not to seek independence in a 1960 referendum, the failure of the Meech Lake Accord which would have granted Québec a "distinct society" status and the more recent rejection almost everywhere in Canada of the Charlottetown Accord has left Canada uncertain of the future of Québec in Canada.

In October, 1995 a razor-thin victory for the "No" in the separation referendum continues the uncertainty about the future of Québec in Canada. (See the **Controversy and Debate** Box, pp. 367, for a discussion of national unity).

IMMIGRATION TO CANADA: A HUNDRED-YEAR PERSPECTIVE

Canada has been, and will probably remain, a land of immigrants. 2.5 million people arrived between 1905 and 1914 such that in 1913 1 in every 17 Canadians was a newcomer. Most of the migrants were from Britain and were expected to maintain the British character of the country. A trickle of Ukrainians and other Europeans arrived to settle farming areas in the West. By 1931 Canada closed the doors especially to Jewish refugees because of a substantial anti-Semitism across the country. After WWII the doors opened again to meet Canada's labour needs and although Europeans were preferred more Asians were permitted entry along with Palestinians and Hungarians in the 1950s. Not until 1962, however, was an official end put to the "White Canada" immigration policy. Educational, occupational, and language skills were the criteria which were formalized as a points system in 1965 in order to meet the needs of the labour market. These changes were followed by waves of immigration from the West Indies and Asia in the 1990s. The Immigration Act of 1976 recognized three classes of people for landed immigrant status: *family class* (immediate family, parents and grandparents), *humanitarian class* (refugees or persecuted and displaced persons) and *independent class* (those admitted on the point system). This stimulated an unmanageable number of refugees and family applicants. In 1996 Asia was the source of 66% of our immigrants and they have settled primarily in Ontario and British Columbia in the cities of Toronto and Vancouver. The **Applying Sociology** Box (p. 359) describes the impact on those cities. Tables 14-4 and 14-5 (p.365) and **Canada Map** 14-1 (p. 366) outline the immigration picture for Canada in 1996.

RACE AND ETHNICITY: PAST AND FUTURE

Canada's future will depend upon forging an identity out of diversity.

KEY CONCEPTS

Define each of the following concepts on separate paper. Check the accuracy of your answers by referring to the text as well as by referring to italicized definitions located throughout the chapter.

assimilation
discrimination
ethnicity
genocide
hyper segregation
institutional completeness
institutional prejudice or discrimination
miscegenation

pluralism
prejudice
race
racism
scapegoat
segregation
stereotypes

STUDY QUESTIONS

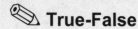 **True-False**

1. T F   Cultural practices, dress, ancestry and language are referred to as objective criteria of ethnicity.

2. T F   A racial or ethnic minority is a category of people, distinguished by physical or cultural traits, who are socially disadvantaged.

3. T F   Prejudice is a rigid and irrational generalization about an entire category of people.

4. T F   The scapegoat theory of prejudice suggests that those who display prejudice exhibit authoritarian personalities.

5. T F   The research by Sowell on intelligence tests found that cultural patterns were better explanations for I.Q. scores than racial or ethnic differences.

6. T F   The visibility of ethnic communities in Canada is affected by their level of institutional completeness.

7. T F   Canada has been fortunate as a nation never to have practised segregation.

8. T F   Toronto has the most diverse visible minority population in Canada.

9. T F   Almost 6% of the population of Canada is of Native descent.

10. T F   In 1999 the state of Nunavut was created in the Northwest Territories.

11. T F   Most immigrants who have come to Canada in recent decades have settled in Ontario and Quebec.

Multiple-Choice

1. Although no society or region of the world lacks genetic mixture, there is especially pronounced racial mixing in

   (a) Africa
   (b) North America
   (c) Oceana
   (d) Middle East
   (e) Japan

2. Race is _____ while ethnicity is _____.

   (a) objective, subjective
   (b) extrinsic, intrinsic
   (c) biological, cultural
   (d) deductive, inductive
   (e) Caucasian, Mongoloid

3. Minority groups have two major characteristics:

   (a) race and ethnicity
   (b) religion and ethnicity
   (c) physical traits and political orientation
   (d) sexual orientation and race
   (e) distinctive identity and subordination

4. Which theory of prejudice suggests that prejudice springs from frustration?

   (a) Scapegoat Theory
   (b) Authoritarian Personality Theory
   (c) Cultural Theory
   (d) Conflict Theory
   (e) Social Distance Theory

5. Thomas Sowell discovered that differences in I.Q. scores for racial or ethnic groups are due to

   (a) biological inheritance
   (b) differences in intellectual aptitude
   (c) racial differences
   (d) people's environment

6. Robert Merton's study of the relationship between prejudice and discrimination revealed one behavioural type that discriminates against persons even though s/he is not prejudiced. This person would be called a(n):

   (a) active bigot
   (b) all-weather liberal
   (c) timid bigot
   (d) fair-weather liberal

7. According to the work of W.I. Thomas, a "vicious cycle is formed by which variables?

   (a) miscegenation and authoritarianism
   (b) race and ethnicity
   (c) pluralism and assimilation
   (d) segregation and integration
   (e) prejudice and discrimination

8. Which pattern of minority/majority interaction is characterized by distinct racial and ethnic minorities who have social parity?

   (a) Pluralism
   (b) Assimilation
   (c) Segregation
   (d) Genocide
   (e) Completeness

9. The _____, which recognized Québec as "a distinct society" failed to be ratified by all provincial legislatures by a 1990 deadline.

   (a) Meech Lake Accord   (d) Victoria Accord
   (b) Charlottetown Accord   (e) Quiet Revolution
   (c) Charter of Rights and Freedoms

10. 66% of the immigrants to Canada in 96/97 were from the geographic region of:

    (a) Europe   (c) Africa
    (b) Caribbean   (d) Asia

✎ Fill-In The Blank

1. The term _____ refers to a category composed of people who share biologically transmitted traits deemed socially significant.

2. The three part scheme of racial classification developed by biologists during the 19th century included _____, _____, and _____.

3. In Canada _____ form a numerical majority but are regarded as minority.

4. Contrary to stereotype, most poor people in Canada are _____.

5. Adorno discovered extreme prejudice in _____ .

6. According to _____ powerful people use prejudice to justify their oppression of minorities.

7. _____ is a process by which minorities gradually adopt patterns of the dominant culture.

8. The Underground Railroad brought escaped slaves to freedom in the Province of _____.

9. The peak ten year period for immigration to Canada was _____.

10. The Immigration Act of 1976 recognized three classes of people eligible for landed immigrant status. They are _____ _____ _____.

Definition and Short-Answer

1. Identify the four explanations of why prejudice exists.

2. Differentiate between the concepts prejudice and discrimination.

3. What are the four types of people identified by Merton's typology of patterns of prejudice and discrimination? Provide an illustration for each.

4. What is institutional prejudice and discrimination? Provide an example.

5. What are the four models representing the patterns of interaction between minority groups and the majority group?

6. In what ways have First Nations people lost their cultural identity?

7. Identify the various waves of immigration to Canada and the reasons for them.

8. Differentiate the concepts of race and ethnicity.

9. What are the major characteristics of minority groups?

10. Are minority groups ever a majority in society?

Answers to Study Questions

True-False

1. T (p. 347)	7. F (p. 355)
2. T (p. 347)	8. T (p. 359)
3. T (p. 348)	9. T (p. 361)
4. F (pp. 349-351)	10. T (p. 362)
5. T (p. 350)	11. F (p. 365)
6. T (p. 353)	

Multiple-Choice

1. d (p. 346)	6. d (p. 352)
2. c (p. 347)	7. e (p. 353)
3. e (p. 347)	8. a (p. 353)
4. a (p. 349)	9. a (p. 363)
5. d (p. 350)	10. d (p. 365)

Fill-In

1. race (p. 345-46)
2. Caucasian, Negroid, Mongoloid (pp. 346)
3. women (p. 348)
4. white (p. 348)
5. authoritarian personalities (p. 351)
6. conflict theory (p. 351)
7. assimilation (p. 354)
8. Ontario (p. 356)
9. 1905 to 1914 (p. 364)
10. family/humanitarian/independent (p. 365)

ANALYSIS AND COMMENT

Go back through the chapter and write down in the spaces below key points from each of the following boxes.

SOCIAL DIVERSITY

"Does Race Affect Intelligence?"
Key Points:

_____

_____

_____

_____

"Black Citizens of Canada: A History Ignored."
Key Points:

_____

_____

_____

_____

APPLYING SOCIOLOGY

"Visible Minorities: Toronto, Vancouver and Montreal."
Key Points:

_____

_____

_____

_____

CONTROVERSY AND DEBATE

"Distinct Societies and National Unity"
Key Points:

_____

_____

_____

_____

SUGGESTED READINGS

Contemporary Sources

Harry H. L. Kitano. *1990 Race Relations.* 4th Ed.
Englewood Cliffs, NJ: Prentice Hall.
This paperback text delves into the issues raised in
this chapter.

George J. Borgas. *Friends or Strangers: The*
Impact of Immigrants on the U.S. Economy. **New**
York: Basic Books.
Do immigrants bring innovation and economic
vitality to a society or merely raise unemployment?
This book paints a multidimensional portrait of
newcomers to the United States and assesses the
economic consequences of immigration.

Herman Belz. *Equality Transformed: A Quarter-*
Century of Affirmative Action. **1991. New**
Brunswick, NJ: Transaction.
This history of racial preferences examines the
complex consequences of affirmative action with
regard to race relations.

Canadian Sources

Peter S. Li. 1988. *Ethnic Inequality in a Class*
Society. **Toronto: Wall and Thompson.**
Christopher McAll. 1990. *Class, Ethnicity, and*
Social Inequality. **Montreal & Kingston: McGill-**
Queen's University Press.
These two books spotlight the centrality of race and
ethnicity to social stratification in Canada.

Valerie Knowles. 1992. *Strangers at Our Gates:*
Canadian Immigration and Immigration Policy,
1540-1990. **Toronto: Dundurn Press.**
This book explores Canada's immigration policy and
details its consequences.

Bissoondath, Neil. 1994. *Selling Illusions: The*
Cult of Multiculturalism in Canada.. **Toronto:**
Penguin Books.
Jeffrey S. Reitz, and Raymond Breton. 1994. *The*
Illusion of Difference: Realities of Ethnicity in
Canada and the United States. **Toronto: C. D.**
Howe Institute.
These two books deal with "illusions" relating to
ethnicity and multiculturalism. The first, by
Bissoondath, questions the goal of preserving cultural
differences at the expense of a Canadian identity.
The second, by Reitz and Breton, looks at
multiculturalism and the American "melting pot" and
asks if these policy thrusts have any impact on the
economic and social incorporation of minorities.

Stanley R. Barrett. 1987. *Is God Racist: The*
Right Wing in Canada. **Toronto: University of**
Toronto Press.
This fascinating account of white, racist, right-wing
organizations in Canada is based upon extensive
interviews.

Mordecai Richler. 1991. *Oh Canada! Oh Quebec! Requiem for a Divided Country.* Toronto: Penguin Books.
Novelist and essayist Mordecai Richler details the experience of being Jewish and Anglophone in Quebec.

Edward N. Herberg. 1989. *Ethnic Groups in Canada: Adaptations and Transitions.* Scarborough, Ontario: Nelson Canada.
This book investigates the social dynamics of race and ethnicity in Canada.

Frank Cassidy, ed. 1991. *Aboriginal Self-Determination.* Montreal: The Institute for Research on Public Policy, 1991.
This book, the edited proceedings of a conference on Aboriginal self-government, contains contributions from a wide range of Native leaders, as well as politicians and academics.

Global Sources

Milton J. Esman and Itamar Rabinovich, eds. 1988. Ethnicity, Pluralism, and the State in the Middle East. Ithaca, N.Y. and London: Cornell University Press.
David K. Shipler. 1986. *Arab and Jew: Wounded Spirits in a Promised Land.* New York: Times Books
This investigation of the resurgence of ethnicity in Israel also demonstrates how ethnicity interacts with social class. If cultural patterns can build community, they can also turn people against one another. Nowhere has this been truer than in the Middle East. The first book examines how ethnicity stands at the core of Middle Eastern social structure. The second book, by a noted foreign correspondent who lived in Jerusalem for five years, explores how stereotypes carry hatred into the lives of each new generation.

Eliezer Ben-Raphael and Stephen Sharot. 1991. *Ethnicity, Religion, and Class in Israeli Society.* Cambridge, U.K.: Cambridge University Press.
John Solomos. 1989. *Race and Racism in Contemporary Britain.* London: Macmillan.
Walter P. Zenner. 1991. *Minorities in the Middle: A Cross-Cultural Analysis.* Albany, NY: SUNY Press.
This global analysis explores the experiences of Jews, Scots, Chinese, and other ethnic categories that have marginal standing in various societies.

CHAPTER 15

- To define and explain the development of the graying of Canada.

- To describe the interrelationship and respective roles of biology and culture in growing old.

- To explain the role of the elderly in cross-cultural and historical perspectives.

- To describe the problems and transitions involved in growing old.

- To explain ageism and its impact on the elderly

- To understand that some cultures are not characterized by ageism.

- To identify the key arguments in the debate over whether the elderly constitute a minority group.

- To describe, compare and contrast the three sociological explanations of aging.

- To describe the changing character of death throughout history and into modern times.

- To understand the ethical issues associated with death.

- To describe the process of bereavement.

- To project the future of a "graying" society.

III CHAPTER REVIEW

This chapter begins with a discussion about the book Final Exit. The author, a founder and director of the Hemlock Society, offers practical assistance for those who wish to take their own lives. The recent case of Sue Rodriguez has brought attention to the issue in Canada and as more people live longer we will be faced with making decisions about whether to assist those who wish to die or not, within the context of escalating medical care costs.

THE GRAYING OF CANADA

A powerful revolution is reshaping Canada. It is referred to as the graying of Canada. In just over a century life expectancy has doubled and the average number of children has declined by half. Figure 15-1 (p.372) shows the changing population pyramid of Canada. In 1996 the population over 65 made up 12.2 percent of the whole but by 2031 the percentage will be 23.8. The two causes of this shift are the tremendous post WWII baby boom, followed by a sharp decline in birth rates. **Canada Map** 15-1 (p. 373) shows the distribution of the over 65 population across Canada. **Global Map** 15-1 (p. 374) shows that aging societies are developed societies.

LIFE EXPECTANCY: GOING UP

Women can expect to live to 81 and men to 75 years. The possible consequences of the massive increase in the elderly population are immense. The old-age dependency rate will double in the next fifty years as the proportion of non-employed adults soars and the costs of health care will rise as well, although there are those who suggest today's seniors are healthier than previous generations.

An Aging Society: Cultural Change

Age segregation will decline and a "culture of aging" is unlikely in such a diverse society.

The "Young Old" and the "Old Old"

The "young old" are between 65 and 75 and are living in reasonable health and financial security while the "old old", those over 75, are increasingly dependent on others. This total older segment of the population, however, will not be growing rapidly until the boomers reach 65.

GROWING OLD: BIOLOGY AND CULTURE

Gerontology is the study of aging and the elderly. This field examines biological processes, personality changes and the impact of culture and social definitions as people age.

Biological Changes

While aging does lead to some bodily deterioration, cultural labels have a major impact upon how we perceive these changes. In Canada's youth oriented society growing old is seen as growing down. Older people do suffer more chronic illnesses and life-threatening diseases such as cancer and heart disease and experience some decline in sensory abilities. Dementia, progressive cognitive impairment, affects 5 to 10 percent of those over 65 years and 20% of those over 80 years, but the vast majority of the elderly population are neither discouraged nor disabled by their physical or mental condition. Patterns of aging vary greatly, however, between social groups. Because women live longer, they suffer more chronic illness and income is positively related to preventative care and perceptions of happiness.

Psychological Changes

Most elderly people do not suffer from mental or psychological problems.. While research suggests that measures of intelligence focussing on sensorimotor coordination do show decline in aged persons, intelligence tests focussing on knowledge show no decline. Verbal and numerical skills may even increase with age. Psychological research has also shown that personality changes little as we grow old.

Aging and Culture

The significance of growing old is a matter of cultural definition. Old is a relative term as **Global Map** 15-2 (p.377) illustrates. In many of the poorer countries the average lifespan is fifty years while a Canadian of sixty years is not identified as old. Advances in medicine and health have made a difference but cultural definition is just as important, as shown in the **Global Sociology** Box (p. 379) and in the **Applying Sociology** Box (p. 378).

Age Stratification: A Global Assessment

Age stratification is defined as the unequal distribution of wealth, power, and privileges among people at different stages of the life course. This varies by societal development and the old seem to generally have more power in societies in which they can accumulate wealth. In *hunting and gathering* societies age is seen as a burden. *Pastoral, horticultural*, and *agrarian* societies on the other hand have the technological capabilities to produce surpluses to enable accumulation to occur. Such societies tend toward *gerontocracy*, a form of social organization in which the elderly have the most wealth, power, and prestige. *Industrialization* tends to create a decline in the relative power and prestige of the aged as the prime source of wealth shifts away from the land and geographical mobility undermines the strength of families. The rapid change in technology also diminishes the expertise of the elderly and they are pushed toward nonproductive roles. Japan is a culture in which the productive role and status of the elderly in the family and labour force has remained intact, providing the aged with greater prestige but even Japan is becoming more like other industrial societies where age means giving up a measure of social importance.

TRANSITIONS AND PROBLEMS OF AGING

Of all life stages old age presents the greatest personal challenges. The body is in some measure of decline and lives are nearing an end.

Finding Meaning

Although some face the end with despair, those who learn to accept their past mistakes and successes fare well. There are illnesses to face but as Table 15-1 (p. 381) indicates most elderly people are at least somewhat happy with life. People who were well adjusted earlier in life tend to be well adjusted as they age.

Social Isolation

Central among the adjustments an individual must make during old age is the accommodation to increased social isolation. Negative stereotypes, retirement, and physical problems diminish social interaction. The most profound social isolation however occurs with the death of a significant other, particularly a spouse.

Almost ¾ of widows and widowers cite loneliness as their most serious problem. Some survivors choose not to live at all. The problem of social isolation falls mostly on women as

Table 15-2 (p. 381) on living arrangements of the elderly shows. Spouses provide emotional support for men but women rely on more varied support, particularly daughters, after their husbands die. (See Figure 15-3, p. 382)

Retirement

Work figures prominently in personal identity. Therefore, loss of work generally entails less income, less prestige and loss of purpose. Some organizations like universities ease the transition and for many older people new challenges like volunteer activities fill the void. Retirement is a recent phenomenon prompted by the need to use fewer workers and to bring in younger workers in a rapidly changing society.

Pension plans have eased the financial burdens in Canada where the aged are now less likely to be poor. While there is a debate about the constitutionality of mandatory retirement only about 1 percent of the workforce would continue past 65 if given the choice. Recently, global restructuring and government downsizing has led to many early retirements and the launching of new careers.

Aging and Income

The image of the elderly as poverty stricken is somewhat unfounded. While retirement leads to a decline in income expenses also decline. But women and people of colour suffer proportionately greater deprivation and the pride of many older citizens leads them to hide even from their families their economic difficulties.

Abuse of the Elderly

Recent surveys indicate that 3-5 percent of the elderly are victimized by maltreatment but the figure is likely much higher because of a reluctance to report the abuse. Much of the abuse appears to be attributable to the stresses of caring for aged parents, especially by the "sandwich generation" of parents who work, raise their children and care for their parents. This is especially the case where the old person has serious health problems.

AGEISM

Ageism refers to prejudice and discrimination against the elderly. While old people are more likely to be mentally and physically impaired, the majority are not. Unwarranted generalizations lead to stereotypes which result in overt (loss of job) and subtle (condescending tones) discrimination. Betty Friedan suggests that older people have much to contribute and would, if negative definitions in the media and elsewhere were to disappear.

The Elderly: A Minority?

Sociologists vary in their opinion concerning the classification of the aged as a minority group. Certain general characteristics of the aged population seem consistent with such a status, however the social disadvantages faced by the elderly are less substantial than those experienced by other categories of people labeled as minorities. Their situation is labeled as an open status, not permanent or exclusive. The old are simply a distinctive segment of the Canadian population.

THEORETICAL ANALYSIS OF AGING

Structural-Functional Analysis: Aging and Disengagement

Disengagement theory links the disengagement by elderly people from positions of social responsibility to the orderly operation of society. This theory, based on Talcott Parson's structural-functional analysis, suggests that the orderly transfer of various statuses and roles from the old to the young provides benefits for both society and individuals with diminished capacity. A problem with this view is that many older people do not want to relinquish their statuses and roles and are quite capably functioning within them. As well, workers cannot freely disengage unless they have financial security and the costs of loss of independence are considerable.

Symbolic-Interaction Analysis: Aging and Activity

Activity theory links personal satisfaction in old age to a high level of activity. Disengagement is viewed as diminishing satisfaction and meaning in life. While disengaging from certain statuses and roles, the elderly shift to new ones based on their own distinctive needs, interests, talents and capabilities. This approach may however underestimate the loss of competency among the aged.

Social-Conflict Analysis: Aging and Inequality

This approach sees different age categories across the life cycle competing for scarce resources. The status of the elderly relative to younger people is viewed as being disadvantaged as a result of the emphasis in capitalist societies on keeping costs down. While focussing our attention on the age stratification which does exist in society, this approach tends to ignore the improvement in social standing of the elderly in recent decades, and focuses upon capitalism when industrialization may be the major culprit.

DEATH AND DYING

The Bible tells us of two certainties: the fact of birth and the inevitability of death. The changing character of death is discussed in this section.

Historical Patterns of Death

Throughout much of human history death was a natural part of everyday life. Disease and catastrophes were widespread. In pre-industrial societies, less productive people (infants and the aged) were sometimes put to death (infanticide/geronticide) for the sake of preserving the group. As societies began to gain some measure of control over death through technological advances, attitudes about death changed. It was no longer an everyday experience in the lives of people. Now old age and death have become fused.

The Modern Separation of Life and Death

Death is now looked at as something unnatural; in a sense, separate from life. Death and dying are now physically removed from everyday activities and typically occur away from the family, in a hospital.

Ethical Issues: Confronting Death

As the capacity to extend life through "heroic measures" and artificial means increases, the question about when life ceases becomes ever more problematic.

Many individuals would like the capacity to choose when their life should end, sometimes as a release from suffering. The **Global Sociology** Box (p. 388) indicates that the Dutch provide people the opportunity of *euthanasia*, but it remains illegal in Canada. Should we allow people the right to end their suffering or is this the "slippery slope" towards forcing death on those who are becoming medically expensive?

Bereavement

It can be argued that Kubler-Ross' stages of death can be applied to the bereavement process. Hospice is a program which helps people, through palliative care, to have better deaths. Bereavement, however, may last a long time and cause profound grief, unless a satisfactory closure to the relationship is attained.

LOOKING AHEAD: AGING IN THE TWENTY-FIRST CENTURY

There are reasons for both concern and optimism as we look ahead. Within the next fifty years one in four Canadians will be over 65 and one in five of them will be over 85. They will require support services which a smaller working population will be hard-pressed to provide (See **Controversy and Debate** box (pp. 389). On the positive side, those seniors will be more healthy and wealthy than previous generations and medical technology will continue to improve.

On balance we will have mounting responsibilities to care for the aged but death will perhaps become again, a natural part of the life course.

KEY CONCEPTS

Define each of the following concepts on separate paper. Check the accuracy of your answers by referring to the text as well as by referring to italicized definitions located throughout the chapter.

Activity theory   euthanasia
Ageism   gerontocracy
Age stratification   gerontology
Disengagement theory

STUDY QUESTIONS

 True-False

1. T F   Presently men can expect to live to be about 75 years of age.

2. T F   Health care spending is 6.5 times greater for those over 75 years than for those
              under 65 years.

3. T F   Among the "older" elderly about 90% are women.

4. T F   The elderly are in better health than in previous generations and are spending
              fewer days in the hospital.

5. T F   Where Natives in Canada strive to maintain cultural traditions, elders are held in
              high esteem.

6. T F   In Abkhasia the residents live long lives despite eating large amount of saturated
              fat and having little physical activity.

7. T F   The most likely source of emotional support for elderly women living without
              their spouses is a son.

8. T F   Over 80% of the elderly live above the low income level cutoff.

9. T F   As the proportion of elderly people rises, so does the incidence of abuse.

10. T F   Death in Canada is physically removed from everyday activities.

 Multiple-Choice

1. The person who fought, right up to the Supreme Court of Canada, for the right to assisted
    suicide when he/she determined that life with ALS was not worth living was

        (a) Robert Latimer   d) Ross Perot
        (b) Sue Rodriguez   e) George Germain
        (c) Austin Bastable

2. By 2031 the percentage of the Canadian population which will be 65 years of age and older will be:

(a) 11.6%   (b) 17.8%   (c) 21.2%   (d) 23.8%

3. Currently life expectancy for females in Canada is:

(a) 64 years   (b) 70 years   (c) 75 years   (d) 81 years

4. Which of the following is a reason that patterns of well being vary greatly within the elderly population?

(a) People with higher incomes are likely to work in a healthful and safe environment, which pays benefits into old age.
(b) Richer people can afford much more preventive medical care.
(c) Women, because they typically live longer than men, suffer more from chronic disabilities than men.
(d) a and b above.
(e) all of the above.

5. In most industrial societies the power and prestige of the elderly is severely eroded. What country is an exception?

(a) Canada   (d) The Netherlands
(b) Japan   (e) France
(c) United States

6. Most elderly males:

(a) live alone   (c) live with extended family members
(b) live in nursing homes   (d) live with their spouse

7. What percentage of the Canadian workforce would work past the age of 65 if given the choice?

(a) 1%   (b) 5%   (c) 15%   (d) 20%   (e) 50%

8. Disengagement theory is a sociological theory of aging that is based upon

(a) structural-functional analysis   (c) social-conflict analysis
(b) symbolic-interaction analysis   (d) social-exchange analysis

9. Which of the following would a social-conflict analysis identify as problems for the aged.

    (a) Employers replace older workers with younger ones in order to keep wages down.
    (b) When a society is concerned with profit, it will devalue those who are less productive.
    (c) There is a lack of diversity in the elderly population.
    (d) (a) and (b) above
    (e) (a) and (c) above

10. The future of aging in our country is likely to include:

    (a) by 2050, one in five seniors will be over 85
    (b) the elderly of the next century will be more vigorous and independent than the elderly today
    (c) the elderly of the next century will have more affluence than the elderly today
    (d) all of the above
    (e) (b) and (c) above

✏️ Fill-In The Blank

1. The period after 1965 during which the birth rate took a sharp turn downward is often called the _____.

2. The ratio of elderly people to working-age adults is called the _____.

3. Erik Erikson suggests that elderly people must resolve a tension of _____ versus _____.

4. The problem of social isolation falls most heavily on _____.

5. Today's middle-aged adults represent a _____ generation who may spend as much time caring for their aging parents as for their own children.

6. _____ refers to prejudice and discrimination against the elderly.

7. Our authors believe the aged should not be identified as a minority group, but rather be considered a _____ segment of the Canadian population.

8. In 1900, about _____ of all deaths in Canada occurred before the age of five.

9. _____ has gone further than any nation in allowing euthanasia.

10. Currently about _____ of the total lifetime medical costs of care for an individual are incurred during the last years of his or her life.

Definition and Short-Answer

1. What is the Hemlock Society? What are your thoughts and feelings about this organization and its purposes? What are some of the broader concerns relating to this issue?

2. Discuss the role of elders in Aboriginal cultures.

3. Define age stratification. How does it vary between hunting and gathering, horticultural, agrarian, and industrial societies?

4. In what ways can a person adjust to old age?

5. Differentiate between activity theory and disengagement theory in terms of how each helps us understand the changing status of the aged in society.

6. Why is elder abuse so common in Canada?

7. Discuss the relative economic condition of the aged in our society today?

8. According to social-conflict theorists, why is the status of the aged diminished in capitalist societies?

9. What are the arguments in the debate concerning whether the aged are a minority group?

10. What are the problems facing Canada as the proportion of aged citizens grows?

11. How will the patterns of inequality in Canada be affected by the Information Revolution?

Answers to Study Questions

True-False

1. T (p. 372)	6. F (p. 379)
2. T (p. 373)	7. F (p. 382)
3. F (p. 375)	8. T (p. 382)
4. T (p. 375)	9. T (p. 383)
5. T (p. 378)	10. T (p. 387)

Multiple-Choice

1. b (p. 371)	6. d (p.381)
2. d (p. 372)	7. a (p. 382)
3. d (p. 372)	8. a (p. 384)
4. e (p. 376)	9. d (p. 385)
5. b (p. 380)	10. d (pp. 389-390)

Fill-In

1. baby bust (p.372)
2. old-age dependency (p. 373)
3. integrity/despair (p. 380)
4. women (p. 381)
5. sandwich (p. 383)

6. ageism (p. 383)
7. distinctive (p. 384)
8. one-third (p. 386)
9. The Netherlands (p. 388)
10. half (p. 389)

ANALYSIS AND COMMENT

Go back through the chapter and write down in the space below key points from each of the following boxes.

APPLYING SOCIOLOGY

"Native Elders: Cultural Custodians."
Key Points:

_____

_____

_____

_____

GLOBAL SOCIOLOGY

"Growing (Very) Old: A Report from Abkhasia."
Key Points:

_____

_____

_____

_____

"Death on Demand: A Report from the Netherlands."
Key Points:

_____

_____

_____

_____

CONTROVERSY AND DEBATE

"Setting Limits: Must We "Pull the Plug" on Old Age?
Key Points:

_____

_____

_____

_____

CYBER. SCOPE

The Information Revolution means loss of manufacturing jobs and an increase in information based jobs. These losses and gains are distributed unevenly in Canada and globally. Males, to some extent, are more likely to be introduced to computers and the young adapt much more readily to the demands of the new information technology.

As well, the Information Revolution is almost entirely a benefit to the industrialized world.

SUGGESTED READINGS

Classic Source

Robert N. Butler. 1975. *Why Survive? Being Old in America.* New York: Harper and Row.
This Pulitzer Prize-winning book launched a growing social movement critical of our society's approach to aging.

Contemporary and Canadian Sources

Robert O. Hansson and Bruce N. Carpenter. 1994. *Relationships in Old Age: Coping With the Challenge of Transition.* New York: Guilford.
This book explores one of the most challenging aspects of growing old: maintaining relationships during a time of transition.

E. Gee and M. Kimball. 1987. *Women and Aging.* Toronto: Butterworths.
A. Martin-Matthews. 1989. "Widowhood as an Expectable Life Event," in V. Marshall, ed., *Aging in Canada: Social Perspectives,* 2nd. Ed., pp. 343-66. Markham, ON: Fitzhenry and Whiteside.
This article and book examine some of the issues facing women as they grow older.

N. Chappell, L. Strain, and A. Blandford. 1986. *Aging and Health Care: A Social Perspective.* Toronto: Holt, Rinehart and Winston.
This is an overview of the health and health services issues confronting the elderly in Canada.

I. Connidis. 1989. *Family Ties and Aging.* Toronto: Butterworths.
This book examines the social and familial relationships of elderly Canadians.

W. Forbes, J. Jackson, and A. Kraus. 1987. *Institutionalization of the Elderly in Canada.* Toronto: Butterworths.
This provides an overview of the living arrangements and institutionalization of elderly Canadians.

S. McDaniel. 1986. *Canada's Aging Population.* Toronto: Butterworths.
This book focuses on the demographic description of Canadian elders.

B. McPherson. 1991. *Aging as a Social Process:*
An Introduction to Individual and Population
Aging, Second Edition. **Toronto: Butterworths.**
This is a comprehensive text on aging in Canada.

Canada. 1988. Canada's Seniors—A Dynamic
Force. Ottawa: **Seniors Secretariat.**
This government publication describes the status and
role of aging Canadians.

CHAPTER 16

The Economy and Work

I CHAPTER OUTLINE

I.   **The Economy: Historical Overview**
    A. The Agricultural Revolution
    B. The Industrial Revolution
    C. The Information Revolution and The Post-industrial Society
    D. Sectors of the Economy
    E. The Global Economy

II. **Comparative Economic Systems**
    A. Capitalism
    B. Socialism
        1. Socialism and Communism
    D. Welfare Capitalism and State Capitalism
    E. Relative Advantages of Capitalism and Socialism
        1. Economic Productivity
        2. Economic Equality
        3. Personal Freedom
    F. Changes in Socialist Countries

III. **Work in the Post-industrial Economy**
    A. The Decline of Agricultural Work
    B. The Dual Labour Market
    C. Labour Unions
    D. Professions
    E. Self-Employment
    F. Unemployment
    G. The Underground Economy
    H. New Information Technology and Work

IV. **Corporations**
    A. Economic Concentration
    B. Foreign Ownership
    C. Conglomerates and Corporate Linkages
    D. Corporations: Are they Competitive?
    E. Corporations and the Global Economy

V.   **The Economy of the Twenty-First Century**
VI. **Summary**
VII. **Critical Thinking Questions**
VIII. **Applications And Exercises**
IX. **Sites To See**

- To explain the history and development of economic activity from the agricultural revolution through the industrial revolution to the post-industrial society.

- To identify and describe the primary, secondary, and tertiary sectors of the economy.

- To compare and contrast the economic systems of capitalism and socialism.

- To identify the differences between welfare capitalism and state capitalism.

- To explain the difference between socialism and communism.

- To identify the advantages and disadvantages of capitalism and socialism on productivity, income, economic, and political factors.

- To describe the general characteristics and trends of work in Canadian post-industrial society.

- To understand the consequences of the shift in post-industrial societies to service work and the attendant problems of unemployment and lower wages.

- To describe the nature of employment in the Canadian economy.

- To compare and contrast corporations and conglomerates and analyze competition and foreign ownership in the Canadian economy.

- To explain the impact of multinational corporations on the world economy.

III CHAPTER REVIEW

This chapter focuses on the economy as a social system which is operating within a complex global market. The opening scenario portrays the difficulties Canadians face in the job market as the economy restructures.

THE ECONOMY: HISTORICAL OVERVIEW

The *economy* is the social institution that organizes production, distribution, and consumption of goods and services. Goods range from basic necessities to luxury items. Services include various activities that benefit others including government services. Modern complex societies are the result of centuries of technological development and social change.

The Agricultural Revolution

Being much more productive than hunting and gathering societies, agrarian societies produce considerable surpluses. The four factors of agricultural technology, productive specialization, permanent settlements, and trade have been important in the development of the economy. In agrarian economies like those which existed in medieval Europe, many people living in cities worked at home, in what is referred to as the *"cottage industry."*

The Industrial Revolution

Five revolutionary changes are identified as resulting from the industrial revolution of Europe beginning in the mid-18th century. These include: new forms of energy, the spread of factories, manufacturing and mass production, specialization, and wage labour. Greater productivity steadily raised the standard of living although the benefits were unequally distributed. The **Social Diversity** box (p. 397) describes the migration of poor rural families in Quebec to the textile factories in Manchester, New Hampshire.

The Information Revolution and the Post-industrial Society

By 1950, Canada was becoming a post-industrial economy, one based on service work and information technology. Machines reduced human production labour and the service industries expanded as manufacturing declined. Finally, an information revolution is being driven by computer technology where ideas and literacy are important and work is being decentralized.

Sectors of the Economy

Three economic sectors exist and their relative balance shifts over history. The *primary sector* is the part of the economy generating raw materials directly from the natural environment. Today in Canada only 4.8 percent of the labour force is involved in this sector. The *secondary sector* is the part of the economy that transforms raw materials into manufactured goods. 22.2% of the labour force is involved in such work. The *tertiary sector* is the part of the economy generating services rather than goods. About 73 percent of our labour force is employed in such work. Figure 16-1 (p. 398) shows the size of sectors by the income of countries and Figure 16-2 (p. 398) indicates the historical shifts in sector activity in Canada.

The Global Economy

Although 191 politically distinct nations exist today, their influence is compromised by the *global economy* which is economic activity spanning many nations. There is a global division of sector activity (see **Global Maps** 16-1 and 16-2, p. 400), products pass through many economies, markets ignore borders and there is an increasing concentration of wealth and economic activity.

COMPARATIVE ECONOMIC SYSTEMS

Capitalism

Capitalism is an economic system in which productive resources are privately owned. This system has three distinctive features: private ownership of property, pursuit of personal profit, and free competition and consumer sovereignty. Although Canada is a capitalist country, the government intervenes in the marketplace and owns resources through Crown corporations.

Socialism

Socialism is an economic system in which productive resources are collectively owned. Its distinguishing characteristics include: collective ownership of property, pursuit of collective goals, and government control of the economy.

➤Socialism and Communism

Communism is a hypothetical economic and political system in which all members of society have economic and social equality. Marx viewed socialism as a transitory stage on the way to communism. However, nowhere has this system been achieved. Such a society, probably even for Marx, is a *utopia*.

Welfare Capitalism and State Capitalism

Several western European democracies have combined a market-based economy with social welfare programs. *Welfare capitalism* is a political and economic system that includes significant government intervention in the economy. Sweden, and Italy are examples. In Japan and other Pacific Rim countries *state capitalism* exists where government and private industry co-operate to facilitate productivity.

Relative Advantages of Capitalism and Socialism

Since no pure examples of capitalism and socialism exist precise objective comparisons are not possible. However, certain crude comparisons can be made keeping the following factors in mind.

➤Economic Productivity

Capitalist societies outproduce socialist societies by a ratio of 2.7 to 1.

➤Economic Equality

While socialist societies have lower overall standards of living they create less income disparity.

➤Personal Freedom

Capitalist societies provide freedom to pursue one's self-interest while socialist societies provide freedom from want. We have yet to devise a system where political freedom and economic equality are both paramount.

Changes in Socialist Countries

The collapse of the Soviet Union has led to sweeping changes in Eastern Europe and the previous Soviet republics. The market reforms are proceeding unevenly and there is some evidence that improvements in living standards are accompanied by increasing economic disparity.

WORK IN THE POST-INDUSTRIAL ECONOMY

The Canadian labour force continues to go through substantial change in the postindustrial period. In 1996, 15 million Canadians were in the labour force, representing two-thirds of those over the age of 15. Male participation is higher than female but the gender gap is closing. Figure 16-3 (p. 404) shows participation rates for selected racial and ethnic categories for 1986 and 1991. Rates are similar for British and French in both years, higher for Asians and Blacks but dropping slightly in 1991 while Native rates are very low.

The Decline of Agricultural Work

Currently, less than 5 percent of the Canadian labour force is involved in farming. Yet, Canadian agriculture is more productive now than it was in the past. More and more production is occurring in corporate agribusinesses as the "family farm" disappears.

The Dual Labour Market

One way to describe the change which is occurring in our economy is to divide work into two different labour markets. The *primary labour market* includes occupations that provide extensive benefits to workers, while the *secondary labour market* includes jobs providing minimal benefits to workers. A growing proportion of new jobs in postindustrial economies fall into the secondary labour market. The workers in these jobs are those most likely to experience alienation and dissatisfaction and are sometimes referred to as the *reserve army of labour*, those last hired during expansion and first fired when the economy contracts.

Labour Unions

Labour unions are organizations of workers that attempt to improve wages and working conditions through strategies including negotiations and strikes. Canadian labour union membership has been remarkably stable with approximately one-third of the labour force involved for the last twenty years. Women's involvement has increased slightly and the highest level of penetration is in the government or public administration where seventy percent belong to unions. There is considerable variation by industry sector and by region of the country. Globally, those countries with social democratic values have higher levels of union participation than those with pro-capitalist values.

Professions

A *profession* is a prestigious, white-collar occupation that requires extensive formal education. Professions share the following characteristics: theoretical knowledge, self-regulated training and practice, authority over clients, and community orientation rather than self-interest.

Many new service occupations are seeking professional standing, a process known as professionalization. This process is initiated by members of an occupational category by labeling their work in a new way. This is followed by the development of a professional association, which initiates a code of ethics and perhaps even schools to train members. In marginal cases, paraprofessional status may be obtained, denoting special training, but lacking extensive theoretical education.

Self-Employment

Self-employment refers to earning a living without working for a large organization. In the early 19th century, about 80 percent of the U.S. labour force was self-employed but then declined precipitously.

In recent years Canada has experienced increases in self- employment so that in 1998 the self- employed made up 16 percent of the labour force. Some professionals are involved but most are small business owners. For the most part these are well-educated, relatively affluent individuals.

While substantial profits are possible, many small businesses go bankrupt during downturns and pension and health-care benefits must be self-provided. As well, these individuals are ineligible for government programs like employment insurance.

Unemployment

While unemployment is found in all societies, it is seen as a natural phenomenon in capitalist societies. It is, however, a problem in socialist societies as well. Canada's unemployment rate in 1993 was 11% but has dropped to 8.1% in December 1997. While part-time work had been increasingly replacing full-time work in 1997, the gains were primarily full-time jobs.

Unemployment rates vary by region (see **Canada Map** 16-1, p. 408) and by race-ethnicity (see Figure 16-4, p. 409). Official unemployment rates, however, understate the problem since "discouraged workers" and the underemployed are not identified. The **Social Diversity** Box (p. 411) also indicates the nature of regional disparity in manufacturing and how the center is likely to remain strong.

The Underground Economy

In violation of government law, there exists an *underground economy*, or economic activity involving income or the exchange of goods and services that is not reported to the government. Such activity ranges from having garage sales and not reporting the money generated, to illegal drug trade. The single largest segment of this underground economy, however, is legally obtained income unreported on income taxes. Perhaps 15-20 percent of the economic activity in Canada is unreported. The imposition of the G.S.T. in 1991 has provided the incentive for under-the-table cash payments.

New Information Technology and Work

Computer technology is changing the character of work. The changes include de-skilling labour, making work more abstract, limiting interaction, and enhancing employer's control of workers. The **Exploring Cyber-Society** box (p. 410) shows clearly how information technology is changing the way all work is done and indeed, what kinds of jobs are created.

CORPORATIONS

A *corporation* is an organization with a legal existence including rights and liabilities apart from those of its members. Most large corporations are owned by thousands of shareholders which theoretically should disperse wealth in society. Clements notes, however, that major stockholders comprise a small economic elite in Canada so that the distribution of wealth in Canada has been unchanged by corporate proliferation.

Economic Concentration

Although many Canadian corporations are small the Canadian economy is dominated by large corporations which, unlike the U.S., includes the banks and other financial institutions. Canada's banks, in fact, are involved in attempts to merge in order to be larger global players. Corporate concentration comes about in Canada because of the power of a small number of people, interlocking directorships, geographic centralization of investment in Ontario and Quebec, and the tendency of corporations, especially after the Free Trade agreement, to expand by acquisition or merger. (Table 16-1, p. 412) shows the top revenue producing companies in Canada for 1999)

Foreign Ownership

Foreign ownership in Canada, primarily by U.S. investment, is so great that some form of federal agency has been in place since the 1970s to monitor foreign control. Concern over whether Canada exercises economic and political sovereignty led to the growth of the National Party of Canada, which has since disbanded.

Conglomerates and Corporate Linkages

A *conglomerate* is a giant corporation composed of many smaller corporations. Beatrice Foods and the Irving empire are examples. (See the **Social Diversity** Box, p. 413). Corporations are also linked by wealthy families; most of whom know each other socially and have business interests in common.

Another type of linkage between corporations is called *interlocking directorates*, or social networks made up of people who simultaneously serve on the boards of directors of many corporations. It is not necessarily against the public interest, but does tend to concentrate power. Not all the linkages are necessarily formal, but the social circles exchange valuable information. More recently, Peter C. Newman has suggested that the arrangements described above are outdated. The new establishment is a meritocracy, based on "what one can do" rather than "whom one knows."

Corporations: Are They Competitive?

The competitive market in Canada is limited to smaller businesses and the self-employed. Large corporations tend to operate within a *non-competitive* sector. Concern over *monopoly*, domination of a market by a single producer, led in the U.S. to an Anti-Trust Act in 1890. No such legislation exists in Canada but monopolies must submit to government legislation.

Monopolies may be controlled but *oligopoly*, domination of a market by a few producers is pervasive. In order to protect the public interest governments provide oversight of much of the Canadian economy. Yet governments and corporations work hand-in-hand to manage the economy, hardly an adversarial relationship.

Corporations and the Global Economy

The largest corporations, centred in the U.S., Canada, Japan and Western Europe now span the Globe. Access to vast markets and cheaper labour (Figure 16-6, p. 415) is a part of the reason. As was noted in Chapter 12 (Global Inequality) there is a substantial debate on the effects of capitalist expansion to the poor countries. Modernization theorists suggest long term advantages of expanded economies while dependency theorists suggest expanded inequality with the rich nations benefiting at the cost of the poor.

THE ECONOMY OF THE TWENTY-FIRST CENTURY

The economy is one of several social institutions designed to meet the needs of societal members. The distribution of resources in Canada is highly unequal and there are two major changes which will impact upon that distribution

The Information Revolution is changing the nature of the labour market but a high proportion of Canadians lack the language and computer skills to effectively participate.

The globalization of economies means that national decisions are often irrelevant to international market conditions. What will Canada and other countries do to respond to these changes? The **Applying Sociology** Box (p. 417) discusses the loss of Canada's brightest to the U.S.

The **Controversy and Debate** box (pp. 418-419) asks whether unfettered market forces need to be balanced by government regulation and in what proportions in order to protect public interest?

KEY CONCEPTS

Define each of the following concepts on separate paper. Check the accuracy of your answers by referring to the text as well as by referring to italicized definitions located throughout the chapter.

capitalism
communism
conglomerates
corporation
economy
global economy
labour unions
monopoly
oligopoly
post-industrial economy
primary labour market
primary sector

profession
professionalization
reserve army of labour
secondary labour market
secondary sector
self employment
socialism
state capitalism
tertiary sector
underground economy
welfare capitalism

STUDY QUESTIONS

 True-False

1. T F   In Canada more than in the United States, governments are involved in the distribution of goods and services.

2. T F   In medieval Europe, people living in cities often worked at home, a pattern called cottage industry.

3. T F   The information revolution is leading to a higher degree of centralization of the workforce.

4. T F   The importance of the primary sector declines with economic development.

5. T F   One consequence of the global economy is that national governments no longer control the economic activity that takes place within their boarders.

6. T F   A purely capitalist economy would operate without interference from the government.

7. T F   Socialist countries have been successful in eliminating the power of all elites

8. T F   The secondary labour market includes jobs providing minimal benefits to workers.

9. T F "Discouraged workers", those who have stopped looking for a job, are still counted as among the unemployed in Canada.

10. T F In 1996 Ontario had the highest percentage of its labour force employed in manufacturing industries.

✎ Multiple-Choice

1. That part of the economy that transforms raw materials into manufactured goods is termed the:

   (a) primary sector
   (b) secondary sector
   (c) manifest sector
   (d) competitive sector
   (e) basic sector

2. Which of the following is *not* a feature of a capitalist economy?

   (a) private ownership of property
   (b) free competition
   (c) pursuit of collective goals
   (d) consumer sovereignty
   (e) pursuit of personal profit

3. An economic and political system in which companies are privately owned but cooperate closely with the government is called

   (a) democratic socialism
   (b) utopian capitalism
   (c) capital oligarchy
   (d) state capitalism
   (e) withered communism

4. Which of the following racial/ethnic groups had the highest percentage participation in the labour force in 1991?

   (a) British
   (b) French
   (c) Asian
   (d) Black
   (e) Native

5. By 1991 the proportion of the Canadian labour force engaged in farming had fallen to

   a) 2%   (b) 5%   (c) 8%   (d) 15%   (e) 22%

6. The highest level of union membership in Canada is found in which of the following areas?

    (a) construction   (c) public administration
    (b) manufacturing   (d) mining

7. Which of the following is *not* a characteristic of professions.

    a) practical knowledge   (d) authority over clients
    b) self-regulated training   (e) community orientation

8. What percentage of the Canadian labour force was in 1998 in the category of self-employed?

    (a) 8   (b) 10   (c) 16   (d) 18   (e) 22

9. Which of the following is *not* one of the ways in which computers are altering the character of work?

    a) making the skills of managers obsolete
    b) giving workers a more "hands-on" relationship with their product
    c) limiting workplace interaction
    d) enhancing employer's control of workers

10. Giant corporations that are clusters of many smaller companies are called:

    (a) megacorporations   (d) monopolies
    (b) multinational corporations   (e) conglomerates
    (c) oligarchies

11. Which of the following statements are *correct* with respect to the recent Canadian "brain drain" to the United States?

    (a) It is made up primarily of highly skilled and educated people.
    (b) Those that left were offered higher incomes.
    (c) Most left because of higher Canadian taxes.
    (d) All of the above
    (e) (a) and (b) above

✎ Fill-In The Blank

1. _____ range from necessities like food to luxuries like swimming pools, while _____ include various activities that benefit others.

2. A _____ is an economy based on service work and information technology.

3. The _____ is the part of the economy generating services rather than goods.

4. In the poor countries of Africa and Asia, as many as three-quarters of all workers are _____ .

5. _____ is an economic system in which productive resources are collectively owned.

6. In Canada the racial or ethnic group least likely to be involved in the labour force is _____ .

7. That part of the labour force which is last hired during expansion and first fired when the economy contracts is called the _____ .

8. An economic activity involving the exchange of goods and services which is not reported to the government is called the _____ .

9. The _____ sector of the economy is actually limited to smaller businesses and self-employed people. Large corporations fall within the _____ sector.

10. _____ theorists claim that multinationals have intensified global inequality.

Definition and Short-Answer

1. What is meant by the term "cottage industry"?

2. What were the five notable changes brought about by the industrial revolution?

3. Define the concept postindustrial economy.

4. What are the basic characteristics of capitalism as reviewed in the text?

5. What are the basic characteristics of socialism as reviewed in the text?

6. What are the relative advantages of capitalism and socialism?

7. What is welfare capitalism? What is state capitalism?

8. Differentiate between the primary and secondary labour markets.

9. What are the basic characteristics of a profession?

10. How is work changed in a post-industrial economy?

11. What is meant by the differentiation between the competitive and noncompetitive sectors of the economy?

12. What will be the long term effects for Canada of the globalization of economies?

Answers to Study Questions

True-False

1. T (p. 396)   6. T (p 401)
2. T (p. 396)   7. F (p. 402)
3. F (p. 399)   8. T (p. 405)
4. T (p. 399)   9. F (p. 409)
5. T (p. 399)   10. F (p. 411)

Multiple-Choice

1. b (p. 399)   7. a (p. 406)
2. c (pp. 400-401)   8. c (p. 406)
3. d (p. 402)   9. b (p. 410)
4. d (p. 404)   10. e (p. 413)
5. b (p. 404)   11. d (p. 417)
6. c (p. 405)

Fill-In

1. goods/services (p. 396)   6. Natives (p. 404)
2. postindustrial economy (p. 398) 7. reserve army of labour (p. 405)
3. tertiary sector (p. 399)   8. underground economy (p. 409)
4. farmers (p. 400)   9. competitive/noncompetitive (p. 414)
5. Socialism (p. 401)   10. dependency (p. 415)

ANALYSIS AND COMMENT

Go back through the chapter and write down in the spaces below key points from each of the following boxes.

SOCIAL DIVERSITY

"The French-Canadians of Manchester, New Hampshire"
Key Points:

_____

_____

_____

_____

_____

"Regional Economic Disparities"
Key Points:

_____

_____

_____

_____

_____

"The Irving Empire"
Key Points:

_____

_____

_____

_____

_____

EXPLORING CYBER-SOCIETY

"Working Through Cyberspace"
Key Points:

_____

_____

_____

_____

_____

APPLYING SOCIOLOGY

"The Brain Drain."

Key Points:

_____

_____

_____

_____

_____

CONTROVERSY AND DEBATE

"The Market: Does the "Invisible Hand" Serve Our Interests or Pick our Pockets?

Key Points:

_____

_____

_____

_____

_____

SUGGESTED READINGS

Classic Sources

Thorstein Veblen. 1953; orig. 1899. *The Theory of the Leisure Class.* **New York: New American Library.**
One of the earliest U.S. sociologists explains how patterns of consumption confer social status on people in an increasingly affluent and upwardly mobile society.

Daniel Bell, 1976. *The Coming of Post-Industrial Society: A Venture in Social Forecasting.* **New York: Harper Collins.**
Daniel Bell was among the first sociologists to recognize and analyze the emerging postindustrial society.

Contemporary Sources

Peter L. Berger. 1986. *The Capitalist Revolution: Fifty Propositions About Prosperity, Equality, and Liberty.* **New York: Basic Books.**
One of sociology's best contemporary thinkers examines the social consequences of capitalism.

James A. Yunker. 1992. *Socialism Revised and Modernized: The Case for Pragmatic Market Socialism.* **New York: Praeger.**
This author envisions how a fusion of capitalist and socialist models--involving public ownership of larger, profit-seeking corporations--would capitalize

Canadian Sources

Wallace Clement. 1975. *The Canadian Corporate Elite.* **Toronto: McClelland & Stewart.**
Diane Francis. 1986. *Controlling Interest: Who Owns Canada?* **Toronto: Macmillan..**
The first title is a Canadian classic dealing with the small group of people who control our economy. The relationships among them are also explored. The second is a highly readable, though disturbing, account of the wealthiest Canadian families and the corporations they control.

Terry Wotherspoon and Vic Satzewich.1993. *First Nations: Race, Class and Gender Relations,* **Scarborough, Ontario: Nelson.**
Jennifer Wells. 1996. "Jobs." *Maclean's,* **March 11, 1996: 12-16.**

Ralph Matthews. 1983. *The Creation of Regional Dependency.* **Toronto: University of Toronto Press.**
The very Canadian problem of regional dependency is given sophisticated treatment here.
on the advantages of both economic systems.

Global Source

Suzan Lewis, Dafna N. Izraeli, and Helen Hootsmans. 1992. *Dual-Earner Families: International Perspectives.* **Newbury Park, CA: Sage.**
This discussion highlights changing economic and family patterns in Hungary, Sweden, Singapore, Japan, India, and elsewhere.

CHAPTER 17

I CHAPTER OUTLINE

I. **Power and Authority**
    A. Traditional Authority
    B. Rational-Legal Authority
    C. Charismatic Authority

II. **Politics In Global Perspective**
    A. Monarchy
    B. Democracy
        1. Democracy and Freedom: Capitalist and Socialist Approaches
    C. Authoritarianism
    D. Totalitarianism
    E. A Global Political System?

III. **Politics in Canada**
    A. Culture, Economics, and Politics
    B. Political Parties
        1. Functions of Political Parties
        2. Political Ideology
        3. Parties on the Political Spectrum
        4. Party Support
    C. Politics and the Individual
        1. Political Socialization
        2. Political Participation
        3. The Participation of Women

VI. **Theoretical Analysis of Power in Society**
    A. The Pluralist Model
    B. The Power-Elite Model
    C. The Marxist Model: Bias in the System Itself

V. **Power Beyond the Rules**
    A. Revolution
    B. Terrorism

VI. **War and Peace**
    A. The Causes of War
    B. The Costs and Causes of Militarism
    C. Nuclear Weapons
    D. Information Warfare
    E. The Pursuit of Peace

VII. **Looking Ahead: Politics in the Twenty-First Century**
VIII. **Summary**
IX. **Critical Thinking Questions**
X. **Applications And Exercises**
XI. **Sites To See**

II LEARNING OBJECTIVES

- To explain the difference between power and authority.

- To distinguish among the three types of authority: traditional, rational-legal, andcharismatic.

- To describe the concepts of political state and nation state.

- To compare and contrast the four principal kinds of political systems and to conceptualize a possible global system.

- To explain the balance between individualism and communal responsibility in Canada.

- To identify what a political party is and the functions political parties serve in Canadian society.

- To contemplate the impact of proportional representation as opposed to the "first past the post" system.

- To understand political ideology and how the parties and their supporters fit on the ideological continuum.

- To describe the nature of change in Native self-government.

- To describe the ways in which people participate in the political system focusing on political socialization and political participation.

- To compare the politics of the U. S. and Canada.

- To compare and contrast the pluralist model of political power and the power-elite model of political power and the Marxist model of political economy.

- To describe the types of political power that exceed, or seek to eradicate, established politics.

- To identify the factors which are involved in creating conditions which increase the likelihood of war.

- To recognize the historical pattern of militarism in the United States, Canada and around the world.

- To identify factors which can be used in the pursuit of peace.

- To conceptualize what political systems will look like in the twenty-first century.

This chapter begins with a description of a spring flood in Manitoba and a decision by Prime Minister Chretien to go ahead with a federal spring election in 1997 despite the political consequences. *Politics* is the institutionalized system by which a society distributes power, sets the society's agenda, and makes decisions.

POWER AND AUTHORITY

Max Weber defined *power* as the ability to achieve desired ends despite resistance from others and it is *government*, a formal organization that directs the political life of a society, which exercises power. Few governments openly force their will, rather they govern through *authority*, power that people perceive as legitimate rather than coercive. Weber identifies three sources of authority.

Traditional Authority

Traditional authority is defined as power legitimated by respect for long-established cultural patterns. This type of power is very common in preindustrialized societies and it has a sacred character. As societies industrialize traditional authority declines, as it does also when a society is characterized by cultural diversity. Yet traditional authority is still expressed in Canadian society by parental dominance over children and the domination of women by men.

Rational-Legal Authority

Rational-legal, or bureaucratic authority, is defined as power legitimated by legally enacted rules and regulations. Bureaucratic authority stresses achievement over ascribed characteristics, and underlies most authority in Canada today. This type of authority resides in the position, not the person occupying it.

Charismatic Authority

Charismatic authority is defined as power legitimated through extraordinary personal abilities that inspire devotion and obedience. It has little to do with social organization. Martin Luther King Jr. and Mahatma Gandhi are obvious examples but so is the "Trudeaumania" of Canadian Prime Minister Pierre Trudeau. The impact of his charisma was released again in the outpouring of emotion at his recent death.

Charismatic movements are very dependent on their leader. The long-term persistence of such a movement requires *routinization of charisma*, the transformation of charismatic authority into some combination of traditional and bureaucratic authority. Christianity is an example of this process, as Christ's charisma was routinized in the tradition and bureaucratic structure of the Roman Catholic Church.

POLITICS IN GLOBAL PERSPECTIVE

In hunting and gathering societies, leaders typically emerge as a result of having some unusual amount of strength, hunting skill or charisma. These leaders exercise only modest power over others, and while having special prestige, they do not have more wealth. In agrarian societies traditional authority develops. As political organization grows it leads to the formation of a *political state*, and the advance of technology significantly increases its power.

During the last several centuries political organizations have evolved toward nation-states. At the present time 191 *nation-states* are recognized but four categories of political systems are seen to exist.

Monarchy

A *monarchy* is a type of political system where power is passed from generation to generation in a single family and is legitimated primarily through tradition. Absolute monarchies flourished in the medieval era but have been mostly replaced today with constitutional monarchies where the monarchs are symbolic heads of state.

Democracy

Democracy refers to a political system in which power is exercised by the people as a whole. In large societies it is not possible for everyone to be directly involved in politics. Therefore, a representative democracy, which places authority in the hands of elected officials who are accountable to the people, develops. This type of system is most common in the relatively rich industrial societies of the world. They are characterized by rational-legal patterns of authority and function as bureaucracies. In Canada large scale bureaucracies, whose members are unelected, make decisions for the rest of us. If they listen to anyone, it is likely the rich.

➤Democracy and Freedom: Capitalist and Socialist Approaches

While the capitalist and the socialist countries have had different political systems for most of this century, both claim to provide freedom for their people. In Canada, the U.S. and Europe, political freedom means the freedom to vote for one's preferred leader and act in one's best financial interest. In the socialist nations, freedom was understood as "having basic needs met" within the context of heavy government control. While capitalism fosters great inequality, the socialist nations reduce inequality while restricting individual freedom. Globally political freedom has increased substantially **(Global Map** 17-1, p. 427) in the past century.

Authoritarianism

Authoritarianism refers to denying popular participation in government. While to some degree this is true for all political systems, as used here, authoritarianism characterizes political systems that are indifferent to people's lives. Saudi Arabia and Ethiopia are current examples. The **Global Sociology** box (p. 428) provides a glimpse of "soft authoritarianism", that stifles dissent while providing security and prosperity.

Totalitarianism

A more restrictive political control characterizes *totalitarianism*, a government that extensively regulates people's lives. Such systems have emerged only within this century as technological means have enabled such governments to rigidly regulate citizen's activities. They bridge the political continuum from the far right, like Nazi Germany, to the far left, like the People's Republic of China.

A Global Political System?

Although economic systems have become global no similar development has taken place politically. The United Nations has played a very limited role in global politics. The very fact, however, that multinational corporations make economic decisions which cannot be controlled by individual nations suggests that these corporations represent a new political order. As well, international non-governmental organizations such as Greenpeace, have sought to advance universal principles.

POLITICS IN CANADA

While Americans opted for life, liberty and the pursuit of happiness, Canadians chose peace, order and good government. While the Americans revolted, Canada evolved with various of the parts coming together over time and quite reluctantly. Table 17-1, (p. 430) reveals the coming together between 1867 and 1949. The provinces have never had uniform relationships with the federal government and many important powers are in provincial hands. In addition one "French speaking" province adds a special dimension. Canada's constitutional review never seems to end.

Canadians are represented in Parliament by a non-elected Senate with 105 seats apportioned on a regional basis and an elected House of Commons with 301 seats distributed roughly on the basis of population. Quebec and Ontario exert enormous power in the House of Commons which troubles other regions of the country.

Culture, Economics, and Politics

While Canadians endorse individualism they are concerned with the good of the collectivity, endorsing interventionist government. Some people think government at all levels should be even more involved in areas like child care and pay equity, for example, while others believe governments already do too much at too great an expense. These differences are in part a reflection of socioeconomic status and regional subcultures and are represented in the policies of Canada's political parties. Figure 17-1 (p. 431) indicates that Canada spends more than the U.S. but less than most European governments on programs.

Political Parties

Political parties are organizations operating within the political system that seek control of the government. Today's political parties (at least some of them) trace their origins to 1840 when Upper and Lower Canada came into being with the "Tory" (Conservative) and "Grit" (Liberal) factions proposing specific policies. A number of other minor parties came into existence after the First World War but only the CCF (now the NDP) has lasted. In recent years close to twenty registered parties have sought election but only the Progressive Conservative, Liberal, New Democratic Party and Social Credit parties have elected M.P.s over an extended period. But recently the Bloc Québecois and the Reform (now Alliance) parties have "regionalised" politics in Canada.

➢Functions of Political Parties

Political parties persist by serving important functions, namely: promoting political pluralism, increasing political involvement, selecting political candidates, forging political coalitions and maintaining political stability.

➢Political Ideology

The *political spectrum* in Canada ranges from communism on the left to extreme conservatism on the right and although political parties contain people of mixed ideological positions they do represent positions in a relatively consistent fashion.

The political left tend to be collectivist and interventionist, the right individualist and non-interventionist although the differences do not always cut so clearly.

➢Parties on the Political Spectrum

Figure 17-2, (p. 435) places Canada's political parties on a left-right continuum.

➢Party Support

Although many Canadians consistently support one political party there is considerable switching from election to election and voting for one party at the provincial level and another at the federal level.

While there used to be some consistent patterns across the country, the 1993 election marked some dramatic changes. The Liberals were the only party with support across the country while regional parties, The Bloc Québecois and the Reform party drew heavy support in Québec and the West respectively. Although there were some shifts in support for the Conservatives and the N.D.P. (they lost support from 1997 to 2000) the overall results are not substantially changed. Figure 17-3 (p. 436) shows the shifts in national voting in the 1988, 1993, 1997, and 2000 elections. Figure 17-4 (p. 438) shows the changing fortunes province by province in the same four elections and Figure 17-5 (p. 439) indicates how popular support is often poorly related to the number of seats won. The **Controversy and Debate** Box (p. 449) suggests that proportional representation would result in fewer majority governments but the "baby" of personal representation by a local M.P. would be thrown out with the "bathwater" of the current "first-past-the-post" system of representation.

Politics and the Individual

How do people acquire political attitudes?

➤Political Socialization

The family is the first agent of political socialization and children of politically involved and upper socioeconomic parents learn more. The educational institution and the mass media are also significant agents of socialization with the media, especially television, playing a dominant role. Opinion polls are also a socializing agent and some concern exists whether they shape rather than reflect public opinion. Adult interest and occupational groups can also become involved in political socialization. The **Applying Sociology** Box (p. 437) shows that image creation in the U.S. and Canada are somewhat different as Gore and Bush competed at a religiosity level while Chrétien and Day attempted to display fitness.

➤Political Participation

Not everyone participates in politics especially those who feel the system does not respond to their needs. The Spicer Commission, in fact, found in 1991 that Canadians have become cynical about politicians and the political process and more recently we have discovered a distrust of all elites. Research in 1965 characterized political participation at three levels, gladiator, transitional and spectator.

In fact approximately 70% of eligible voters turn out to Canadian federal elections as compared to 50-55 percent in the U.S. but participation at provincial and municipal levels is less.

The **Social Diversity** Box (pp. 432-433) notes the Natives have become much more concerned to participate politically to protect interests that have been long ignored.

➤The Participation of Women

Women acquired the right to vote in federal elections and most provincial elections by 1918. Since then Agnes McPhail ran successfully for parliament in 1921, a female cabinet member was named in 1957, Audrey McLaughlin became a party leader in 1989 and Kim Campbell became prime minister in 1993. Although women are still underrepresented in Parliament they have moved from 5% of M.P.s in 1980 to 21% in 2000.

THEORETICAL ANALYSIS OF POWER IN SOCIETY

The Pluralist Model

This approach is linked to the structural-functional paradigm. The *pluralist model* is an analysis of politics that views power as dispersed among many competing interest groups.

In *The Vertical Mosaic*, John Porter identifies five competing elites but notes that these elites are highly integrated and accommodate each others interests.

The Power-Elite Model

The *power-elite model* is an analysis of politics that views power as concentrated among the rich. The term power-elite was introduced by C. Wright Mills in 1956. He perceived American society, its economy, government, and military, as being dominated by a coalition of the super rich.

Clement's examination of economic power in Canada concludes that Canada is ruled by an economic or corporate elite which is becoming increasingly powerful. Networks bind economic, political and bureaucratic elites who have a vested interest in maintaining the capitalist system.

The Marxist Model: Bias in the System Itself

The Marxist political-economy model explains politics in terms of a society's economic system. The capitalist system shuts out those politically who do not exercise economic power.

Table 17-2 (p. 444) summarizes the three models of power. There is research data to support all three but Figure 17-6 (p. 443) indicates that the majority of Canadians support the power elite theory. It is worth noting, however, that the elite do not always get their way. Labour unions and feminists have successfully taken on big business and won favourable policy changes. **Exploring Cyber-Society** (p. 442) discusses the power of media communications to influence political decision-making.

POWER BEYOND THE RULES

Revolution

Political revolution is the overthrow of one political system in order to establish another. While reform involves change within a system, revolution means change of the system itself. No political system is immune to revolution. Several general patterns characterize revolutions. These include: rising expectations, non-responsiveness of the government, radical leadership by intellectuals, and establishing a new legitimacy. Canada recently experienced revolutionary potential when Quebec almost voted to begin a process to sovereignty.

Terrorism

Terrorism, is the use of violence or the threat of violence by an individual or group as a political strategy. Four insights are offered about terrorism. First, it elevates violence to a legitimate political tactic. Second, it is especially compatible with totalitarian governments as a means of sustaining widespread fear and intimidation to reach what is called *state terrorism*. Third, extensive civil liberties make democratic societies vulnerable to terrorism. Canada experienced terrorism in the 1960's at the hands of the FLQ and in 1970 when prime minister Pierre Trudeau suspended civil liberties to deal with the crisis. Four, one person's terrorist is another person's freedom fighter; definition is important.

WAR AND PEACE

War is defined as organized armed conflict among people of various societies. *Peace* implies the absence of war, although not necessarily all conflict. Over 100,000 Canadians lost their lives in World Wars I and II.

The Causes of War

War, according to research, is not the result of some natural human aggressive tendency, it is a product of society. The following factors are identified by Quincy Wright as promoting war: perceived threats, social problems, political objectives, moral objectives, and the absence of alternatives.

The Costs and Causes of Militarism

The cost of militarism runs far greater than actual war. To fund it, governments must divert resources away from social needs. Globally 5 trillion dollars is spent annually on militarism; in the U.S. 19 percent of government spending goes to the military and related activities. Despite the collapse of the Soviet Union and the cold war, U. S. expenditures remain high.

Some argue that the U. S. economy has relied on militarism to generate corporate profits and suggests that the result is a *military-industrial complex*, a close association between the federal government, the military, and defence industries. As well regional conflicts have helped maintain militarism.

Nuclear Weapons

The destructive capability of the 25,000 nuclear weapons in existence today is incredible. As well, *nuclear proliferation,* the acquisition of nuclear weapons technology by more and more societies, continues to place us all at risk.

Information Warfare

Computers may affect warfare by paralyzing an enemy's fighting capacity. The most technologically sophisticated weapon systems may be the most vulnerable to a cyber-attack.

The Pursuit of Peace

Several approaches can be used to reduce the danger of nuclear war. These include: deterrence, high-technology defense, like the strategic defense initiative, diplomacy and disarmament, and resolving underlying conflict. Canada has played a dominant role as peace-keeper in many conflicts as a part of United Nations forces.

LOOKING AHEAD: POLITICS IN THE TWENTY-FIRST CENTURY

Just as global economies have rapidly changed so also are global political processes albeit more slowly. The Information Revolution provides information that governments cannot exclude from their boundaries, the limiting character of Cold War thinking is declining and new centres of political power are likely to arise. One hopes that amid this sea of change we will learn to resolve our conflicts and enlist the powers of peace.

KEY CONCEPTS

Define each of the following concepts on separate paper. Check the accuracy of your answers by referring to the text as well as by referring to italicized definitions located throughout the chapter.

authoritarianism

authority

charismatic authority

democracy

government

marxist political economy model

military-industrial complex

monarchy

nuclear proliferation

pluralist model

political economy

political parties

political revolution

politics

power

power-elite model

rational-legal authority

routinization of charisma

state terrorism

terrorism

totalitarianism

traditional authority

war

STUDY QUESTIONS

 True-False

1. T F   The spring flood in Winnipeg in 1997 caused the prime minister to delay the federal election.

2. T F   Traditional authority is compelling only so long as everyone shares the same heritage and world view.

3. T F   Any organization governed by rational-legal authority faces a crisis of survival upon the loss of its leader.

4. T F   According to Freedom House, in 1999 40% of the world's people were politically

free.

5. T F   The former Soviet Union denied most citizens telephone directories, fax machines and accurate city maps.

6. T F   The United States taxes its citizens more heavily than does Canada in order to support its vast social programs.

7. T F   If the Charlottetown accord had been approved, the inherent right to self government by aboriginal peoples would have been given constitutional recognition.

8. T F   Candidates for the American presidency are more likely than candidates for Canadian prime minister to don the mantle of religiosity.

9. T F   In the 2000 federal election in Canada 50% of the successfully elected candidates were women.

10. T F   Research by Wallace Clement supports the power-elite model of how power is distributed in Canada.

✎ Multiple-Choice

1. Who defined power as the likelihood that a person can achieve personal ends in spite of possible resistance from others?

   (a) C. Wright Mills   (c) Max Weber
   (b) Alexis de Tocqueville   (d) Robert Lynd

2. Which of the following is not one of the general contexts in which power is commonly defined as authority?

   (a) traditional   (c) charismatic
   (b) rational-legal   (d) democratic

3. The survival of a charismatic movement depends upon _____, according to Max Weber.

   (a) pluralism   (c) legality
   (b) political action   (d) routinization of charisma

4. Which of the following are *correct* observations about government and life in Singapore?

    (a) It has been characterized as a filthy society.
    (b) The People's Action Party has ruled without opposition for the past fifteen years.
    (c) The government provides security and prosperity.
    (d) Critics of the government charge that the system amounts to "hard democracy."

5. Which Canadian political party saw its support fall to 8.5% of the national vote in 2000?

    (a) Progressive Conservative   (d) Alliance
    (b) Liberal   (e) Bloc Québecois
    (c) N.D.P.

6. With which general sociological paradigm is the pluralist model associated?

    (a) exchange   (c) symbolic-interaction
    (b) structural-functional   (d) social-conflict

7. Which idea below does not represent the power-elite model of power?

    (a) power is highly concentrated
    (b) voting cannot create significant political changes
    (c) the state and capitalists act as one.
    (d) wealth, social prestige, and political office are rarely combined

8. Which of the following is *not* one of the common traits of revolution?

    (a) rising expectations   (c) leadership from the masses
    (b) unresponsive government   (d) establishing a new legitimacy

9. Quincy Wright has identified which of the following circumstances as conditions which lead humans to go to war?

    (a) perceived threats   (d) all of the above
    (b) social problems   (e) a and b above
    (c) moral objectives

10. When a few highly skilled operators with sophisticated electronic equipment interferes with communications necessary to conduct military adventures, the activity is called

    (a) techno-deterence   (d) tech-wreck
    (b) S.D.I.   (e) information warfare
    (c) peacekeeping

11. When the number of seats awarded to a party mirrors their portion of the popular vote the system is called

(a) first-past-the-post   (d) proportional representation
(b) triple E   (e) populist representation
(c) democratic population

✎ Fill-In The Blank

1. _____ is the ability to achieve desired ends despite the resistance from others.

2. Power widely perceived as legitimate rather than coercive is referred to as _____.

3. _____ authority is power legitimized by legally enacted rules and regulations.

4. The transformation of charismatic authority into some combination of traditional and bureaucratic authority is called _____.

5. _____ is a political system in which a single family rules from generation to generation.

6. _____ is political control denying the majority participation in a government that extensively regulates people's lives.

7. The triple concept of Triple E Senate stands for _____, _____ and _____.

8. Free-trade with the U.S. is not supported by the political _____ in Canada.

9. The first female to win federal political office in Canada was _____.

10. The acquisition of nuclear weapons technology by more and more nations is referred to as _____.

Definition and Short-Answer

1. Differentiate between the concepts of power and authority.

2. Differentiate among Weber's three types of authority.

3. Four types of political systems are reviewed in the text. Identify and describe these systems.

4. How are politics different in Canada and the U.S.?

5. What are the functions served by political parties?

6. How do people acquire political attitudes?

7. Differentiate between the pluralist, power-elite and Marxist models concerning the distribution of power in Canada.

8. What are the four general traits identified in the text concerning revolutions?

9. What are the five factors identified in the text as promoting war?

10. Several approaches to pursuing peace are addressed in the text. What are these approaches?

11. How will global politics operate in the next century?

Answers to Study Questions

True-False

1. F (p. 423)   6. F (p. 431)
2. T (p. 424)   7. T (p. 433)
3. F (p. 425)   8. T (p. 437)
4. T (p. 427)   9. F (p. 440)
5. T (p. 429)   10. T (p. 443)

Multiple-Choice

1. c (p. 423)   7. d (p. 442)
2. d (pp. 424-425) 8. c (pp. 444-445)
3. d (p. 425)   9. d (p. 446)
4. c (p. 428)   10. e (p. 448)
5. c (p. 436)   11. d. (p. 449)
6. b (p. 441)

Fill-In

1. power (p. 423)   6. totalitarianism (p. 429)
2. authority (p. 424)   7. equal, effective, elected (p. 430)
3. rational/legal (p. 424)   8. left (p. 434)
4. routinization of charisma (p. 425)   9. Agnes MacPhail (440)
5. monarchy (p. 425)   10. nuclear proliferation (p. 447)

ANALYSIS AND COMMENT

Go back through the chapter and write down in the spaces below key points from each of the following boxes.

GLOBAL SOCIOLOGY

" Soft Authoritarianism or Planned Prosperity? A Report From Singapore."
Key Points:

_____

_____

_____

_____

_____

SOCIAL DIVERSITY

"Native Self-Government"
Key Points:

_____

_____

_____

_____

_____

APPLYING SOCIOLOGY

"Canada and the United States: Two Snapshots of Politics."
Key Points:

_____

_____

_____

_____

_____

EXPLORING CYBER-SOCIETY

"Who Decides? The Impact of Modern Communications."
Key Points:

_____

_____

_____

_____

_____

CONTROVERSY AND DEBATE

"Reforming Canada's Political System: Throwing Out the Baby With the Bath Water"
Key Points:

_____

_____

_____

_____

_____

SUGGESTED READINGS

Classic Sources

Alexis de Tocqueville. 1969 (orig. 1834-40).
Democracy in America. **Garden City, NY: Doubleday-Anchor Books.**
This classic analysis of politics and society is based on a journey through the United States made by a brilliant French aristocrat in the early 1830s. Many of de Tocqueville's insights remain as fresh and valuable today as when he wrote them.

Hannah Arendt. 1958. *The Origins of Totalitarianism.*   **Cleveland: Meridian Books.**
This classic description of totalitarianism and its rise in the modern world is written by a woman deeply influenced by her captivity in a Nazi death camp during World War II.

John Porter. 1965. *The Vertical Mosaic: An Analysis of Social Class and Power in Canada.*

Contemporary Sources

Lyman Tower Sargent, ed. 1995. *Extremism in America: A Reader.* **New York: New York University Press.**
This collection of essays probes radical political organizations that advocate violence such as the Oklahoma City bombing.

Mary Ann Glendon. 1991. *Rights Talk: The Impoverishment of Political Discourse.* **New York: The Free Press.**
Among the questions posed by this provocative book: Should we claim more and more "rights?" What does this focus on the individual do to our sense of political responsibility for others?

Toronto: University of Toronto Press.
Wallace Clement. 1975. *The Canadian Corporate*
Elite; Economic Power in Canada. **Toronto:**
McClelland and Stewart.
The exercise of power by multiple or single elites is
the topic of these two Canadian classics.

Canadian Sources

Raymond Breton. 1992. *Why Meech Failed:*
Lessons for Canadian Constitution Making.
Toronto: C. D. Howe Institute.
This thoughtfully analytical and easy-to-read book is a
must for political sociologists.

Sylvia B. Bashevkin. 1993. *Toeing the Lines:*
Women and Party Politics in English Canada. **2**nd.
Ed. Toronto: Oxford University Press.
This book provides a comprehensive analysis of
women's political participation in Canada.

J. Anthony Long and Menno Boldt, eds. 1998.
Governments in Conflict? Provinces and Indian
Nations in Canada. **Toronto: University of**
Toronto Press.
This collection of articles deals with many aspects of
Native policy, rights, land claims and self-
government.

Frederick J. Fletcher, ed. *Media and the Voters in*
Canadian Election Campaigns. **Vol. 18 of the**
Research Studies of the Royal Commission on
Electoral Reform and Party Financing. Ottawa
and Toronto: RCERPF/Dundurn.
A current debate concerns the effects of the media on
our political system.

Global Sources

Patrick Garrity and Steven A. Maaranen, eds.
Nuclear Weapons in the Changing World:
Perspectives from Europe, Asia, and North America.
New York: Plenum, 1992.
This collection of essays by experts examines nuclear-
weapons issues from the points of view of nations in
various regions of the world.

Cynthia Enloe. 1990. *Bananas, Beaches, and*
Bases: Making Feminist Sense of International
Politics. **Berkeley, CA: University of California**
Press.
This feminist analysis of the world political scene
maintains that gender is at the center of global power
structures.

CHAPTER 18

Family

II LEARNING OBJECTIVES

- To define the basic concepts of kinship, family, family unit, marriage, and family of affinity.

- To cross-culturally compare and contrast extended and nuclear families marriage patterns, residential patterns, patterns of descent, and patterns of authority.

- To describe the four functions of the family from the structural-functional perspective.

- To explain the link between family and social inequality using the social-conflict perspective.

- To identify the contributions that symbolic-interaction analysis and social-exchange analysis have made to the sociological knowledge of the family.

- To describe the life course of the average Canadian family.

- To explain the impact of social class, race, ethnicity, and gender socialization on the family.

- To describe the problems and transitions that seriously affect family life: divorce, remarriage, spousal and child abuse.

- To describe the composition and prevalence of alternative family forms: one-parent families, cohabitation, gay and lesbian couples, and singlehood.

- To explain the impact, both technologically and ethically, of new reproductive techniques on the family.

- To identify five sociological conclusions about the family as we enter the twenty-first century.

III CHAPTER REVIEW

It is estimated that 20 to 30 percent of lesbian women are mothers. Though they often face difficulty in retaining custody of their children, definitions of family in Canada are changing quickly. As well in Canada more divorce and increased numbers of children born to unmarried mothers means that fully half of children born today will live with a single parent at some point. As more women enter the workforce, Canadians are concerned about a decline in family life but immense change has previously occurred and families did manage to adjust.

THE FAMILY: BASIC CONCEPTS

The family is a social institution that unites individuals into cooperative groups that oversee the bearing and raising of children while *kinship* is a social bond based on blood, marriage or adoption that joins individuals into families. Recently in Canada we have regarded a family unit as a social group of two or more people, related by blood, marriage or adoption, who usually live together. Two different types of families are outlined. A *family of orientation* is the family into which a person is born and receives early socialization, while a *family of procreation* is a family within which people have or adopt children of their own. In most societies, families begin with *marriage*, or a socially approved relationship involving economic cooperation and allowing sexual activity and childbearing, that is expected to be relatively enduring. The significance of marriage for childbearing is evident in the labels *illegitimacy* and *matrimony,* which have, however, recently declined in importance as illegitimacy has increased. Controversy exists today in terms of how the family, both structurally and functionally, is to be understood, and how it is to be defined officially. For instance, *families of affinity*, or groups whose members are drawn together and who think of themselves as a family, such as gay or lesbian couples, are becoming more common. Clearly wider definitions of the family are a product of the debate on "family values."

The Family: Global Variety

In preindustrial societies the *extended* or *consanguine* families included parents, children and other kin while in industrial societies the focus is upon the *nuclear* or *conjugal family* composed of one or two parents and their children. While extended families are not irrelevant in Canada the *nuclear family* is most important. The **Global Sociology** box (p. 455) describes a growing method of becoming parents, international adoption.

Marriage Patterns

Norms identify categories of people suitable for marriage for particular individuals. *Endogamy*, refers to a normative pattern of marriage between people of the same social group or category. It is differentiated from the norm of *exogamy*, or marriage between people of different social groups or categories. All societies enforce varying degrees of each type. *Monogamy* means marriage that joins one female and one male. Serial monogamy refers to a number of monogamous marriages over one's lifetime. *Polygamy* is defined as marriage that unites three or more people. Polygamy takes one of two forms. One type is called *polygyny*, by far the most common, referring to a marriage that joins one male with more than one female. The second type is called *polyandry*, referring to marriage that joins one female with more than one male. **Global Map** 18-1 (p. 456) looks at marital forms in global perspective.

Residential Patterns

Where people live after they are married also varies cross- culturally. *Neolocality*, a residential pattern in which a married couple lives apart from the parents of both spouses, is the most common form in industrial societies. In preindustrial societies residing with one set of parents is more typical. *Patrilocality* is a residential pattern in which a married couple lives with or near the husband's family. *Matrilocality* is a residential pattern in which a married couple lives with or near the wife's family. This latter pattern is rare.

Patterns of Descent

Descent refers to the system by which kinship is traced over generations. Industrial societies follow the *bilateral descent* system of tracing kinship through both males and females. Preindustrial societies typically follow one of two patterns of unilineal descent. The more common, *patrilineal descent,* is a system tracing kinship through males. *Matrilineal descent* refers to a system of descent tracing kinship through females. Patrilineal systems are typical of pastoral or agrarian societies, while matrilineal systems are common in horticultural societies.

Patterns of Authority

The universal presence of patriarchy is reflected in the predominance of polygyny, patrilocality, and patrilineal descent. No known society is clearly matriarchal, but Canada is moving toward more egalitarian family patterns.

THEORETICAL ANALYSIS OF THE FAMILY

Functions of the Family: Structural-Functional Analysis

The structural-functionalists focus on several important social functions served by the family.

➤**Socialization**

The family serves as the primary agent in the socialization process. Children are typically socialized for different kinds of roles and learning never stops as adults learn from socializing their children.

➤**Regulation of Sexual Activity**

Some restrictions on sexual behaviour is characteristic of every culture. Every society has some type of *incest taboo*, a cultural norm forbidding sexual relations and marriage between certain kin. However, the specific kinship members who are subject to the taboo varies greatly cross-culturally. The significance of the incest taboo is primarily social rather than biological. It minimizes sexual competition, helps integrate the larger society and establishes specific linkages of rights and obligations between people.

➤**Social Placement**

Many ascribed statuses are determined at birth through the family. Transmission of social standing through the family is universal.

➤**Material and Emotional Security**

Families provide for the physical, emotional and financial support of its members. People living in families tend to be healthier than those living alone.

Structural-functionalists tend to under-emphasize problems in families, and underestimate the great diversity of family forms.

Inequality and the Family: Social-Conflict Analysis

The focus of the social-conflict approach to the study of the family is how this institution perpetuates patterns of social inequality.

➤ **Property and Inheritance**

Social class divisions are preserved by the inheritance of wealth.

➤ **Patriarchy**

Patriarchal values maintain the sexual and economic subordination of women. Despite the fact that women have increased their participation in the paid labour force they still do most of the housework and child rearing.

➤ **Race and Ethnicity**

These continue to be strong endogamous characteristics of marriage.

Constructing Family Life: Micro-Level Analysis

The structural-functional and social-conflict paradigms provide a macro-level perspective from which to understand the institution of the family while micro-level approaches explore how individuals shape their family life.

➤ **Symbolic-Interaction Analysis**

Symbolic-interaction analysis is used to study how specific realities are constructed within specific families. Varying experiences and perceptions of different family members are stressed but emotional bonds are forged over time.

➤ **Social-Exchange Analysis**

Social-exchange theory draws attention to the power of negotiation within families. People are seen as exchanging socially valued resources with each other. As gender roles are converging, so also is what males and females have to exchange.

While providing a meaningful counterbalance to the macro-level approaches, the micro-level is limited in its ability to allow us to see the social and cultural forces impacting upon the family.

STAGES OF FAMILY LIFE

Family life is viewed as dynamic, consisting of changing patterns over its life cycle.

Courtship

Preindustrial societies typically are characterized by arranged marriages where the kinship group determines marriage partners. See **Global Sociology** Box (p. 460) for a description of child marriage.

In industrial societies personal choice in mate selection dominates, with tremendous emphasis on *romantic love*. This is particularly true in North America.

Romantic Love

Romantic love is a less stable foundation for marriage than are social and economic considerations. Although most people like to think that contemporary marriages are purely a matter of individual choice, *homogamy* is a reality, where individuals marry those who are socially like themselves.

Settling In: Ideal and Real Marriage

Marriage and family tend to be idealized by most, with real life experiences never meeting expectations, including sexuality. Those who have the most fulfilling sexual relationships experience the most marital satisfaction. Figure 18-1 (p. 462) shows the amount of sexual activity by marital status. Although rates of extramarital sexuality are increasing, most Canadians are opposed to it.

Childrearing

Childrearing creates major transitions for families, some of them problematic. Despite the demands children make of families, most Canadians still desire them albeit at reduced numbers than the past as indicated in Table 18-1, (p. 462). Children are certainly now a considerable economic liability compared to pre-industrial times. As well, women have entered the labour force and husbands resist accepting responsibility for household tasks. Figure 18-2, (p. 463) indicates that the age for mothers having children has steadily increased in the last 20 years.

Because parents have less time for their children, parenting has changed and problems like *latchkey kids* have arisen. (See the **Social Diversity** Box, p. 464 for a discussion of disciplining children).

The Family in Later Life

With life expectancy increasing, the number of years a couple live together without children during what is known as the "empty nest" years is increasing. Many new challenges are faced by couples during these years. The departure of children and the maintenance of relationships with them, the increased value of companionship in marriage, and death of one's spouse are major events in later life. An additional adjustment is required of "boomers" who may still be raising children while caring for elderly parents. The problem of this "sandwich generation" is often exacerbated by the return to the family nest of children who had previously left.

CANADIAN FAMILIES: CLASS, RACE AND GENDER

Social Class

Social class has a major impact on the family, including determining a family's economic security, and range of opportunities. Further, research by Lillian Rubin illustrates how social class affects the relationship of spouses, with middle-class couples being more open and expressive with each other. Differences in socialization patterns between classes also impact upon children's achievement.

Ethnicity and Race

➤Native Canadian Families

There are many native bands and Inuit and Métis settlements in Canada with perhaps 42 percent of Natives living in urban areas. To talk of family patterns of Natives is therefore problematic. What we do know, however, is that many of the family traditions of extended kin solidarity, familistic values, respect for elders and welfare of children have been weakened by church and state attempts to Christianize and Canadianize Native children, to the point that Native culture is at risk.

➤Mixed Marriages

Racially mixed marriages are increasingly accepted in Canada (see Table 18-3 p. 466) but some resistance still exists.

Gender

Jessie Bernard succinctly suggests that in reality there are two marriages: a female marriage and a male marriage. Even today, despite considerable change in female roles in the society men tend to dominate in marriages and experience health and happiness advantages while women experience poorer mental health and lesser levels of happiness than single women do but if both share household and child-care responsibilities their mental health improves..

TRANSITION AND PROBLEMS IN FAMILY LIFE

Divorce

As Figure 18-3, (p. 468) indicates the divorce rate in Canada has increased dramatically since 1968, when the Divorce Act was liberalized. Further changes in 1985 further enhanced the increasing rate. The societal factors which appear to have influenced the rate of divorce are emphasis on the individual, the subsiding of romantic love, the increasing independence of women, the stress of dual career marriages and the social ease of obtaining a divorce. The divorce rate has declined slightly in the last few years but that may be partially explained by the aging of the "boomer" generation.

➤Who Divorces?

Divorce is more common among young couples (especially teen and young marriages resulting from an unexpected pregnancy), the lower classes, couples with dissimilar social backgrounds and those where women have successful careers. Further, people who have divorced once are more likely to divorce again than people in their first marriages. See **Canada Map** 18-1, (p. 470) for varying rates by province.

➤Divorce as Process

Paul Bohannan has suggested divorce involves different adjustments for men and women. These include *emotional, legal, psychic, community, economic*, and *parental*. Divorce has a negative impact upon children especially with respect to maintaining contact with both parents and self-blame. Another problem for children is the low rate of compliance with court ordered support payments. With respect to support, custody and access, British Columbia has extended the same privileges and responsibilities to gay and lesbian couples.

Remarriage

About 80 percent of people who divorce in Canada remarry. Remarriage rates are higher for men than for women and the chances of the remarriage being successful are less than first marriages. Remarriage often creates a *blended family* consisting of a biological parent and stepparent, along with children of their respective first marriages and any children of the blended marriage.

Family Violence

Many families are characterized by *family violence*, or emotional, physical, or sexual abuse of one family member by another. The family has been characterized as one of the most violent institutions in our society.

➤Violence Against Women

Violence transcends the boundaries of social class. Common stereotypes of abusers are brought into question through the use of empirical data. One-fifth of all couples are estimated to have relationships characterized by at least some violence each year, and the seriousness of abuse is greater for wives than for husbands.

Traditionally, women have had few options and the violent marriage acts as a trap for many women. The traditional view of domestic violence as a private concern of families has also hindered the effectiveness of programs and policies, but more communities are establishing shelters and "stalker" legislation in Canada assists police in protecting women and their children.

➤Violence Against Children

While the level of abuse against children is unknown because so little of it is reported we do know that it is extensive and inflicts both physical and emotional harm. Large numbers of children simply run from family abuse and these runaways are getting younger. Most abused children suffer guilt as they are sure they must be responsible for the abuse. 90 percent of the abusers are estimated to be men and the majority were themselves abused as children.

ALTERNATIVE FAMILY FORMS

One-Parent Families

Over the last thirty-five years there has been a dramatic increase in single parent families. Figure 18-4, (p. 471) indicates that in 1996 14.6% of families were headed by single parents, over 80% of them by a mother. (See Figure 18-5, p. 472 for the percentage of births to unmarried women). Almost 12% of children in Canada live in these families and many of them live in relative poverty. The poverty, rather than emotional distress, probably accounts for the lower level of success for these children.

Cohabitation

Cohabitation is the sharing of a household by an unmarried couple. Most cohabiting couples do not marry and most relationships are of short duration. Figure 18-6, (p. 472), shows couples living common law by province. The **Applying Sociology** Box (p. 473) indicates that although cohabitation is unstable, increasing portions of Canadians are choosing this structural alternative.

Gay and Lesbian Couples

In 1989 Denmark became the first country to legalize homosexual marriages. In the U.S. some legal benefits of marriage have been conferred on gay and lesbian couples and in Canada some churches offer a marriage ceremony while some employers offer spousal benefits to homosexual unions. Interpersonal relationships mirror those of heterosexual unions and the unions may include children who have been legally adopted.

Singlehood

While singlehood is often seen as a transitory stage increasing numbers of people are choosing to remain single. Women who choose to delay entry into the marriage market find a decreasing number of available men.

NEW REPRODUCTIVE TECHNOLOGY AND THE FAMILY

The impact of new reproductive technology on the family in recent years has been significant, with many benefits having been realized. However, the new technology has brought with it many difficult ethical problems.

In vitro fertilization is a process involving the union of the male sperm and the female ovum in glass rather than in the woman's body. The benefits are twofold. First, couples who otherwise could not conceive may be able to use this technique. Second, the genetic screening of sperm and eggs reduces the incidence of birth defects.

Several ethical issues have been created and some of these are discussed in the **Controversy and Debate** Box (p. 475)

LOOKING AHEAD: FAMILY IN THE TWENTY-FIRST CENTURY

Family life has changed dramatically and will continue to do so. Five changes are likely in the next century. First, divorce will be increasingly accepted. Second, family forms will be highly variable. Third, more children will grow up without ties to their fathers. Fourth, both parents will work. Fifth, new reproductive technology will continue to affect family life.

KEY CONCEPTS

Define each of the following concepts in the space provided or on separate paper. Check the accuracy of your answers by referring to the text as well as by referring to italicized definitions located throughout the chapter.

bilateral descent	Marriage
cohabitation	matrilineal descent
descent	matrilocality
endogamy	monogamy
exogamy	neolocality
extended family	nuclear family
family	patrilineal descent
family of orientation	patrilocality
family of procreation	polyandry
family unit	polygamy
family violence	polygyny
homogamy	romantic love
kinship	serial monogamy

STUDY QUESTIONS

 True-False

1. T F   By some estimates 20% to 30% of lesbian women are mothers.

2. T F   A form of marriage joining one female with two or more males is called polygyny.

3. T F   Neolocality is a residential pattern most common in hunting and gathering societies.

4. T F   Every known culture has some type of incest taboo.

5. T F   Your textbook notes that romantic love makes for a less stable foundation for marriage than do social and economic considerations.

6. T F   The "sandwich generation" are echo generation mid-lifers who are now caring for their boomer parents while still raising their own children.

7. T F   The involvement of church and state in Native lives tended to assist them to adjust to the Canadian culture.

8. T F   In the 1985 Divorce Act "marriage breakdown" was made the only reason for divorce.

9. T F   We have recently discovered in Canada that 50% of child abusers are women.

10. T F   Cohabitation rates are higher in Québec than any other province.

11. T F   Test-tube babies are, technically speaking, the result of the process of in vitro fertilization.

Multiple-Choice

1. The expression "Families of affinity" refers to _____.

   (a) People who are married
   (b) People who are married with children
   (c) People with legal ties who feel they belong together
   (d) People with blood ties who feel they belong together
   (d) People with or without legal or blood ties who feel they belong together

2. Exogamy and endogamy are cultural norms relating to:

   (a) marriage patterns   (d) residence patterns
   (b) descent regulations   (e) authority patterns
   (c) beliefs about romantic love

3. A marriage form that unites one man with two or more women is termed:

   (a) monogamy   (c) polyandry
   (b) polygyny   (d) endogamy

4. Which of the following is not a descent pattern?

(a) matrilineal
(b) patrilineal
(c) bilateral

(d) neolocal
(e) all are descent patterns

5. Critiques of the structural-functional approach to studying the family suggest which of the following:

(a) problems of family life are minimized
(b) diversity of family life is ignored
(c) the impact of socialization is ignored

(d) a and b above
(e) b and c above

6. The type of sociological analysis of the family that holds that the family serves to perpetuate patriarchy is:

(a) social-exchange analysis
(b) social-conflict analysis

(c) structural-functional analysis
(d) symbolic-interaction analysis

7. The _____ analysis explores how individuals shape and experience family life.

(a) macro-level
(b) micro-level
(c) felicitous

(d) mechanical
(e) multivariate

8. Marriage between people with the same social characteristics is called

(a) heterogamy
(b) homogamy
(e) Connubial

(d) courtship
(e) mechanical solidarity

9. With respect to extramarital sexual relationships Reginald Bibby found that _____ of adults viewed such behaviour as always wrong.

(a) 1/4   (b) 1/2   (c) 3/4   (d) almost all

10. Which of the following is *not* one of the reasons that divorce rates are so high in Canada?

(a) People in families do not work and play together often.
(b) Our culture bases marriage on romantic love.
(c) Women are not so financially dependent on men.
(d) Divorce still carries a powerful stigma.

11. Which of the following factors is *not* associated with approval of premarital sex and cohabitation?

    (a) high levels of education   (d) Canadian born
    (b) Catholicism   (e) living in Ontario
    (c) church attendance

✎ Fill-In The Blank

1. Between 1981 and 1990 adoptions of children born in Canada declined almost __ %.

2. The _____ family is based on blood ties.

3. _____ is the normative pattern referring to marriage between people of the same social group or category.

4. A system tracing kinship through both women and men is a _____ descent pattern.

5. Social exchange analysis depicts courtship and marriage as forms of _____ .

6. Many experts agree that couples with the most fulfilling _____ experience the greatest satisfaction in their marriage.

7. In 1989 _____ became the first country to legalize same-sex marriages.

8. Test-tube babies are a product of _____ .

9. Family life in the twenty-first century is likely to be _____ rather than monolithic in sociologists' view.

10. The absence of fathers is increasingly seen as _____ to children.

Definition and Short-Answer

1. What are the four basic functions of the family according to structural-functionalists?

2. Define and describe the three patterns of descent outlined in the text.

3. Why do families have fewer children now than in the past?

4. Why has the divorce rate increased in recent decades in Canada?

5. What are the four stages of the family life cycle which are outlined in the text? Describe the major events which occur during each stage.

6. Six adjustments to divorce are identified by Paul Bohannan. Identify and describe each.

7. What impact does divorce have on children?

8. In what ways are middle-class and working-class marriages different according to research cited in the text?

9. What are the characteristics of cohabitation in Canada?

10 . What are the five conclusions being made about marriage and family in the twenty-first century?

Answers to Study Questions

True-False

1. T (p. 453)	7. F (p. 465)
2. F (p. 457)	8. T (p. 467)
3. F (p. 457)	9. F (p. 471)
4. T (p. 458)	10. T (p. 473)
5. T (p. 461)	11. T (p. 474)
6. F (p. 463)	

Multiple-Choice

1. e (p. 455)	7. b (p. 459)
2. a (p. 455)	8. b (p. 461)
3. b (p. 456)	9. c (p. 462)
4. d (p. 457)	10. d (p. 467)
5. d (p. 458)	11. e (p. 473)
6. b (p. 458)	

Fill-In

1. 50 (p. 455)	6. sexual relationships (p. 462)
2. consanguine (p. 455)	7. Denmark (p. 473)
3. endogamy (p. 455)	8. in vitro fertilization (p. 474)
4. bilateral (p. 457)	9. variable (p. 475)
5. negotiation (p. 459)	10. harmful (p. 476)

ANALYSIS AND COMMENT

Go back through the chapter and write down in the spaces below key points from each of the following boxes.

SOCIAL DIVERSITY

"Child Discipline, Child Abuse?"
Key Points:

_____

_____

_____

_____

GLOBAL SOCIOLOGY

"Early to Wed: A Report from Rural India"
Key Points:

_____

_____

_____

_____

"International Adoption"
Key Points:

_____

_____

_____

_____

APPLYING SOCIOLOGY

"Cohabitation Among Canadians"
Key Points:

✍

_____

_____

_____

_____

_____

_____

CONTROVERSY AND DEBATE

"The New Reproductive Technologies."
Key Points:

✍

_____

_____

_____

_____

_____

SUGGESTED READINGS

Classic Source

Michael Young and Peter Willmott.1992 (orig.
1957). *Family and Kinship in East London.*
Berkeley, CA.: University of California Press.
One of the best studies of the working-class family,
this account of the lives of "Eastenders" reveals the
power of class to shape family life.

Contemporary Canadian Sources

Pat Armstrong and Hugh Armstrong. 1984. *The
Double Ghetto: Canadian Women and Their
Segregated Work.* Toronto: McClelland &
Stewart.
This book describes and analyses the gendered nature
of the Canadian labour force.

Maureen Baker, ed. 1989. *Families: Changing
Trends in Canada.* 2nd ed. Toronto: McGraw-
Hill Ryerson.

Margrit Eichler. 1988. *Families in Canada Today:
Recent Changes and Their Policy Consequences.*
2nd ed. Toronto: Gage.
Emily Nett. 1993. *Canadian Families Past and
Present.* Toronto: Buterworths.
These three books provide various overviews of the
nature and condition of the family in Canadian
society. The first and fourth are general texts. The
second and third focus on policies that affect the
family and on feminist understandings of families.

Margrit Eichler. 1989. "Reflections on
Motherhood, Apple Pie, the New Reproductive
Technologies and the Role of Sociologists in
Society." *Society/Societe* 13(1): 1-5.
This article critiques some aspects of new
reproductive technologies.

Patrick Johnston. 1983. *Native Children and the
Child Welfare System.* Toronto: Lorimer.

293

Linda MacLeod. 1987. *Battered But Not Beaten...Preventing Wife Abuse in Canada.* Ottawa: Canadian Advisory Council on the Status of Women.
These books focus on "problems" within the Canadian family. The first examines Native children. The second discusses violence in the family. The third portrays the extent of poverty in Canada.

Global Sources

William J. Goode. *World Changes in Divorce Patterns.* New Haven, Conn.: Yale University Press, 1993.
This global survey explains how divorce is affected by economic patterns such as industrialization; it also explores variation in divorce by class.

Mark Mathabane. *African Women: Three Generations.* New York: HarperCollins, 1994.
This personal look at three women--a grandmother, a mother, and a sister--by a South African details the struggles common to women under a system of racial oppression.

CHAPTER 19

Religion

I CHAPTER OUTLINE

I.   **Religion: Basic Concepts**
    A. Religion and Sociology

II. **Theoretical Analysis of Religion**
    A. Functions of Religion: Structural-Functional Analysis
    B. Constructing the Sacred: Symbolic Interaction Analysis
    C. Inequality and Religion: Social Conflict Analysis

III. **Religion and Social Change**
    A. Max Weber: Protestantism and Capitalism
    B. Liberation Theology

IV. **Types of Religious Organization**
    A. Church and Sect
    B. Cult

V.   **Religion in History**
    A. Religion in Preindustrial Societies
    B. Religion in Industrial Societies

VI. **World Religions**
    A. Christianity
    B. Islam
    C. Judaism
    D. Hinduism
    E. Buddhism
    F. Confucianism
    G. Religion: East and West

VII. **Religion in Canada**
    A. Religious Affiliation
    B. Religiosity
    C. Religion and Social Stratification
        1. Social Class   2. Ethnicity

VIII. **Religion in a Changing Society**
    A. Secularization
    B. Civil Religion
    C. Religious Revival
    D. Religious Fundamentalism
        1. The Electronic Church

IX. **Looking Ahead: Religion in the Twenty-First Century**

X.   **Summary**

XI. **Critical Thinking Questions**

XII. **Applications And Exercises**

XIII. **Sites To See**

- To define the basic concepts of religion; faith, profane, sacred, and ritual.

- To explain the aspects of religion that sociology addresses.

- To identify and describe the three functions of religion as developed by Emile Durkheim.

- To identify and describe the view that religion is socially constructed.

- To identify and describe the role religion plays in maintaining inequality.

- To identify the relationship between religious values and economic development including political activism which aims to right social inequality.

- To compare and contrast the basic types of religious organizations: church (two types), sect, and cult.

- To distinguish between preindustrial and industrial societies in terms of religious beliefs and practices.

- To identify and describe the size, location, and type of belief system of the major world religions: Christianity, Islam, Hinduism, Buddhism, Confucianism, and Judaism.

- To explain religious affiliation, religiosity, and the correlates of religious affiliation in Canada.

- To describe the pattern of secularization in Canadian society.

- To identify and describe religious revival in North American society, especially religious fundamentalism.

- To understand the relationship between science and religion.

III CHAPTER REVIEW

A religious student goes to a prestigious university and finds secular life a challenge to his principles. The role of religion in a secular society has fuelled a long-standing debate.

RELIGION: BASIC CONCEPTS

Durkheim suggested human beings distinguish between the *profane*, meaning ordinary elements of everyday life, and the *sacred*, or that which is defined as extraordinary, inspiring a sense of awe, reverence, and even fear. This differentiation, according to Durkheim, is the key to religious belief. *Religion* is therefore a system of beliefs and practices based upon a conception of the sacred. The sacred is approached through *ritual,* or formal ceremonial behaviour.

Religion and Sociology

Because religion transcends everyday experience its truth cannot be tested by science. It is a matter of *faith*, belief anchored in convictions, not scientific evidence. Sociology is concerned with the social correlates of religious practices and the consequences of religious activity for social life.

THEORETICAL ANALYSIS OF RELIGION

Functions of Religion: Structural-Functional Analysis

Durkheim argued society has an existence of its own, beyond the lives of the people who create it. Society and the sacred are inseparable in Durkheim's view. He believed that the power of society was understood by people through their creation of sacred symbols. In technologically simple societies a *totem* is an object within the natural world that is imbued with sacred qualities which can transform individuals into a collectivity. He saw religion as providing three major functions for society.

➤**Social Cohesion**

Religion unites members of a society through shared symbolism, values, and norms.

➤**Social Control**

Every society promotes some degree of social conformity. Cultural norms, for example, are justified using religious doctrine.

➤**Providing Meaning and Purpose**

Religion provides people with a sense of meaning and purpose by addressing the ultimate issues of life.

A weakness in the structural-functional view is that it down-plays the dysfunctions of religion, particularly its role in producing destructive social conflict.

Constructing the Sacred: Symbolic-Interaction Analysis

Peter Berger, operating from the symbolic-interaction view, theorized that religion is a socially constructed reality much as the family and economy are. The sacred can provide a permanence for society as long as society's members ignore the recognition that the sacred is socially constructed.

Inequality and Religion: Social Conflict Analysis

The social-conflict view of religion draws attention to the social ills perpetuated by religion through justifying inequality and suggesting that a better life will come. Even sexual misconduct by priests was buried by the Catholic Church in Canada. The **Social Diversity** Box, (pp. 482-483) addresses the question of the extent to which religion favours males. The conflict perspective, however, ignores the extent to which religion can promote positive social change.

RELIGION AND SOCIAL CHANGE

Max Weber: Protestantism and Capitalism

Max Weber contends that Calvinism was the engine of change for industrialization in Western Europe. The doctrine of predestination led Protestants to demonstrate that they possessed God's favour by working hard and becoming prosperous. But the fruits of the labour were to be reinvested by the thrifty Calvinists, providing the foundation for industrial capitalism.

Liberation Theology

Liberation theology is a fusion of Christian principles with political activism, often Marxist in character. This view originated in the 1960s, and asserts that not only is the teaching of Christianity necessary for liberation from human sin, but the Church must help people liberate themselves from poverty. Adherents message is simple, inequality contradicts Christian morality, and poverty is preventable. The costs of this theology to its practitioners have been high, many have met with death.

TYPES OF RELIGIOUS ORGANIZATION

Church and Sect

A *church* is a formal religious organization that is well integrated into the larger society. Two types of church organization are the *ecclesia*, a church that is formally allied with the state, and a *denomination*, or a church that recognizes religious pluralism. The Catholic Church of the Roman Empire and the Anglican Church of England are examples of ecclesia. The Baptist, Methodist , and Catholic churches in Canada are examples of denominations.

A *sect*, distinct from a church, is a type of religious organization that stands apart from the larger society. Sects tend to lack the formal organization of a church and they exalt the personal experience of divine power. Leaders are often those people who manifest *charisma*, or extraordinary personal qualities which attract followers.. Proselytizing is important to obtain new members through *conversion*, a personal transformation resulting from new religious beliefs. Sects tend to reject the established society and sect members tend to be people of lower social standing than those in churches but some movement in membership does take place and as the churches lose membership, the sects often gain a sprinkling of affluent members.

Cult

Cults are religious organizations substantially outside a society's cultural traditions. They offer messages that are seen as new and are often judged by outsiders as deviant. Many cults, however, become more church-like over time.

RELIGION IN HISTORY

Religion in Pre-industrial Societies

Archaeological research suggests religious ritual has existed for at least 40,000 years. Among hunting and gathering societies religion typically takes the form of *animism*, or the belief that natural objects are conscious forms of life that can affect humanity. In such cultures, a shaman, or religious leader may be recognized, however not as a full-time position. With technological development religion moves out of the family and emerges as a distinct social institution.

Religion in Industrial Societies

With industrialization, science begins as a force which diminishes the scope of religious power and thinking. Yet science has not caused religion to be eliminated as it cannot answer certain fundamental questions about the reason for human existence.

WORLD RELIGIONS

Religion is found virtually everywhere in the world. Many of the thousands of religions are highly localized, but a few may be termed *world religions* because they have millions of followers and are known throughout the world.

Christianity

Christianity is the world's largest religion with two billion followers. Christianity is based on *monotheism*, or religious beliefs recognizing a single divine power. When this view first emerged it challenged the Roman Empire's tradition of *polytheism*, or religious beliefs recognizing many gods. Eventually Christianity become the official religion of the Roman empire but over the centuries there have been several divisions within Christianity. The **Global Maps** 19-1 through 19-4 (pp. 489 and 490) show us four major world religions in global perspective.

Islam

Islam is the world's second largest religion with more than one billion followers called Muslims. This religion is based on the life of Muhammad, born in Mecca in 570. He is seen as a prophet, not a divine being. Islam means "submission and peace." While divisions exist, there are five pillars of Islam: recognition of Allah as the one true God and Muhammed as God's messenger, ritual prayer, giving alms to the poor, regular fasting, and making at least one pilgrimage to Mecca. Muslims are obligated to defend their faith occasionally, justifying holy wars. As in most religions, women's lives are dominated by men.

Judaism

A small religion with only 14 million adherents, Judaism, nonetheless, has a special relationship with North America where 6 million Jews reside. Judaism has a long history and is animist in origin. After Moses led the exodus from Egypt, Judaism became monotheistic, recognizing one all-powerful God. A belief in the "covenant" suggests to Jews they have a special relationship with God. Their teachings emphasize moral behaviour in the world rather than the personal salvation of Christianity. There are divisions of Judaism based upon greater or lesser adherence to traditional practices but all Jews share an awareness of rejection which more recently is expressed through anti-Semitism. Also in Canada, Jews have experienced discrimination in the occupational and educational institutions. The University of Toronto has recently added two chairs in Jewish studies since Jewish culture is so important to an understanding of the development of Western civilization..

Hinduism

Hinduism is probably the oldest religion, coming into existence about 4500 years ago. It has about 793 million followers. Hinduism and Indian society are closely fused, so unlike Islam and Christianity it has not diffused widely to other nations. Since it is not linked to the life of one person, beliefs and practices vary greatly. All Hindus generally believe that a force termed dharma confronts all people with moral responsibility. Karma, a belief in the spiritual progress of a person's soul and involving reincarnation, is also a fundamental aspect of this religion. Hinduism is neither monotheistic nor polytheistic.

Buddhism

Buddhism emerged in India about 2500 years ago and currently has 325 million adherents. Siddharta Gautama was its founder. After years of travel and meditation he reached "bodhi," or enlightenment. Followers began spreading his teachings, called the *dhamma*. Buddhists see existence as suffering and reject the idea of wealth as a solution to human problems. Reincarnation is also a belief in this religion. The answer to world problems lies in personal transformation toward a spiritual existence.

Confucianism

Confucianism was the official religion of China from 200 BCE until the beginning of this century. This religion was shaped by Kung-Fu-Tzu (Confucius) who lived in the 6th and 5th centuries BCE. This religion is based on the concept of the jen, humaneness. Lacking a clear concept of the sacred, it is more a disciplined way of life than a religion.

Religion: East and West

Although all religions have a conception of a higher moral force or purpose, Western religions (Christianity, Islam, Judaism) have a clear focus on God and celebrate their faith in congregations while Eastern religions (Hinduism, Buddhism, Confucianism) focus on ethical codes and celebrate their faith in society itself.

RELIGION IN CANADA

Although Canada has experienced remarkable institutional changes religion continues to play a central role.

Religious Affiliation

About 90 percent of adults identify with a particular religion. Historically Canada was fairly evenly divided between Protestants and Catholics but now Catholics are in the majority at 45 percent. Figure 19-1, (p 493) outlines religiosity in Canada and elsewhere.

About 24 percent go to church at least once a week and one third claims to pray daily. Canada has no official religion as the separation of church and state is enshrined in the Constitution. With respect to maintenance of religious affiliation, mothers' influence is tremendously important.

Religiosity

Religiosity is the importance of religion in a person's life. Charles Glock has identified five distinct dimensions of religiosity; *experiential, ritualistic, ideological, consequential*, and *intellectual.*

The majority of Canadians (81%) claim to believe in God, 74 percent believe in miracle healing, 61 percent believe in angels and 49 percent believe in hell. However, fully 12 percent claim no religion at all (see **Canada Map** 19-1, p 494) and church attendance figures continue to drop. As well, some who attend church may not be particularly religious. Although the data are not clear, the majority of people in Canada are probably somewhat religious. See the **Applying Sociology** Box (p. 495) for a picture of children's attendance at religious services.

Religion and Social Stratification

➤**Social Class**

Protestants tend to have somewhat higher social positions than Catholics, and Jews, despite being fairly recent immigrants, have a high social standing, probably as a result of commitment to education and achievement. Table 19-1 (p. 496) demonstrates that religious stratification can be measured by average income levels.

➤**Ethnicity**

Religion is strongly linked with ethnicity world-wide and some of those identities are continued in Canada. However, nearly all ethnic groups in Canada display some religious diversity.

RELIGION IN A CHANGING SOCIETY

Secularization

A pattern of social change in Canada and elsewhere is *secularization,* a historical trend away from the supernatural and the sacred. As scientific explanation has been accepted, religious explanation has declined. The Quiet Revolution in Québec is a perfect example of the loss of influence of the Catholic church. Some dimensions of religiosity are in decline such as a belief in life after death but affiliation with a religious perspective may be increasing. While conservatives decry the loss of faith, progressives hail the loss of stifling beliefs such as the inferior position of women.

Civil Religion

There remains in industrial societies "civil religion", a quasi-religious loyalty binding individuals in essentially secular societies. Various patriotic symbols evoke religious feelings such as the belief that life in Canada is the best in the world. As well, the flag, the national anthem and social programs infuse most Canadians with a sense of collective identity.

Religious Revival

As mainline churches lose membership, sect-like organizations grow.

Religious Fundamentalism

Religious fundamentalism is a conservative religious doctrine that opposes intellectualism and worldly accommodation in favour of restoring a traditional other-worldly focus. Fundamentalism has spread rapidly in the U.S. and Canada especially among Protestants but it is gaining favour with Catholics and Jews as well.

Five characteristics identify fundamentalists: a literal interpretation of scripture, less tolerance for religious diversity, an emphasis on the personal experience of God's presence, an adversity to secularization and an endorsement of conservative political goals.

➤**The Electronic Church**

Fundamentalist churches have made substantial use of the mass media to gain converts. Some religious programming has produced enormous monetary donations and some of it has been grossly misused. The **Exploring Cyber-Society** Box (p. 498) examines the practice of finding God online.

LOOKING AHEAD: RELIGION IN THE TWENTY-FIRST CENTURY

Secularization is not squeezing out religion from our society. If anything, processes of change appear to be creating more need for religious faith. The **Controversy and Debate** Box, (p. 499) examines the tension between religion and science.

KEY CONCEPTS

Define each of the following concepts or on separate paper. Check the accuracy of your answers by referring to the text as well as by referring to italicized definitions located throughout the chapter.

animism
charisma
church
civil religion
cult
denomination
ecclesia
faith
fundamentalism
liberation theology

monotheism
polytheism
profane
religion
religiosity
ritual
sacred
sect
secularization
totem

STUDY QUESTIONS

 True-False

1. T F   Faith is belief anchored in conviction rather than scientific evidence

2. T F   Reform Judaism upholds the traditional prohibition against women serving as rabbis.

3. T F   According to Weber, Calvinism was a key factor in the development of capitalism in Western Europe.

4. T F   Denominations deteriorate in societies that formally separate church and state.

5. T F   Christianity is an example of polytheism.

6. T F   In Arabic, the word *Islam* means both "submission" and "peace".

7. T F   Canada, unlike most of the Western democracies, has never been guilty of anti-Semitism.

8. T F   Eastern religions tend to make less clear-cut distinctions between the sacred and the secular.

9. T F   Ideological religiosity concerns an individual's degree of belief in religious doctrine; while consequential religiosity has to do with how much religious beliefs influence a person's daily behaviour.

10. T F   A quasi-religious loyalty binding individuals with a basically secular society is called civil religion.

✎ Multiple-Choice

1. _____, according to Durkheim, is that which is defined as extraordinary, inspiring a sense of awe, reverence, and even fear.

   (a) the sacred   (c) religion
   (b) the profane   (d) jen

2. A totem—an object imbued with sacred qualities—is characteristically found within which of the following societies?

   (a) technologically simple   (c) heathen
   (b) modern advanced   (d) agrarian

3. Liberation theology, developed in the late 1960s, advocates a blending of religion with:

   (a) family   (c) economy
   (b) education   (d) politics

4. Which of the following is true of sects?

   (a) They are not different from churches in their social composition
   (b) They typically attract people of high social standing
   (c) They do not appeal to people who perceive themselves as outsiders
   (d) They discount the beliefs of other.
   (e) They do not promise personal fulfilment as the church might

5. The religious view that elements of the natural world are conscious life forms that affect humanity is called:

   (a) religion   (d) charisma
   (b) ecclesia   (e) proselytization
   (c) animism

6. Which of the following world religions has the most followers?

   (a) Islam
   (b) Christianity
   (c) Buddhism
   (d) Hinduism

7. Buddha's teachings were called

   (a) dharma
   (b) nirvana
   (c) moksha
   (d) dhamma
   (e) jen

8. Confucianism still influences the _____ way of life.

   (a) Indian
   (b) Chinese
   (c) Pakistani
   (d) Egyptian
   (e) Mesopotamian

9. What percentage of Canadians claim a religious preference.

   (a) 10%   (b) 25%   (c) 42%   (d) 79%   (e) 90%

10. Frank Jones has found that _____ of Canada's children attend religious services weekly.

    (a) 11%   (b) 18%   (c) 23%   (d) 35%   (e) 56%

11. Fundamentalism in North America has made its greatest gains amongst:

    (a) Catholics
    (b) Pluralists
    (c) Muslims
    (d) Taoists
    (e) Protestants

✎ Fill-In The Blank

1. Durkheim labelled the ordinary elements of everyday life the _____.

2. According to Marx, religion was the _____ of the people.

3. John Calvin advanced the doctrine of _____.

4. A _____ is a church, independent of the state, that accepts religious pluralism.

5. A belief in many Gods is referred to as _____.

6. Most Christians live in _____ or the _____.

7. _____ is the second largest religion in the world, with one billion followers who are called _____.

8. _____ differs from most other religions by not being linked to the life of any single person.

9. A historical trend away from the supernatural and the sacred is referred to as _____.

10. New information technology may usher in an age of _____ - churches.

Definition and Short Answers

1. Is sociology a threat to religious institutions?

2. What are the three major theoretical sociological perspectives on the role of religion in society?

3. What does Max Weber say about the development of capitalism in Western Europe?

4. What is the major difference between sects and cults?

5. Identify the major characteristics of the world religions.

6. What is the position of religion in contemporary society?

7. How does the development of "civil religion" relate to the secularization process?"

12. What will religiosity look like in the Canada of 2005?

13. What is the likelihood of the development of a cyber-church?

Answers to Study Questions

True-False

1. T (p 480)   6. T (p 488)
2. F (p 483)   7. F (p 489)
3. T (p 484)   8. T (p 492)
4. F (p 485)   9. T (p 493)
5. F (p 487)   10. T (p 496)

Multiple-Choice

1. a (p 479)   7. d (p 491)
2. a (p 48058)   8. b (p 492)
3. d (p 484)   9. e (p 493)
4. d (p 485)   10. c (p 495)
5. c (p 486)   11. e (p 497)
6. b (p. 487)

Fill-In

1. profane (p. 479)
2. opium (p.483)
3. predestination (p. 484)
4. denomination (p. 485)
5. polytheism (p. 487)

6. Europe/Americas (p. 487)
7. Islam/Muslims (p. 488)
8. Hinduism (p. 490)
9. secularization (pp. 495-496)
10. cyber (p. 498)

ANALYSIS AND COMMENT

Go back through the chapter and write down in the spaces below key points from each of the following boxes.

SOCIAL DIVERSITY

"Religion and Patriarchy: Does God Favour Males?"
Key Points:

_____

_____

_____

_____

APPLYING SOCIOLOGY

"Are Children Going to Religious Services?"
Key Points:

_____

_____

_____

_____

CONTROVERSY AND DEBATE

"Does Science Threaten Religion?"
Key Points:

_____

_____

_____

_____

_____

EXPLORING CYBER-SOCIETY

"The Cyber Church: Logging On to Religion."
Key Points:

_____

_____

_____

_____

_____

SUGGESTED READINGS

Classic Source

Max Weber. 1958. *The Protestant Ethic and the Spirit of Capitalism.* **New York: Charles Scribner's Sons.**
This is the classic account of the power of religion to effect sweeping social change.

W. E. Mann. 1955. *Sect, Cult and Church in Alberta.* **Toronto: University of Toronto Press.**
This is the first sociological study of religion in Canada. It focuses on the growth of various religious groups in Alberta between the 1920s and 1940s.

Contemporary Sources

Helen Rose Ebaugh. 1993. *Women in the Vanishing Cloister: Organizational Decline in Catholic Religious Orders in the United States.* **New Brunswick, N.J.: Rutgers University Press.**

This account, written by a nun-turned-sociologist, explores the drop in the number of women in Catholic religious orders since the 1960s.

Wade Clark Roof. 1992. *A Generation of Seekers: The Spiritual Journeys of the Baby Boom Generation.* **New York: HarperCollins.**
Mounting evidence points to a return to religion for many members of the generation of young people who came of age in the 1960s.

Canadian Sources

Tom Harpur. 1994. *The Uncommon Touch: An Investigation of Spiritual Healing.* **Toronto: McClelland Stewart.**
This is a review of spiritual healing from a historical and cross-cultural perspective.

Reginald W. Bibby. 1987. *Fragmented Gods: The Poverty and Potential of Religion in Canada.* **Toronto: Irwin.**
This is a comprehensive analysis of religion in Canada based on three national surveys conducted in 1975, 1980, and 1985.

George A. Mori. 1990. *Religious Affiliation in Canada: Canadian Social Trends.* **Ottawa: Statistics Canada.**
This is a government publication that provides a demographic review of religion in Canada.

John R. Williams, ed. 1984. *Canadian Churches and Social Justice.* **Toronto: Lorimer.**
This book examines views on social justice of a variety of religious groups in Canada.

Reginald W. Bibby. 1993. *Unknown Gods.* **Toronto: Stoddart.**
This book explains why Canadian churches are in a state of decline and makes some future predictions.

Global Sources

Richard W. Bulliet. 1994. *Islam: The View From the Edge.* **New York: Columbia University Press.**
Although the heart of Islam lies in the Middle East, Muslims live in North America and around the world. This book examines how Islam differs in its central and peripheral settings.

Christian Smith. 1991. *The Emergence of Liberation Theology: Radical Religion and Social Movement Theory.* **Chicago: University of Chicago Press.**
This account of liberation theology among politically active Catholics during the 1960s assesses the movement's successes and failures.

CHAPTER 20

$\boxed{\textbf{Education}}$

I CHAPTER OUTLINE

I.   **Education: A Global Survey**
       A. Schooling and Economic Development
       B. Schooling in India
       C. Schooling in Japan
       D. Schooling in Great Britain
       E. Schooling in Canada

II.   **The Functions of Schooling**
       A. Socialization
       B. Cultural Innovation
       C. Social Integration
       D. Social Placement
       E. Latent Functions of Schooling

III. **Schooling and Social Inequality**
       A. Social Control
       B. Testing and Social Inequality
       C. Streaming and Social Inequality
       D. Unequal Access to Higher Education
       E. Credentialism
       F. Privilege and Personal Merit

IV.   **Problems in the Schools**
       A. School Discipline
       B. Dropping Out
       C. Value for Our Money
       D. Academic Standards
       E. Education and the World of Work

V.   **Education for Tomorrow**
VI.   **Summary**
VII. **Critical Thinking Questions**
VIII. **Applications And Exercises**
IX.   **Sites To See**

II LEARNING OBJECTIVES

- To understand how the role of education changes in response to economic development

- To compare and contrast schooling in Great Britain, Japan, India and Canada.

- To identify and describe the functions of schooling.

- To explain how education supports social inequality through social control, testing, and streaming.

- To describe the problems associated with unequal access to higher education and credentialism.

- To identify and analyze the problems facing Canadian education today: discipline, drop-out rates, academic standards, the relationship between education and the world of work, and whether there is measurable value received for money expended.

- To describe the changes in society that the educational system will have to face, namely; an increasingly diverse population, a revolution in technology and a global political and economic restructuring.

III CHAPTER REVIEW

We are introduced to the Matsuo family of Yokohama, Japan. Education in Japan is very competitive, and rigorous application of the student to its demands is critical through primary and secondary levels to even hope to achieve high enough scores on national tests to get into a national university. Many children go to the *Juku*, or "cram school," several days a week after their regular day at school.

Education refers to the various ways in which knowledge including factual information and skills as well as cultural norms and values, is transmitted to members of society. An important kind of education in industrial societies is *schooling*, or formal instruction under the direction of specially trained teachers.

EDUCATION: A GLOBAL SURVEY

Schooling and Economic Development

While children today in Japan, Canada and other industrialized societies can expect to be in school at least until they are eighteen years of age, in preindustrial times there was no formal system of education. In 1830 in Canada, for example, half the children's total exposure to school was approximately one year.

In hunting and gathering societies all knowledge was passed on by the family. In agrarian societies schools were available but only for the elite. During the Middle Ages the church expanded schooling with the establishment of universities but again, they were primarily for the ruling elite.

In preindustrial societies today there is marked diversity in schooling affected by religion and various distinctive cultural traditions but all low-income countries have high rates of illiteracy (see **Global Map** 20-1, p. 504) while industrial societies expect that everyone will receive at least basic educational skills.

Schooling in India

Despite the existence of child labour laws many of India's children work in factories for long hours in order to supplement family income. As a result less than half receive secondary level education leaving the majority illiterate. As well, patriarchal attitudes leave girls receiving less education than boys.

Schooling in Japan

Mandatory education laws began in 1872. The cultural values of tradition and family are stressed in the early grades. In their early teens, students begin to face the rigorous and competitive exams of the Japanese system. Test scores determine whether a person will go to university or college, rich and poor alike. Some 90 percent of Japanese students graduate from high school, a much higher rate than Canada. However, only 30 percent go on to the post secondary level compared to 55 percent in Canada. Japanese mothers of school age children participate in the labour force at considerably lower rates than Canadian mothers in order to devote themselves to the educational success of their children. The results of their system seem impressive, particularly in the areas of math and science.

Schooling in Great Britain

Schooling in Great Britain has long been associated with the elite. Traditional social distinctions still exist, with many children from wealthy families attending public schools, the equivalent of our private boarding schools. Expansion of the university system has allowed all children to compete for Britain's government funded university system. However, graduates of the elite schools of Oxford and Cambridge have considerable economic and political power in Britain. Quite clearly, the examples from India, Japan and Great Britain indicate how social and cultural patterns help shape educational participation.

Schooling in Canada

In Canada, church controlled schools were started in the early French settlements and by 1636 the Jesuits started a college which became Laval. Gradually other universities were added in English Canada and boarding schools became the first step in a secondary school system. Prior to Confederation both Catholic and Protestant school systems were in place and by 1920 compulsory education to 16 years was adopted. Mass education was, in part, a response to the requirements for a skilled and literate workforce.

But, official literacy and functional literacy are not the same. While absolute illiteracy has been minimized in industrial societies (see **Global Map** 20-1, p. 504), functional literacy and numeracy skills in Canada, those needed for effective daily living, are not possessed by fully 15 percent of adult Canadians. Twenty-eight percent of Canadians aged 16-24 cannot read a simple newspaper article and 44% are not functionally numerate. Only 20-22% of Canadians function at the highest literacy levels (prose, document and quantitative scales) and this is true for only 8-13% of Qu■becers, 23-26% of Ontarions and 25-35% in the Western provinces. Even so, educational attainment has grown tremendously; between 1961 and 1986 the proportion of Canadians between 25 and 44 years of age with some post-secondary education has moved from 8 to 55 percent and in 1999, 17% of Canadians had completed university degrees.

In the 1800s in Canada education was seen as a precondition to economic growth and widespread participation was the goal. Full public funding for elementary and secondary education has gradually been established in both the public and Catholic systems. The majority of funding for colleges and universities also is supplied by government.

Canada ranks only behind Sweden in public expenditures for education which fits the goal of universality; however Canada is behind both the U.S. and the Netherlands in proportion of citizens with university degrees.

Canada has long valued a *practical* education. The educational philosophy of John Dewey played a role in this development as *progressive education*, that which meets current needs was adopted. Despite this, Canada is lagging behind many other nations in number of engineering degrees awarded. There is some recent change as engineering, mathematics and science degrees increase while social sciences and humanities degrees decline.

THE FUNCTIONS OF SCHOOLING

Structural-functional analysis focuses our attention on the functions which educational systems satisfy for society.

Socialization

As societies become more technologically advanced, social institutions must emerge beyond the family to help socialize members of the society to become functioning adults. Important lessons on cultural values and norms are learned in schools at all levels along with basic mathematical and language skills. As compared to the United States, the Canadian classroom focuses on cooperative activities and the celebration of diversity.

Cultural Innovation

Education is not merely a transmission of culture, it is also a factor in the creation of culture through critical inquiry and research. Marshall McLuhan, in 1972, foresaw the use of the electronic media to create classrooms without walls.

Social Integration

Through the teaching of certain cultural values and norms, people become more unified. This is a particularly critical function in culturally diverse societies.

This social integration has met with mixed success however, in Canada and elsewhere. What is recognized is that education is necessary for success and while cultural traditions can be protected, certain linguistic and other skills must be learned in order to survive in the larger society. In a bilingual society, French is a useful occupational tool, and the response has been an increase in French immersion programs, but enrolments are quite low.

Social Placement

Schooling operates as a screening device to place people in the society according to their aptitudes and abilities. Ideally the "brightest and best" take the challenging tasks.

Latent Functions of Schooling

Schools serve as babysitters for younger children, and by occupying the time of teenagers, keeps them from engaging in higher rates of socially disruptive behaviours. Lasting relationships are also established in school.

The structural-functionalists stress the ways in which education supports the operation of the industrial economy. One weakness of this approach however is that it fails to focus on how the quality of education varies greatly for different groups of people.

SCHOOLING AND SOCIAL INEQUALITY

Social-conflict analysis views schooling as a perpetuation of social stratification in Canada.

Its clear that gender, race and ethnicity have been good predictors of participation rates and subjects studied. There has, however, been a real effort in recent years to rid curriculum and textbooks of gender bias and negative racial or ethnic stereotypes. Certainly women and francophones have increased their participation rates at the post-secondary level. Social class is linked to educational aspirations and the opportunity to use computers in the home.

Regional variations in educational attainment are outlined in **Canada Map** 20-1, p. 512.

Social Control

Social-conflict analysis views social control as an outcome of schooling because youth are socialized to accept the status quo. The term *hidden curriculum* refers to the content of schooling that subtly espouses certain ideas. Compliance, punctuality, and discipline are part of the hidden curriculum, which are seen to support the capitalist system.

Testing and Social Inequality

Standardized tests have traditionally been used for streaming and placement purposes. These tests, however, are weighted in favour of those students from middle and upper class backgrounds.

Streaming and Social Inequality

Streaming is the categorical assignment of students to different types of educational programs. The idea is to provide education appropriate to a student's aspirations and aptitudes.

Critics suggest that streaming simply replicates the stratification system, students from affluent families expect to be in university bound streams and those from modest backgrounds expect to learn a trade. Many schools are now more cautious about streaming.

Unequal Access to Higher Education

In Canada higher education is regarded as the path to occupational achievement. Figure 20-2 (p. 513) indicates that Canada ranks fifth among OECD countries in university enrolment. Of those individuals who do not enter post-secondary institutions, some enter the labour force, others find the cost prohibitive and yet others cannot master the material.

While females now are more likely than males to attend university, working class people are grossly under-represented. Figure 20-3, p. 516, shows that Asians and Blacks are over-represented in higher education while Natives are least likely to attend. The **Social Diversity** Box, (pp. 514-515), outlines the oppressive education received by natives in residential schools.

Clearly educational attainment is positively related to occupational success as indicated in Figure 20.4, (p. 516).

Credentialism

Credentials serve to help ensure that properly trained people acquire important jobs in a complex society but they also serve a gate-keeping role to ensure that the "right kind" of people get the good jobs.

Privilege and Personal Merit

An important theme of social-conflict analysis is that schooling turns social privilege into personal merit. University is seen as a rite of passage for children of wealthier families, while children from modest beginnings must struggle to overcome the lack of resources. The **Applying Sociology** Box (p. 517) demonstrates that family structure and parents' educational achievement are strong predictors of educational attainment.

The social-conflict approach focuses on education in terms of social inequality. However, it ignores the social mobility provided by education and the challenge to the inequalitarian system offered in educational curricula.

PROBLEMS IN THE SCHOOLS

Canadians are increasingly dissatisfied with the quality of education their children are receiving. Table 20-1, p. 519 indicates the level of dissatisfaction across the country. Despite this finding, 68 percent of Canadians favour increased government funding to all educational sectors. More parents, however, are enrolling their children in private schools.

School Discipline

There is a concern with discipline in Canadian schools. Assaults upon students and teachers are common but the largest concern is with the lack of respect shown to teachers whose major concern is often a matter of maintaining control.

Dropping Out

While some students are disruptive still more are simply dropping out. The rate for Canada is 18 percent but varies considerably by province. (See Table 20-2, p. 519)There are several social factors related to dropping out, many of them class based. Aboriginals have the highest rate while immigrants have the lowest. Those that do drop out of school are at a tremendous disadvantage in a credential-based society.

Value for Our Money

Canada spends more money on education than any other leading industrialized country without any accompanying evidence that the quality of education is better. Demographer David Foot suggests that we simply ignored basic demographics; when elementary school enrolment declined by 20% we did not reduce expenditures at that level and increase them at the secondary level. By so doing we inflated budgets without necessarily increasing the quality of education. In fact our students compare unfavourably with students from other countries in international standardized tests.

Academic Standards

There has been a growing concern in the United States and Canada about a decline in educational standards. Few students write or think in complex ways and many high school graduates are functionally illiterate. (See the **Social Diversity** box, p. 522). Canadians fare poorly on international tests but many countries have only their elite students take such tests. Nonetheless, the feeling persists that Canadian standards of academic excellence have declined in recent years.

Education and the World of Work

While its clear that the educational system must develop technical skills in students what seems to be missing is the development of skills to integrate and use information, adapt to change, take reasonable risks and conceptualize the future.

EDUCATION FOR TOMORROW

In a society characterized by diversity, in the midst of a technological revolution and competing in a global economy, the educational institution must be a catalyst, an adaptive mechanism and a force for maintaining continuity in a period of change. While computers and the internet can improve the overall quality of learning (See **Exploring Cyber-Society** p. 520) they are not a panacea or a replacement for a plan to provide quality universal schooling. Look at the **Controversy and Debate** box (p. 524) for another view on educational open-mindedness being challenged by political correctness.

KEY CONCEPTS

Define each of the following concepts in the space provided or on separate paper. Check the accuracy of your answer by referring to the text as well as by referring to italicized definitions located throughout the chapter.

credentialism   hidden curriculum
education   schooling
functional illiteracy   streaming

STUDY QUESTIONS

 ## True-False

1. T F   Throughout the world, just half of all children attend secondary school.

2. T F   In Japan university is limited to only the best students.

3. T F   Between 1971 and 1986 the proportion of Canadians with a university degree rose from 7 to 55%.

4. T F   Although Canada produces few engineers compared to societies like Japan and Germany, there is a clear shift toward engineering, math and science degrees.

5. T F   In Canadian schools as opposed to American schools, there is less emphasis on a unified cultural identity, and more on respect for the many cultures that make up the Canadian mosaic.

6. T F   Hidden curriculum refers to categorically assigning students to different types of education programs.

7. T F   Women are now as likely as men to attend university.

8. T F   Native children educated in residential schools were, for the most part, cared for compassionately.

9. T F   According to Collins, credentials work as a gatekeeping strategy.

10. T F   Between 1986 and 1996, the percentage of Aboriginals who earned university degrees increased from 2 to 10 percent.

11. T F   Canada spends more than 20% of its gross national product on education.

Multiple-Choice

1. The extra, intensive schooling received by Japanese elementary school children in the afternoon takes place within the:

    (a) huanco
    (b) mitchou
    (c) taruko
    (d) juku
    (e) kiturya

2. What percentage of high school graduates in Japan enter university?

    (a) 10%   (b) 20%   (c) 30%   (d) 40%   (e) 50%

3. What percentage of Canada's adult population are found to be functionally illiterate?

    (a) 5%   (b) 10%   (c) 15%   (d) 20%   (e) 30%

4. John Dewey endorsed _____ which reflected people's changing concerns and needs.

    (a) functional education
    (b) private schools
    (c) progressive education
    (d) cultural integration
    (e) affiliative education

5. Which of the following functions of formal education helps to forge a population into a single, unified society?

    (a) socialization
    (b) social integration
    (c) social placement
    (d) cultural innovation

6. The subtle presentations of political or cultural ideas in the classroom is called

    (a) the hidden curriculum
    (b) streaming
    (c) social placement
    (d) cultural innovation
    (e) persuasion

7. Which OECD country has the highest proportion of women 17-34 years of age enrolled in university?

    (a) Austria
    (b) United States
    (c) Spain
    (d) Canada
    (e) Australia

8. The requirement that a person hold some particular diploma or degree as a condition of employment is called:

(a) overeducation
(b) under-education
(c) hidden effects
(d) credentialism
(e) oligarchy

9. David Foot claims that the inflated cost of Canada's educational system is the result of a failure to

(a) decertify teacher's unions
(b) eliminate boards of education
(d) analyse demographic trends
(d) permit more private schools
(e) none of the above

10. Which of the following societies has the lowest level of functional illiteracy?

(a) Canada
(b) United States
(c) Germany
(d) Sweden
(e) Poland

✎ Fill-In The Blank

1. In India only about _____ of the people are literate.

2. Many wealthy families in England send their children to what the British call _____, the equivalent to Canadian private boarding schools.

3. Literacy is lowest in _____ and highest in the Western provinces.

4. _____ schools are now seen as a significant factor in the oppression of native Indian children.

5. The _____ and _____ communities have higher levels of educational attainment than the English or the French.

6. The level of dissatisfaction with the quality of education is highest in the provinces; _____ and _____.

7. The _____ people experience a 40 percent drop out rate from school.

8. According to the National Literacy Secretariat only _____ % of Canadians have sufficient literacy and numeracy skills to deal adequately with everyday tasks.

9. The education system in Canada is expected to play an _____ role by fostering a Canadian identity that overrides our differences.

10. Many think that the open mindedness of universities is being compromised by _____ .

Definition and Short-Answer

1. Describe the four basic functions of education as reviewed in the text.

2. What are the latent functions of schooling?

3. How does streaming relate to social inequality?

4. What are the relationships between level of schooling and employment?

5. What are the problems in the school system that lead to parental dissatisfaction?

6. How must education change in order to fit more readily with the world of work?

7. Compare the educational systems of Canada, Japan, Great Britain and India.

8. How have Aboriginals been disadvantaged by the educational system in Canada?

Answers to Study Questions

True-False

1. T (p. 504)   7. T (p. 513)
2. T (p. 506)   8. F (pp. 514-515)
3. F (p. 507)   9. T (p. 516)
4. T (p. 508)   10. F (p. 517)
5. T (p. 508)   11. F (p. 519)
6. F (p. 511)

Multiple-Choice

1. d (p. 503)   6. a (p. 511)
2. d (p. 506)   7. c (p. 513)
3. c (p. 507)   8. d (p. 516)
4. c (p. 508)   9. c (p. 520)
5. b (p. 508)   10. d (p. 522)

Fill-In

1. 1/2 (p. 505)
2. public schools (p. 506)
3. Québec (p. 507)
4. residential (pp. 514-515)
5. Asian / black (p. 516)

6. Ontario and B.C. (p. 519)
7. Aboriginal (p. 519)
8. 63 (p. 522)
9. integrative (p. 523)
10. political correctness (p. 524)

ANALYSIS AND COMMENT

Go back through the chapter and write down in the space below key points from each of the following boxes.

APPLYING SOCIOLOGY

"Explaining Educational Attainment."
Key Points:

_____
_____
_____
_____
_____

CONTROVERSY AND DEBATE

"Is Political Correctness Undermining Education?"
Key Points:

_____
_____
_____
_____

SOCIAL DIVERSITY

"Functional Illiteracy: Must We Rethink Education?"
Key Points:

_____
_____
_____
_____

"An Education of Repression", Canada's Indian Residential Schools

Key Points:

_____

_____

_____

_____

EXPLORING CYBER-SOCIETY

"Welcome to Cyber-School."

Key Points:

_____

_____

_____

_____

SUGGESTED READINGS

Classic Source

John Dewey. 1963; orig. 1938. *Experience and Education.* **New York: Collier.**
In this short book--originally presented as a series of lectures--Dewey sketches his vision of progressive education.

Contemporary Sources

Allan Bloom. 1987. *The Closing of the American Mind: How Higher Education Has Failed Democracy and Impoverished the Souls of Today's Students.* **New York: Simon & Schuster.**
Dinesh D'Souza. 1991. *Illiberal Education: The Politics of Race and Sex on Campus.* **New York: The Free Press.**
The first of these books is a best-seller that helped launch the current debate over "political correctness" on the university campus. The second echoes these conservative sentiments, indicting "PC" for undermining higher education.

Dorothy C. Holland and Margaret A. Eisenhart. 1990. *Educated in Romance: Women, Achievement, and College Culture.* **Chicago: University of Chicago Press.**
These researchers investigate how a "culture of romance" erodes the career aspirations of women on university campuses.

Canadian Sources

Ratna Ghosh and Douglas Ray, eds. 1991. *Social Change and Education in Canada.* **Toronto: Harcourt Brace Jovanovich.**
This is an excellent reader for detailed and concise explorations of current educational issues.

John Porter, Marion Porter, and Bernard R. Blishen. 1982. *Stations and Callings.* **Toronto: Methuen.**
This report of a large-scale cross-sectional study argues that Canada' s Meritocratic educational system does not benefit the majority of working-class children.

Terry Wotherspoon, ed. 1987. *The Political Economy of Canadian Schooling.* **Toronto: Methuen.**
This collection of articles approaches the sociology of education from a critical perspective, showing how schools perpetuate inequalities.

Sid Gilbert, Lynn Barr, Warren Clark, Mathew Blue, and Deborah Sunter. 1993. *Leaving School.* **Ottawa: Government of Canada.**
A national survey comparing school leavers and high school graduates on a wide range of variables is the basis of this provocative publication.

Global Source

Nelly P. Stromquist, ed. *Women and Education in Latin America: Knowledge, Power and Change.* **Boulder, Co.: Lynne Rienner, 1992.**
This book is a collection of thirteen essays that focus on the educational opportunities for women in this important world region.

CHAPTER 21

I CHAPTER OUTLINE

I. **What is Health?**
   A. Health and Society
II. **Health: A Global Survey**
   A. Health in History
   B. Health in Low Income Countries
   C. Health in High Income Countries
III. **Health in Canada**
   A. Social Epidemiology: The Distribution of Health
   1. Age and Sex   2. Social Class and Race
   B. Health and Society: Three Examples
   1. Cigarette Smoking
   2. Eating Disorders
   3. Sexually Transmitted Diseases
      a. Gonorrhea
      b. Genital Herpes
      c. AIDS
   C. Ethical Issues: Confronting Death
IV. **The Medical Establishment**
   A. The Rise of Scientific Medicine
   B. Holistic Medicine
   C. Paying for Health: A Global Survey
   1. Medicine in Socialist Societies   2. Medicine in Capitalist Societies
   D. Medicine in Canada
V. **Theoretical Analysis of Health and Medicine**
   A. Structural-Functional Analysis
   1. The Sick Role   2. The Physician's Role
   B. Symbolic-Interaction Analysis
   1. The Social Construction of Illness
   2. The Social Construction of Treatment
   C. Social-Conflict Analysis
   1. The Access Issue
   2. The Profit Motive
   3. Medicine as Politics
VI. **Looking Ahead; Health and Medicine in the Twenty-first Century**
VII. **Summary**
VIII. **Critical Thinking Questions**
IX. **Applications And Exercises**
X. **Sites To See**
XI. **Cyber.Scope**
   A. New Information Technology and Social Institutions

- To understand the ways in which the health of a population is shaped by society's cultural patterns, its technology and social resources, and its social inequality.

- To know the ways that health differs historically and in low and high income countries today.

- To explain how age, sex, race, and social class affect the level of health of individuals in our society.

- To identify and describe the issues of eating disorders, cigarette smoking, and sexually transmitted diseases to world health today.

- To explain the ethical issues related to dying and death.

- To compare and contrast scientific medicine with holistic medicine.

- To compare and contrast medical care in socialist and capitalist societies.

- To understand the characteristics of Canada's health care system.

- To describe, compare, and contrast the three sociological paradigms and their contributions to understanding health and medicine.

- To understand the impact of information technology on social institutions.

III CHAPTER REVIEW

The chapter opens with a description of the impact of television on Fiji. Prior to television, Fijian girls were unconcerned with controlling their weight; after television, 62% reported they had dieted in the previous month. Eating disorders can be seen to be socially constructed by the society. What is considered healthy is, at least partly, a matter of social definition.

WHAT IS HEALTH?

Health is defined as a state of complete physical, mental, and social well-being. Therefore, it is viewed as much a *social* as a *biological* issue.

Health and Society

Health is shaped by several factors in a society; its cultural patterns such as standards of health and ideas of moral goodness, its technological development and level of inequality.

HEALTH: A GLOBAL SURVEY

Health in History

Health as a social issue is demonstrated by the significant increase in well-being over the course of history. The simple technology of hunting and gathering societies made it difficult to maintain a healthful environment. As many as one-half of the people in such societies died by age twenty, and few lived passed the age of forty.

The agricultural revolution increased surpluses, but also inequality, so only the elite enjoyed better health. Urbanization during medieval times created horrible health problems and life expectancy was low.

Health in Low Income Countries

Abject poverty leads to poor nutrition and is linked to poor sanitation, contaminated drinking water and infectious diseases. Combined with a lack of trained medical personnel (See **Global Map** 21-1, p. 531) health is poor and life expectancy low for most residents of low income countries. The **Global Sociology** Box on page 530 describes the impact of poverty on many people in Africa. When medical technologies are introduced to these countries and infectious diseases are reduced, the population often soars bringing on yet more poverty!

Health in High Income Countries

Early industrialization was characterized by crowded, filthy cities where disease was rampant. By the late 1800s medical advances reduced the impact of infectious diseases and sewer systems were separated from drinking water. In the longer term industrialization has delayed death considerably although the diseases of affluence, cancer and heart disease, are very much with us.

HEALTH IN CANADA

Social Epidemiology: The Distribution of Health

Social epidemiology is the study of how health and disease are distributed throughout a society's population. Examined are the links between health and physical and social environments.

➤**Age and Sex**

Health of Canadians of all ages has improved during this century, with the exception of young adults, who are victims of more accidental deaths. Those children today characterized by poor diets and lack of exercise, however, will be the heart patients of the future. While women live longer than men they do suffer more illnesses. The socialization of men produces aggression and risky behaviours.

➤Social Class and Race

There is a strong relationship between social class and health. Infant mortality is twice as high among the poor as it is among the affluent: Table 21-1, (p. 532) shows that an index of health is higher for those in upper income brackets.

Native Canadians live a shorter life than non-Native Canadians, approximately 6 years less. Natives and non-Natives who live in poverty are condemned by a substandard diet and minimal medical care. There is also evidence that AIDS is spreading more quickly in the Native population.

Health and Society: Three Examples

➤ Cigarette Smoking

Cigarette smoking is the leading preventable cause of illness and death in Canada and is increasingly seen as deviant behaviour. The percentage of smokers has declined from 45% in 1960 to 24% in 1994. (See **Canada Map** 21-1, p. 533 for provincial smoking rates.) Smoking appears to be stress related as divorced/separated, unemployed, and armed forces individuals are especially likely to smoke as are those who are less educated. Women now smoke almost as much as men and lung cancer now competes with breast cancer as a leading cause of death.

Since smoking is such a health risk advertising is constrained and smoke-free environment laws are increasing. The tobacco companies have conceded smoking is harmful to health and have agreed to no longer target young people in advertisements.

➤ Eating Disorders

These disorders involve intense forms of weight control in order to become very thin. 95% are women and most are white and middle-class. The cultural ideal of thinness for women is espoused by affluent families and the mass media who provide unrealistic standards of beauty.

➤ Sexually Transmitted Diseases

Increased concern about *venereal diseases* occurred during the 1960s at the beginning of the "sexual revolution". They are viewed by many as not just an illness, but also a punishment for immorality.

Sexually transmitted diseases (STDs) represent an exception to the general decline in infectious diseases during this century.

Gonorrhea

Gonorrhea is almost always transferred through sexual contact and is much more common among poor people and visible minorities.

Genital Herpes

This virus infects large numbers of Canadians. Although not as serious as gonorrhea , there is currently no cure available.

AIDS

The most serious STD is AIDS, caused by the human immunodeficiency virus, HIV, which attacks the immune system and renders a person susceptible to a wide range of diseases.

The first case in Canada was reported in 1982. By 1993, 6,197 deaths due to AIDS were reported in Canada and approximately 1 in 1,000 Canadians is infected with HIV. By the end of 1999, 16,913 AIDS cases were reported and 54,000 were living with HIV.

Women and children are increasingly infected as are men and women in the Aboriginal communities.

Globally, HIV infects 40 million people, half under the age of 25. Two thirds of cases are in Africa where HIV is spread primarily by heterosexual contact.

Transmission almost always occurs through blood, semen or breast milk. It is not spread through casual contact; although this disease is deadly it is also difficult to acquire. It can be spread through unprotected sex, sharing needles and using drugs or alcohol in the sense that it impairs judgement. Abstinence from sex or sharing an exclusive relationship with an uninfected person are sure ways to avoid transmission of HIV. Canada's blood supply is now routinely screened for HIV.

In Canada prevalence is much higher in gay and bisexual men (anal sex is a high risk factor) but heterosexual contact also involves risk. It is estimated that 10-15% of gay and homosexual men are HIV positive and that perhaps 9% of infections occur through heterosexual contact.

AIDS is a major social and medical crisis costing our society a fortune in direct costs of treatment and research and much more in lost productivity.

Some drugs extend the lives of AIDS patients but do not cure them; education is still the best defence.

Ethical Issues: Confronting Death

The issue of death has become a major ethical concern. Questions addressed include: When does death occur? Do people have a right to die? And, what about mercy killing?

Medical and legal experts presently define death as an irreversible state involving no response to stimulation, no movement or breathing, no reflexes, and no indication of brain activity.

The Sue Rodriguez case in B.C. goes to the heart of the issue of whether people have a right to die. The current Criminal Code retains a prohibition against assisting a suicide but Rodriguez, who had Lou Gehrig's disease and little time to live, wished for a physician-assisted death when she neared the end. The Supreme Court of Canada ruled 5-4 against her request. In the end an anonymous physician helped her to die.

Euthanasia, assisting in the death of a person suffering from an incurable disease, is a contentious issue in Canada. Support for positive euthanasia is growing but active euthanasia provokes controversy as the Robert Latimer case indicates. He is now serving a 10 year prison term for murdering his daughter.

THE MEDICAL ESTABLISHMENT

Medicine is an institutionalized system for combating disease and improving health. For most of human history, the individual and family were responsible for health care. In preindustrial societies, traditional healers, from herbalists to acupuncturists, provide for the health needs of their society's members. Medicine emerges within technologically complex societies as people fill specialized roles as healers.

The Rise of Scientific Medicine

Scientific medicine dominates health care in Canada, meaning the logic of science is applied to research and treatment of disease and injury.

In colonial Canada, medicine was the domain of herbalists, druggists, midwives, and ministers. These medical people knew little by today's standards and the surgeons of the time probably killed as many as they saved.

Gradually specialists came to know more about anatomy, physiology and biochemistry and medicine came under self-regulating medical societies. Doctors established in 1865 the General Council of Medical Education and Registration in Upper Canada and the Canadian Medical Association in 1867. By these activities they won control of the certification process and relegated other health practitioners such as naturopaths to fringe roles.

Medicine became a male, higher social level background preserve. Even in 1992, more than 80 percent of physicians were men and 97 percent of nurses were women.

Holistic Medicine

Holistic medicine is an approach to health care that emphasizes prevention of illness and takes account of the whole person within a physical and social environment. The following are major concerns of the holistic approach: patients are people, individual responsibility for health is stressed instead of dependency on medicine, a personal treatment environment is sought, and the goal of holistic medicine is optimum health for all.

Paying for Health: A Global Survey

➢**Medicine in Socialist Societies**

In societies like the People's Republic of China and the former Soviet Union, government directly controls medical care. Medical costs are paid for by public funds, and medical care is distributed equally among all.

The People's Republic of China is still a relatively poor agrarian society which is just beginning to industrialize. With over 1 billion people, reaching everyone within one system is difficult. Barefoot doctors, equivalent to paramedics in America, bring modern methods to millions of rural residents in China but traditional healing arts remain strong in China.

The former Soviet Union is struggling to formulate a new medical care system within the switch from a state-dominated economy to a market system.

Currently medical care is paid for by taxes and people receive their care at a local government health facility. Physicians, mainly women, are poorly paid and the health care system is in crisis, providing standardized, impersonal care.

➤Medicine in Capitalist Societies

In capitalist societies citizens provide for health care with their own resources with varying levels of government assistance.

Sweden

This is a socialized medical system where the system and the facilities are owned and operated by the government and most physicians are salaried employees.

Great Britain

Britain has a dual system where everyone is eligible for care provided by the National Health Service, but where more extensive and expensive care can be privately purchased.

Japan

Japan has a private system but where most of the costs are covered by government or privately run plans. (See Figure 21-2, p. 541 for the extent of "socialized medicine" in various countries)

The United States

For the most part medicine in the US is a private, profit-making industry where more money brings better care. It is called a *direct-fee system* where patients pay directly for the services of physicians and hospitals. The poor in the US fare badly compared to their counterparts in Europe and Canada accounting for the relatively high death rates among both infants and adults. It is the most expensive medical care system in the world, yet leaves 44 million Americans with no medical insurance at all.

Medicine in Canada

The governments pay doctors and hospitals, who operate privately, for the services they provide according to a schedule of fees set annually after consultation with professional medical associations. See the **Controversy and Debate** Box (p. 546) for a discussion of multiple payers and the possibility of a two-tier system developing.

In 1961 the Hall Commission on Health Service recommended a health scheme with universality, portability, comprehensive coverage and administered on a non-profit basis. This plan was adopted across Canada in 1972.

The Canadian system has the advantage of providing care to everyone at a societal cost less than exists in the US (see Table 21-1, p. 542). Critiques of the system say it is not as technically advanced as the American system and responds more slowly to medical need.

THEORETICAL ANALYSIS OF HEALTH AND MEDICINE

Structural-Functional Analysis

Structural-functionalism provides a view of illness as dysfunctional for society.

➤The Sick Role

The key concept in structural-functionalist analysis of illness is the *sick role*, or patterns of behaviour that are socially defined as appropriate for those who are ill. As explained by Talcott Parsons, the sick role has three characteristics, including: (1) a sick person is exempted from routine responsibilities, (2) a sick person must want to be well, and (3) a sick person must seek competent help.

➤The Physician's Role

The physician is expected to cure illness. According to Parsons, a hierarchy exists in which physicians expect compliance from their patients. This hierarchy is being challenged, however, as patients demand more meaningful information from physicians about their illness.

Critics suggest that Parson's model does not deal with a more prevention-oriented approach to health and applies to acute rather than chronic illnesses.

Symbolic-Interaction Analysis

Health and medical care are seen as human creations based on social definitions.

➤The Social Construction of Illness

The health of any person must be put into the context of the general health of the society. The definition of health and healthy life-styles varies cross-culturally and historically. Further, definitions of illness are negotiated within particular social situations, what may be illness to a person in one situation, may be seen as a mere inconvenience in another..

➤The Social Construction of Treatment

Research by Joan Emerson involving gynaecological exams is used to illustrate how physicians "craft" their physical surroundings to make specific impressions on others.

A problem with the symbolic-interaction approach is that it minimizes an objective sense of health and illness.

Social-Conflict Analysis

➤The Access Issue

Social-conflict analysis suggests that capitalist systems allocate health-care resources in an unequal fashion. This problem is obvious in the U.S. but may become more problematic in Canada as federal and provincial funding for health care is diminished.

➤The Profit Motive

It is argued that the profit motive encourages unsafe medical practices, needless tests, unnecessary surgery and the over-prescribing of drugs.

➤Medicine as Politics

Medicine has not been as politically neutral is it claims when it opposes government supported health programs, ignores the impact of inequality on health, practices racial and sexual discrimination and focuses on biological rather than social causes of illness. Clearly health and medicine are social issues and can be evaluated from the perspective of all three major theoretical perspectives in sociology. The **Applying Sociology** Box (p. 544) argues for a more complete eclectic approach to enhance our understanding of how health care works.

LOOKING AHEAD:
HEALTH AND MEDICINE IN THE TWENTY-FIRST CENTURY

Health and health care are improving, especially in the industrialized world, and people recognize that they can personally influence their health through quitting smoking, eating sensibly and exercising regularly.

The major problem to be tackled is inequality within societies and between societies as the poor receive less adequate medical care.

The **Cyber.scope** Box (pp. 550-551) deals with the influence of information technology on all social institutions including medicine.

KEY CONCEPTS

Define each of the following concepts in the space provided or on separate paper. Check the accuracy of your answers by referring to the text as well as by referring to italicized definitions located throughout the chapter.

direct-fee system	medicine
eating disorder	sick role
health	social epidemiology
holistic medicine	socialized medicine

STUDY QUESTIONS

 True-False

1. T F   The health of any population is dependent upon the surrounding societal structures.

2. T F   Poverty is the leading cause of death in low income countries.

3. T F   Researchers today, in studying the links between health and physical and social environments are interested in comparing the health of similar categories of people.

4. T F   40% of people who suffer from anorexia nervosa are men.

5. T F   HIV/AIDS infection is increasing in Canada among women, children and Aboriginals.

6. T F   Support for passive euthanasia is growing in North America.

7. T F   The United States is unique among the industrialized societies in lacking government programs that ensure basic medical care to every citizen.

8. T F   Health expenditures in Canada have dropped between 1993 and 1997 as measured by percentage of GNP.

9. T F   The "social construction of treatment" of illness is a product of the structural-functional theory.

10. T F   The funding of Canada's universal medicare is public, yet its delivery is almost entirely private.

 Multiple-Choice

1. Which of the following is *not* one of the ways in which society shapes health as outlined in your text?

    (a) People judge their health as compared to others
    (b) People pronounce as "healthy" what they hold to be morally good
    (c) Cultural standards of health change over time
    (d) Health relates to a society's technology
    (e) Health relates to a society's religious values

2. "Kwashiorkor" is a term in west Africa which refers to

   (a) female genital circumcision
   (b) changes in cultural values toward medicine
   (c) mothers weaning a first child on the birth of a second
   (d) holistic medicine practised in the villages
   (e) none of the above

3. Death in high-income countries among young people is rare except for

   (a) the mentally retarded   (d) all of the above
   (b) accidents   (e) b and c above
   (d) AIDS

4. Which of the following statements is (are) accurate with respect to cigarette smoking in Canada?

   (a) Quitting is difficult because nicotine is highly addictive.
   (b) Smoking rates are higher in Ontario than Québec.
   (c) By 1994, only 40% of Canadians were smokers.
   (d) Some 5 million Americans die prematurely each year as a result of cigarette smoking.
   (e) All of the above are accurate.

5. With respect to eating disorders which of the following statements is *not* accurate?

   (a) Of those who suffer from anorexia nervosa most are from affluent families
   (b) University women want to be thinner than most men actually want them to be
   (c) Messages about thinness do not come from parents.
   (d) The overall result of gendered images of women's bodies is low self-esteem

6. The institutionalization of scientific medicine by the CMA resulted in:

   (a) expensive medical education   (d) all of the above
   (b) domination of medicine by males   (e) a and b only
   (c) an inadequate supply of physicians in rural areas

7. Which of the following is *not* among the foundations of holistic health care?

   (a) an emphasis on the environment in which the person lives.
   (b) an emphasis on providing a professional setting for appropriate treatment
   (c) an emphasis on patient responsibility
   (d) an emphasis on achieving the highest well-being for everyone.

8. Which country has the highest amount of "socialized medicine"?

   (a) Canada   (d) United States
   (b) Japan   (e) Norway
   (c) Sweden

9. Which of the following is *not* one of the basic characteristics of the recommendations of the Hall Commission which became law in Canada in 1972?

   (a) universality   (c) portability
   (b) partial coverage of most procedures (d) non-profit administration

10. Which of the following theoretical paradigms in sociology utilizes concepts like "sick role" and "physician's role" to explain health behaviour?

    (a) social-conflict   (d) exchange
    (b) symbolic-interaction   (e) materialism
    (c) structural-functionalist

11. Which of the following is *unlikely* as a result of the new information technology?

    (a) A return to use of coins for international currency.
    (b) More democracy because of the unrestricted access to information.
    (c) Families may be able to spend more time together.
    (d) Routine health checks done at home.
    (e) Virtual experiences for people with physical and mental limitations.

✎ Fill-In The Blank

1. Health is as much a _____ as a biological issue.

2. Canadians today tend to die of diseases of affluence, _____ and _____.

3. _____ is the study of the distribution of health and disease.

4. Death from _____ exceeds the combined death roll from alcohol, cocaine, heroin, homicide, suicide, automobile accidents and AIDS.

5. _____ are an exception to the general decline in infectious diseases during the past century.

6. _____ medicine is an approach to health care that emphasizes prevention of illness and takes account of the whole person within the physical and social environments.

7. When patients pay directly for physicians services it is called a _____.

8. One limitation of the sick-role concept is that it applies to acute conditions better than it does to _____illness.

9. As long as there is a single _____, there cannot be created a two-tier health care system.

10. Life expectancy for the world as a whole has been _____.

Definition and Short-Answer

1. It is pointed out in the text that the health of any population is shaped by important characteristics of the society as a whole. What are the five characteristics identified? Provide an example of each.

2. How have the causes of death changed in Canada over the last century in terms of which ones account for most deaths?

3. Compare the health care conditions of low-income and high-income countries.

4. What is social epidemiology? Provide two illustrations of patterns of health found using this approach.

5. How are cigarette smoking, eating disorders and sexually transmitted diseases socially explained?

6. What are the two types of euthanasia? Discuss the Rodriguez and Latimer cases to illustrate. Relate these cases to the "ethical issues confronting death" as reviewed in the chapter.

7. What is meant by the "sick role"?

8. Describe the characteristics of holistic medicine. How do they differ from those of scientific medicine?

9. How do health care systems operate in socialist societies? Provide specific examples.

10. In what ways does the health-care system of the United States differ from health-care systems in other capitalist societies?

11. What are social-conflict analysts' arguments about the health care systems in the United States and Canada?

12. Discuss how symbolic-interactionists help us understand our health system and our sense of health and illness.

13. How might a two-tier health system be created in Canada?

Answers to Study Questions

True-False

1. T (pp. 527-528)
2. T (p. 528)
3. F (p. 530)
4. F (p. 534)
5. T (p. 535)

6. T (p. 537)
7. T (p. 540)
8. T (p. 541)
9. F (pp. 543-544)
10. T (p. 546)

Multiple-Choice

1. e (pp. 527-528
2. c (p. 530)
3. e (p. 530)
4. a (pp. 533-534)
5. c (p. 534)
6. d (p. 538)

7. b (p. 538)
8. e (p. 541)
9. b (p. 542)
10. c (p. 542)
11. a (pp. 550-551)

Fill-In

1. social (p. 527)
2. cancer and heart disease (p. 530)
3. social epidemiology (p. 530)
4. cigarette smoking (p. 534)
5. S.T.D.s (p. 535)

6. holistic (p. 538)
7. direct-fee system (p. 540)
8. chronic (p. 543)
9. payer (p. 547)
10. rising (p. 547)

ANALYSIS AND COMMENT

GLOBAL SOCIOLOGY

" Killer Poverty: A Report from Africa."
Key Points:

_____
_____
_____
_____
_____

APPLYING SOCIOLOGY

"Hi……..; How are You?"
Key Points:

_____
_____
_____
_____
_____

CONTROVERSY AND DEBATE

"Two-Tiered Health Care: Threat, Fact, or Fiction?"
Key Points:

_____
_____
_____
_____
_____

CYBER.SCOPE

"New Information Technology and Social Institutions."
Key Points:

_____
_____
_____
_____
_____

SUGGESTED READINGS

Classic Sources

Elisabeth Kubler-Ross. 1969. *On Death and Dying.*
New York: Macmillan.
This study of the orderly process of dying illustrates
how social research can assist terminally ill patients.

Michel Foucault. 1975. *The Birth of the Clinic: An
Archaeology of Medical Perception.* New York:
Vintage Books.

This history of medicine emphasizes not scientific developments but the cultural forces that gradually changed how people thought about illness and health care.

Contemporary Sources

Clyde B. McCoy and James A. Inciardi. 1995. *Sex, Drugs, and the Continuing Spread of AIDS.* Los Angeles, Ca.: Roxbury.
The "second wave" of the AIDS epidemic is placing poor people at risk, according to this book.

Susan Sherwin. 1992. *No Longer Patient: Feminist Ethics and Health Care.* Philadelphia: Temple University Press.
This author argues that ethical issues in medicine should be resolved in a feminist context.

Peter E. S. Freund and Meredith B. McGuire. 1991. *Health, Illness, and the Social Body.* Englewood Cliffs, N.J.: Prentice Hall.
This book probes many of the issues raised in this chapter

Canadian Sources

B. Singh Bolaria and Harley D. Dickenson, eds. 1994. *Sociology of Health Care in Canada.* 2nd ed. Toronto: Harcourt Brace.
This is a reader with extensive coverage of a wide variety of issues related to the Canadian medical care system. For the most part the writers are from a variety of social science disciplines

Joel Lexchin. 1984. *The Real Pushers: A Critical Analysis of the Canadian Drug Industry.* Vancouver: New Star Books.
This is a critical study of the pharmaceutical industry in Canada.

Juanne Nancarrow Clarke. 1985. *It's Cancer: The Personal Experiences of Women Who Have Received a Cancer Diagnosis.* Toronto: IPI Publishing.
This is based on qualitative interviews with women about the impact of cancer on their lives.

Juanne NancarrowClarke. 1996. *Health, Illness and Medicine in Canada.* Toronto: Oxford University Press.
This is an overview of medical sociology and the sociology of health and illness from a paradigmatic perspective.

Global Sources

Kaja Finkler. 1994. *Women in Pain: Gender and Morbidity in Mexico.* Philadelphia: University of Pennsylvania Press.
Women in low-income countries face especially serious threats to health.

Bruce Kapferer. 1990. *A Celebration of Demons.* New York: Berg.
Describing rituals of exorcism in Sri Lanka, the book above explores forms of healing that defy understanding in Western terms

CHAPTER 22

Population, Urbanization and the Environment

II LEARNING OBJECTIVES

- To learn the basic concepts used by demographers to study population; fertility, mortality and migration.

- To describe, compare, and contrast the Malthusian theory and the demographic transition theory.

- To explain how populations differ in industrialized societies and less developed societies.

- To compare and contrast the first cities of the world, preindustrial cities in Europe and industrial-capitalist cities in Europe.

- To trace the transformation of North America into an urban civilization from colonial settlement through urban expansion and the metropolitan era to urban decentralization.

- To understand the relationship between suburbs and central cities and to understand inter-regional population movement.

- To compare and contrast the characteristics of rural and urban life by explaining the theoretical views of Toennies, Durkheim, Simmel, and the Chicago school.

- To describe the key ideas of urban ecology and the related models of city structure.

- To understand the causes of urbanization in low-income countries and the future prospects of cities in those countries.

- To understand the nature of ecology and the natural environment.

- To describe the impact of technology on the environment.

- To comprehend the limits of growth.

- To understand the impact of industrial growth on water and air.

- To recognize the relationship between rain forests and global warming.

- To recognize the ways of creating a sustainable world.

III CHAPTER REVIEW

As population increases and the urban population becomes ever more dependent on "intensive livestock operations," the environment is compromised and water pollution becomes an increasing reality.

DEMOGRAPHY: THE STUDY OF POPULATION

Demography is the study of human population, investigating the size, age, sex composition and migration patterns of given populations. It is a quantitative discipline, however crucial questions about the consequences of these variables are analyzed which have great qualitative significance. Several basic concepts central to demographic analysis are discussed in the following sections.

Fertility

Fertility is the incidence of childbearing in a society's population. A female's childbearing years last from the beginning of menstruation to menopause. But, *fecundity*, or potential child- bearing, is greatly reduced by health and financial constraints, cultural norms, and personal choice.

A typical measurement used for fertility is the *crude birth rate*, or the number of live births in a given year for every 1000 people in a population. In 1996, 379,295 live births occurred in Canada (population 29 million) for a crude birth rate of 12.7. **Canada Map** 22-1, (p. 554) shows birth rates across Canada. The term "crude" relates to the fact that comparing such rates can be misleading because it doesn't focus on women of childbearing age, and doesn't consider varying rates between racial, ethnic, and religious groups. It is however easy to calculate and provides a measure of a society's overall fertility. Figure 22-1, (p. 555) shows that crude birth rates in industrial societies are low in world context.

Mortality

Mortality is the incidence of death in a society's population. The *crude death rate* refers to the number of deaths in a given year for every 1000 people in a population. In 1996, Canada's crude death rate was 7.2, low by world standards.

The *infant mortality rate*, refers to the number of deaths within the first year of life for each 1000 live births in a given year. The infant mortality rate in Canada in 1996 was 6.1. Figure 22-1 (p. 555) compares fertility, mortality, infant mortality and life expectancy rates for countries around the world. Significant differences exist between industrialized and less developed nations.

Life expectancy, or how long a person, on average, can expect to live, is negatively correlated with a society's infant mortality rate. For males born in Canada in 1996 life expectancy is 76 years and for females 83 years, 3 and 4 years longer than in the U. S. See Figure 22-1 (p. 555)

Migration

Migration is defined as the movement of people into and out of a specified territory. Some is involuntary, such as the historical existence of slave trading, while most is voluntary and based on various "push-pull" factors like dissatisfaction and attraction.

Movement into a territory is termed *in-migration,* and is measured by the number of people entering an area for every 1000 people in the total population. Movement out of an area, termed *out-migration*, is measured by using the number of people leaving an area for every 1000 people in the population. The difference between the two figures is termed *net-migration rate.*

Population Growth

Migration, fertility, and mortality each affect a society's population size. ***The natural growth rate*** of a society is determined by subtracting the crude death rate from the crude birth rate. This figure for Canada in 1996 was 5.5 per thousand, or 0.55 percent annually. The projected rates for different world regions during the 1990s are presented in **Global Map** 22-1 (p. 556). Industrialized regions, Europe, North America and Oceania have very low rates, while the low-income regions— Asia, Africa and Latin America have relatively high rates. An annual growth rate of 2 percent (as found in Latin America) doubles a population in 35 years. In some parts of Africa, the growth rate is 3 percent which doubles the population in 24 years. This calculation is called "doubling time."

Population Composition

The ***sex ratio*** refers to the number of males for every 100 females in a given population. In Canada in 1996 the sex ratio was 96.5. A more complicated descriptive device is the ***age-sex pyramid*** which is a graphic representation of the age and sex composition of a population. Figure 22-2, (p. 557) presents the age-sex pyramids for Canada for the years 1971-1991. Figure 22-3, (p. 558) compares the age-sex pyramids for Sweden and Kenya. For Canada the ***baby boom*** and ***baby bust*** birth cohorts lead to a bulge gradually moving up the pyramid from 1971-1991.

The pyramid for Sweden indicates low birth and death rates while the pyramid for Kenya indicates very high birth and death rates.

HISTORY AND THEORY OF POPULATION GROWTH

Until relatively recently in human history, societies desired high birth rates as they were needed to offset high death rates.

The growth of the world's population from 1700 through to the year 2100 is portrayed in Figure 22-4 (p. 559). A critical point in world population growth occurred in about 1750 as the earth's population turned upward. In the 20th century alone the world's population has increased fourfold. Currently there are more than 6 billion people on earth. Around 1800 the world population reached 1 billion, in 1930 it reached 2 billion, in 1962 it reached 3 billion, in 1974 it reached 4 billion, and in 1987, 5 billion. By 2050 the world's population is projected to reach 8 to 9 billion.

Malthusian Theory

In the late 18th century Thomas Malthus developed a theory of population growth in which he warned of disaster. He predicted population would increase according to a geometric progression, while food production would only increase in arithmetic progression.

Birth control he felt was immoral and abstinence unlikely.

For several reasons his projections have not been realized. First, the birth rate in Europe began to drop in the 19th century as children became less of an economic asset. He also underestimated human ingenuity, specifically in terms of technological applications in solving food production and population related problems.

But his warnings still need to be taken seriously. Technology has caused problems for the environment, and population growth in the low-income nations remains very high. Even if their population growth rate is reduced, any rate of increase in the long-range can be dangerous.

344

Demographic Transition Theory

Demographic transition theory has now replaced Malthusian theory and is the thesis that population patterns are linked to a society's level of technological development. Figure 22-5 (p. 559) illustrates four stages of technological change, and the related birth and death dates. Stage 1 is represented by the preindustrial agrarian society with high birth rates and high death rates. Stage 2, represented by industrialization, marks the beginning of the demographic transition, with high birth rates continuing, but death rates dropping significantly. In stage 3, the fully industrialized society, birth rates begin to drop significantly and death rates remain stable and low. In Stage 4, the post-industrial economy, birth rates continue to drop and death rates remain steady.

The lower birth rate in the third stage is related to a higher standard of living, resulting in children being a greater economic burden. Smaller families are also more functional as a higher percentage of women work outside the home. In the post-industrial society population may actually decrease.

This view provides far more optimism than Malthusian theory. It has been incorporated into modernization theory. Dependency theorists have therefore been critical of this view, as they predict continued poverty in the pre-industrial world and continued high birth rates leaving the industrialized "haves" and the non-industrialized "have-nots".

Global Population Today: A Brief Survey

➤The Low-Growth North

Shortly after industrialization began the population growth in Europe and North America peaked at 3 percent annually. It has been generally declining since, and since 1970 has not been above 1 percent. The Canadian birth rate is now below 2.1 children per woman, a point which is called *zero population growth*, a level of reproduction that maintains population at a steady state. The rate in 1996 was 1.64, so low that without immigration, Canada's population will eventually decline.

➤The High-Growth South

Most of the poor societies of the southern hemisphere have reached Stage 2 of the Demographic Transition Theory. Birth rates remain high but mortality rates are falling dramatically because of the importation of medical technology from the industrialized nations. Part of the answer is provided in the **Social Diversity** Box on p. 561 where declining fertility is seen as attached to elevated standing for women. Some progress on declining fertility is observable but mortality continues to decline as well.

URBANIZATION: THE GROWTH OF CITIES

For most of human history people have lived in small, nomadic groups. Urbanization, the concentration of humanity into cities, can be traced to three urban revolutions.

The Evolution of Cities

The first urban revolution occurred about 12,000 years ago with the emergence of permanent settlements.

➤ The First Cities

The enabling factor for the growth of cities was a material surplus produced by advancing technology.

The first city is argued to have been Jericho, just north of the Dead Sea, coming into existence about 10,000 years ago. By 3000 B.C.E. there were several cities within the Fertile Crescent in present day Iraq and along the Nile in Egypt.

➤ Preindustrial European Cities

Urbanization began in Europe about 5,000 years ago on Crete and spread throughout Greece. As Greek civilization faded the militaristic Roman Empire expanded throughout Europe and Northern Africa.

➤ Industrial European Cities

Increasing commerce in the Middle ages created an affluent urban middle-class or **"bourgeoise"** as it came to be known, which rivaled the power of the nobility. The second urban revolution was under way by about 1750. Industrial productivity caused cities to grow rapidly.

Besides population changes, the physical layouts of cities were transformed. Broad boulevards for transportation dominated the urban landscape.

Urban social life began to change as well, as crowding, impersonality, inequality, and crime became more and more characteristic of cities.

The Growth of North American Cities

Over tens of thousands of years Native North Americans established few permanent settlements. Cities were first established by the Spanish at St. Augustine in Florida in 1565, by the English at Jamestown, Virginia in 1607, and by Champlain at Quebec in 1608. Many others were established over the next 150 years as trade expanded and more settlers arrived in the new world. By 1991 both the U.S. and Canada have more than ¾ of their population living in urban areas.

➤ Colonial Settlement: 1624-1850

The quiet villages of northeastern U.S. were transformed during the 17th century. They became thriving towns with wide streets.

Canadian growth was later in this period. Figure 22-6, (p. 564) shows a map of York (Toronto) in 1793.

The first U.S. census in 1790 counted a population of 4 million but by the time of Confederation in Canada (1867) the American population was 40 million and 20 percent urban while Canada's population was 3 million, with 18 percent urban. Table 22-1, (p. 565) shows Canada's population growth and levels of urbanization from 1871 to 1996.

➤Urban Expansion

Transportation development encouraged the growth of towns and cities. B.C. joined Confederation at the promise of a transcontinental railway. By 1931, 50 percent of Canadians were living in cities.

➤The Metropolitan Era

As the Industrial Revolution picked up momentum cities grew rapidly. Table 22-2, (p. 565) describes the growth of cities in Canada. This early growth marked the coming of the *metropolis*, a large city that socially and economically dominates the surrounding area. Canada now has 25 CMA's (Census Metropolitan Areas) which have populations of at least 100,000 spread out among one or more municipalities with economic and community ties.

Suburbs and Central Cities

Since about 1940 *suburbs*, urban areas beyond the political boundaries of a city, have been flourishing. People began moving out from the central core to seek space to have families beyond the commotion of the city. As well racial and ethnic intolerance led the middle-class whites in American cities to flee, leaving the central city to decay without their tax dollars. Suburbanites tend to spend their dollars in suburban shopping malls rather than "main street" of the city.

In Canada the decay of the central core has not been so obvious partly because of the creation of metropolitan areas where some political functions and tax dollars are shared between municipalities. Just recently six municipalities merged to create the new city of Toronto.

When several metropolitan areas bump into each other they form a *megalopolis*, a vast urban region containing a number of cities and their surrounding suburbs. The Boston to Washington area is an example as is the "Golden Horseshoe" in Canada stretching from Oshawa through Toronto to St. Catharines, an area that contains 1/3 of Canada's population.

Inter-Regional Population Movement

All countries experience internal population movement. In the U.S. it is Snowbelt to Sunbelt as cities like Detroit and Chicago lose population and San Antonio and Phoenix gain.

In Canada there is considerable movement between the provinces as indicated in Table 22-3, (p. 567). Quebec and the Atlantic provinces have consistently lost population between 1956 and 1996 as have Manitoba and Saskatchewan. Ontario and Alberta have fluctuated while only B.C., Canada's equivalent of the sunbelt, has shown consistent gain.

URBANISM AS A WAY OF LIFE

Ferdinand Toennies: Gemeinschaft and Gesellschaft

This German sociologist of the late 19th century differentiated between two types of social organization. The first *gemeinschaft* refers to a type of social organization with strong solidarity based on tradition and personal relationships. It describes social settings dominated by primary groups and small villages. Its meaning is similar to Durkheim's mechanical solidarity. In contrast, *gesellschaft* is a type of social organization with weak social ties and individual self-interest. This represents city dwellers, and is similar to Durkheim's concept of organic solidarity.

Emile Durkheim: Mechanical and Organic Solidarity

Durkheim analyzed what held people together and he drew different conclusions than Toennies as he saw the bonds of interdependent specialization in a positive light whereas Toennies saw *gesellschaft* relationships as inferior.

Georg Simmel: The Blase Urbanite

This German sociologist used a micro-level analysis of how urban life shaped the behaviour and attitudes of people. He argued city dwellers needed to be selective in what they responded to because of the social intensity of such a life. They develop then a blasé attitude out of necessity.

Observing the City: The Chicago School

The first major sociology program in the U.S. at the Chicago School saw the city as a focus for sociological interpretation of urban life. While relationships between people who occupied specialized positions might be pleasant, self-interest rather than friendship was the reason for the interaction.

Urban Ecology

Urban ecology is the study of the link between the physical and social dimensions of cities. One important issue is why cities are located where they are. Another issue concerns the physical design of cities. Several models explaining urban form exist including the concentric zone model, the sector model, the multi-centered model, social area analysis, and integrated analysis.

Urban Political Economy

Urban political economy is a conflict model which suggests that the powerful make decisions about city life including moving it from the Maritime provinces to Montréal and now to Toronto.

Jane Jacobs, who lives in Toronto suggests that sustaining economic development is not as simple as the availability of capital and political will.

URBANIZATION IN POOR SOCIETIES

A major urban revolution began in 1950 when about 25 percent of poor societies were urbanized. Most of the future growth will take place in less economically developed societies; where conditions in cities may not support positive lives.

ENVIRONMENT AND SOCIETY

The human species has prospered but only by placing increasing demands on the earth. *Ecology* is the study of the interaction of living organisms and the natural environment. Often we have compromised the natural environment in order to meet our own interests and desires.

The Global Dimension

The *ecosystem* is composed of the interaction of all living organisms and their natural environment. What happens in Brazil has an impact on Canada.

Technology and the Environmental Deficit

Increasingly industrial technology has impacted the environment such that we are running up an *environmental deficit*, profound and negative long-term harm to the natural environment caused by human focus on short-term material affluence. We make social decisions which have environmental effects. Presumably we can make social decisions to undo those effects.

Culture: Growth and Limits

➤The Logic of Growth

This is an optimistic view of the future where technology improves our lives. Critics of this optimism suggest that improving our lives uses up finite resources.

➤The Limits to Growth

This is a thesis which suggests that we are quickly consuming the earth's finite resources and the future holds starvation and industrial decline. Either we change the way we live, or calamity will force change upon us.

Solid Waste: The Disposable Society

The average North American disposes two kilograms of materials daily. We consume a disproportionate share of the planet's natural resources and we throw huge portions away. More efficient use and systematic recycling is in order.

Water and Air

➤Water Supply

Water is the lifeblood of the global ecosystem but soaring population and complex technology has reduced our global ready supply of water. Water consumption needs to be curbed.

➤Water Pollution

Not only water must be protected but also the *quality* of that water is a concern. Pollution, such as acid rain can devastate forests and lakes.

➤Air Pollution

The deadly mix of automobile exhaust and coal-fired plants can plague the environment. Rich nations have reduced noxious outputs but poorer nations, relying on dirty fuels will increasingly pollute the air. The **Applying Sociology** Box (p. 576-577) indicates that Canada, while on the face of it, environmentally friendly, in reality is not.

The Rain Forests

These regions of dense forestation help to cleanse the atmosphere of carbon dioxide which, we think, leads to global warming. We are, however, losing rain forests at an accelerating rate, suggesting that both global warming and declining biodiversity will compromise our future life on this planet.

Environmental Racism

It is often the poorest in a society which bear the brunt of environmental pollution.

LOOKING AHEAD: TOWARDS A SUSTAINABLE WORLD.

Population growth and unabated urbanization in poorer countries leads to massive urban problems. The environmental deficit mortgages our future. The answer, perhaps, is to formulate an *ecologically sustainable culture*, a way of life that meets the needs of the present generation without threatening the environmental legacy of future generations. This can be accomplished by controlling the world's population growth, conserving finite resources and reducing waste. The **Controversy and Debate** Box (p. 581) suggests that the task is substantial but manageable.

KEY CONCEPTS

Define each of the following concepts in the space provided or on separate paper. Check the accuracy of your answers by referring to the text as well as by referring to italicized definitions located throughout the chapter.

age-sex pyramid
crude birth rate
crude death rate
demographic transition theory
demography
ecology/ecologically sustainable culture
ecosystem
environmental deficit
environmental racism
fertility
gemeinschaft
gesellschaft
greenhouse effect

infant mortality rate
life expectancy
megalopolis
metropolis
migration
mortality
natural environment
rain forests
sex ratio
suburbs
urbanization
urban ecology
zero population growth

STUDY QUESTIONS

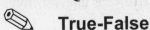 **True-False**

1. T F   The infant mortality rate is the number of deaths in the first year of life for each thousand live births in a given year.

2. T F   The net result of in-migration and out-migration is known as the total migration rate.

3. T F   According to demographic transition theory, population growth patterns are linked to a society's level of technological development.

4. T F   The 1994 Cairo Conference on Population and Development suggested that giving women more choices tends to reduce the fertility rate.

5. T F   Today, more than three-quarters of Canadians live in urban areas.

6. T F   There are now 10 Census Metropolitan Areas in Canada.

7. T F   Ecology is the study of resources necessary to sustain life.

8. T F   According to the limits of growth thesis, we are quickly consuming the earth's finite resources.

9. T F   So lax are environmental regulations in Canada that Ontario ranks third among North America's polluters.

10. T F   Rain forests have been found to be irrelevant to maintaining good air quality.

✎ Multiple-Choice

1. The incidence of childbearing in a society's population is called

(a) demography
(b) fecundity
(c) crude growth
(d) fertility
(e) infant occurrences

2. The first city to have ever existed is argued to be:

(a) Athens
(b) Tikal
(c) Rome
(d) Cairo
(e) Jericho

3. By 1931 in Canada _____ % of the population was living in cities.

4. Which province shows consistent interprovincial migration gains every five-year interval from 1957 to 1996?

(a) Newfoundland
(b) British Columbia
(c) Ontario
(d) Québec
(e) Alberta

5. Durkheim observed, that in urbanized societies social organization was based upon

(a) sameness
(b) gemeinschaft
(c) difference
(d) gesellschaft
(e) ritual

6. The study of the interaction of living organisms and the natural environment is called

(a) technology
(b) ecology
(c) environment
(d) growth
(e) deficit

7. The logic of growth suggests

(a) a belief in progress
(b) science will make our lives more rewarding
(c) new discoveries will make life better
(d) all of the above
(e) b and c above

8. North Americans dispose of _____ of solid waste every day.

   (a) ½ kilogram
   (b) ¾ kilogram
   (c) 1 kilogram
   (d) 1 ½ kilograms
   (e) 2 kilograms

9. The pattern by which environmental hazards are greatest for poor people, especially minorities, is called

   (a) pattern prejudice
   (b) limited biodiversity
   (c) racism
   (d) environmental racism
   (e) sustainable culture

10. An ecologically sustainable culture depends on which of the following strategies?

   (a) Controlling the world's population
   (b) Development of new resources
   (c) Reducing waste
   (d) a and b above
   (e) a and c above

✎ Fill-In The Blank

1. _____ is the potential for childbearing.

2. Canadian females born in 1996 can expect to live _____ years.

3. In Stage 2 of the demographic transition, _____ rates fall dramatically.

4. A large city that socially and economically dominates the surrounding area is called a _____.

5. The model of urban development where cities lose their single centre is called a _____.

6. An _____ is a system composed of interaction of all living organisms and their natural environment.

7. A profound and negative long-term harm to the natural environment caused by a focus on short-term material affluence is called _____.

8. A rise in the earth's average temperatures due to an increasing concentration of carbon dioxide in the atmosphere is called a _____.

9. The world's population increases by _____ annually.

Definition and Short-Answer

1. What are the three basic factors which determine the size and growth rate of a population? Define each of the three concepts.

2. Differentiate between Malthusian theory and demographic transition theory as perspectives on population growth.

3. Describe the population trends in low-growth and high-growth countries.

4. Differentiate between the concepts of metropolis and megalopolis.

5. Differentiate between the population theories of the Chicago School and George Simmel.

6. What will the major urbanization patterns in the twenty-first century look like?

7. What is meant by the "environmental deficit?"

8. How environmentally friendly is Canada?

9. What can be done to form an ecologically sustainable future?

Answers to Study Questions

True-False

1. T (p. 555)	6. F (p. 564)
2. F (p. 557)	7. F (p. 571)
3. T (p. 559)	8. T (p. 573)
4. T (p. 561)	9. T (p. 576)
5. T (p. 563)	10. F (p. 578)

Multiple-Choice

1. d (p. 554)	6. b (p. 571)
2. e (p. 562)	7. d (p. 572)
3. b (p. 564)	8. e (p. 573)
4. b (p. 566)	9. d (p. 579)
5. c (p. 567)	10. e (p. 580)

Fill-In

1. fecundity (p. 554)	6. ecosystem (p. 571)
2. 83 (p. 555)	7. environmental deficit (p. 572)
3. death (p. 559)	8. greenhouse effect (p. 578)
4. metropolis (p. 564)	9. 77 million (p. 581)
5. multi-centred model (p. 568)	

ANALYSIS AND COMMENT

Go back through the chapter and write down in the spaces below key points from each of the following boxes.

CRITICAL THINKING

"Empowering Women: The Key to Controlling Population Growth."
Key Points:

_____

_____

_____

_____

_____

APPLYING SOCIOLOGY

"Environmentally Friendly Canada, Eh."
Key Points:

_____

_____

_____

_____

_____

CONTROVERSY AND DEBATE

"Will People Overwhelm the Earth?: The Environmental Challenge."
Key Points:

_____

_____

_____

_____

_____

SUGGESTED READINGS

Classic Sources

Ehrlich, Paul R. 1968. *The Population Bomb.* **New York: Ballantine Books.**
This brief book, its reputation tarnished by some predictions that did not come to pass, nevertheless was crucial in igniting the contemporary debate over increasing global population.

Ferdinand Toennies. 1963; orig. 1887. *Community and Society. (Gemeinschaft und Gesellschaft).* **New York: Harper & Row.**
This classic comparison of rural and urban social organization--widely cited but rarely read--introduced many of the themes that have shaped urban sociology ever since.

Contemporary Sources

Anthony Downs. 1994. *New Visions for Metropolitan America.* **Washington, D.C.: Brookings Institute.**
This analysis examines the core cultural and political values that underlie U.S. cities and urges us to rethink our ideas about how cities should work.

Stephanie Golden. 1992. *The Women Outside: Meaning and Myths of Homelessness.* **Berkeley: University of California Press.**
The author argues that our understanding of the urban problem of homelessness--especially when it involves women--is distorted by a pejorative cultural mythology about the poor.

Canadian Sources

Michael Goldberg and John Mercer. 1986. *The Myth of the North American City.* **Vancouver: University of British Columbia Press.**
This book provides a wide-ranging comparison of urban development in Canada and the United States.

Peter McGahan. 1982. *Urban Sociology in Canada.* **Toronto: Butterworths.**
This overview of research on urban communities in Canada covers a broad range of topics.

S. Dasgupta. 1987. *Rural Canada.* **Toronto: Mellon.**
This book examines rural social structures and change.

David K. Foot. 1996. *Boom, Bust & Echo: How to Profit From the Coming Demographic Shift.* **Macfarlane: Walter & Ross.**
Professor Foot asks us to consider the impact of the baby boom and bust cycles on education, real estate, the corporate world, retail sales and leisure activities.

Global Sources

Belgin Tekce, Linda Oldham, and Frederic Shorter. 1994. *A Place to Live: Families and Health Care in a Cairo Neighbourhood.* **Cairo, Egypt: American University in Cairo.**
This study of an "unofficial" settlement of more than 60,000 immigrants to Cairo conveys the challenge of regulating urban growth in a poor country.

David Hakken with Barbara Andrews. 1993. *Computing Myths, Class Realities: An Ethnography of Technology and Working People in Sheffield, England.* **Boulder, Colo.:** Westview Press.
This community study examines changes within an English manufacturing city during a time of economic decline.

CHAPTER 23

I CHAPTER OUTLINE

- To identify the problems associated with studying collective behaviour from a sociological perspective.

- To explain the general characteristics of collectivities that distinguish them from social groups.

- To distinguish among the concepts of crowds, mobs and riots.

- To describe, compare and contrast contagion theory, convergence theory, and emergent-norm theory in terms of how each orients researchers in the study of collective behaviour.

- To describe, compare, and contrast the various dispersed collectivities: rumour, gossip, public opinion, propaganda, mass hysteria, panic, fashion, and fads.

- To understand how crowds and mobs relate to social change.

- To identify and describe the four sources of social movements in Canada.

- To compare and contrast the five theories of social movements: deprivation theory, mass-society theory, structural-strain theory, resource mobilization theory and "new social movements" theory

- To identify the relationship between gender and participation in social movements.

- To describe the four stages of a social movement.

- To explain the relationship between social movements and social change.

III CHAPTER REVIEW

This chapter opens with a description of Elijah Harper's blockage of the ratification of the Meech Lake Accord and the confrontation of Natives and the Quebec police and the Canadian Army. It is argued that a social movement was galvanized by these events.

A major focus of this chapter is *social movements*, or organized activity that encourages or discourages social change. Social movements are one of the most important types of *collective behaviour*, referring to activity involving a large number of people, often spontaneous, and typically in violation of established norms.

STUDYING COLLECTIVE BEHAVIOUR

Studying collective behaviour is difficult for several reasons, including its wide-ranging nature, its *complexity*, and the fact that it is often *transitory*. It is pointed out that this is perhaps true for all issues studied by sociologists. However, a particularly significant problem here is limited theoretical analysis in this domain of social inquiry.

A *collectivity* is a large number of people who interact little if at all in the absence of well-defined and conventional norms. Two types of collectivities are (1) localized collectivities, referring to people in physical proximity to one another, and (2) dispersed collectivities, meaning people influencing one another, often from great distances.

These collectivities are distinguished from social groups on the basis of three characteristics, including limited social interaction, unclear social boundaries, and weak or unconventional norms.

Localized Collectivities: Crowds

A *crowd* is a temporary gathering of people who share a common focus of attention and whose members influence one another.

Herbert Blumer identifies four types of crowds, based in part on their level of emotional intensity. These include: the *casual* crowd, or a loose collection of people who have little interaction; the *conventional* crowd, resulting from deliberate planning of an event and conforming to norms appropriate to the situation; the *expressive* crowd, which forms around an event that has emotional appeal; and an *acting* crowd which is a crowd energetically doing something. Crowds can change from one type to another. A fifth type, or *protest* crowd, not identified by Blumer, is a crowd which has some political goal, like the 4000 Quebec residents who clashed with the police when protesting the bridge takeover during the Oka crisis.

Mobs and Riots

When an acting crowd becomes violent it is classified as a *mob*, a highly emotional crowd that pursues some violent or destructive goal. Lynching is a notorious example in the history of the United States. The freeing of the slaves, which provided blacks with political rights and economic opportunities were perceived by whites as a threat. Lynching was used as a form of social control to exert white supremacy over blacks.

A violent crowd with no specific goal is termed a *riot*, or a social eruption that is highly emotional, violent, and undirected. Throughout history riots have resulted from a collective expression against social injustice. In 1907, as a response to steady Chinese immigration and a sudden influx of Japanese, a riot broke out in Vancouver against Japanese individuals and their businesses. Sometimes riots can result from positive feelings as they did in Montreal after the "Canadiens" won the Stanley Cup in 1993.

Crowds, Mobs, and Social Change

Although crowds and mobs can be seen as a threat to those in power, not all call for social change, some resist it.

Explaining Crowd Behaviour

➢Contagion Theory
One of the first social scientists to try and explain such behaviour was Gustave Le Bon, who developed *contagion theory.* This theory maintains that a crowd can exert a hypnotic effect on its members. Anonymity of a crowd creates a condition in which people lose their identity and personal responsibility to a collective mind.

Critics claim that many crowds do not take on a life of their own separate from the thoughts and actions of their members. Rather specific structural features may be found to be responsible for the behaviour.

➤**Convergence Theory**

This theory leads researchers to see the motives which drive collective action as emerging prior to the formation of a crowd. The argument is that people of like-mind come together for a particular purpose and form a crowd. As opposed to contagion theory, which focuses our attention on irrational forces, this perspective provides a view of rational processes creating a crowd.

➤**Emergent-Norm Theory**

Ralph Turner and Lewis Killian developed this theory, and argue like convergence theorists, that crowds are not merely irrational collectivities. However, they further suggest that patterns of behaviour emerge within the crowds themselves.

This view fits into the symbolic-interaction approach to the study of social life. Crowd behaviour is seen, in part, as a response to its members motives, but that norms emerge and guide behaviour within the development of the crowd itself.

DISPERSED COLLECTIVITIES: MASS BEHAVIOUR

Mass behaviour refers to collective behaviour among people dispersed over a wide geographic area

Rumour and Gossip

Rumour, or unsubstantiated information spread informally, often by word of mouth is one example. Rumour has three essential characteristics, including thriving on a climate of ambiguity, being changeable, and being difficult to stop. The **Social Diversity** Box, (p. 590) illustrates how the rumour of the death of a famous person can be self-sustaining.

Closely related to rumour is *gossip*, or rumour about the personal affairs of others. Gossip is referred to as being more localized than rumour. It can be an effective means of social control.

Public Opinion and Propaganda

Public opinion is a form of highly dispersed collective behaviour. No one "public opinion" exists on key social issues, but rather is represented by a diversity of opinion.

A public grows larger and smaller over time as interest in a particular issue changes. The women's movement is used as an illustration. Certain categories of people are argued to have more social influence than others when it comes to shaping public opinion.

Propaganda is defined as information presented with the intention of shaping public opinion. It can be accurate or false, positive or negative. Various forms exist from politics to advertising to pronouncements on the Charlottetown Accord.

Panic and Mass Hysteria

A *panic* is a form of localized collective behaviour by which people react to some stimulus with emotional, irrational, and often self-destructive behaviour. Generally some threat provokes a panic, as in the case of a fire in a crowded theatre.

Mass hysteria is a form of dispersed collective behaviour in which people respond to a real or imagined event with irrational, frantic behaviour. The 1938 CBS radio broadcast of a dramatization of the novel *War of the Worlds*, is an example which illustrates how mass hysteria can emerge.

Fashions and Fads

Fashion is defined as a social pattern favoured for a time by a large number of people. Fashions are transitory and occur for two reasons, the future-orientation of people in industrial societies and the socially mobile who use consumption patterns to evaluate social standing.

American sociologist Thorstein Veblen originated the term *conspicuous consumption*, referring to the practice of spending money with the intention of displaying one's wealth to others.

A *fad* is an unconventional social pattern that is enthusiastically embraced by a large number of people for a short time. They are sometimes referred to as crazes. While fads are truly "passing fancies," fashions tend to reflect fundamental human values and social patterns that evolve over time.

SOCIAL MOVEMENTS

Three characteristics differentiate social movements from other types of collective behaviour: a higher degree of internal organization; typically longer duration, often spanning many years; and the deliberate attempt to reorganize or defend society itself.

Social movements are a common phenomenon in the high level of diversity of industrial societies. In Canada social movements often spring from four sources: the fact of Québec, the disparate regions, Native peoples and their struggle for self-government and the ethnic and racial minorities in an officially multicultural society.

Types of Social Movements

Social movements are classified by who is changed and by how much.

Four types of social movements are identified based on these dimensions. Figure 23-1 (p. 594) presents a model of the different types identified along these two dimensions. These types include: *alternative social movements*, which pursue limited change for certain individuals (planned parenthood being an example); *redemptive social movements*, which focus on a limited number of individuals, but seek to change them radically (fundamentalist church organizations are an example); *reformative social movements*, which seek limited social change for the entire society (proponents and opponents of abortion are an example); and *revolutionary social movements*, which seek basic transformations of the entire society (the Québec separatists are an example).

Explaining Social Movements

➤Deprivation Theory

Deprivation theory holds that social movements arise as people react to feeling deprived of things they consider necessary or believe they deserve.

Relative deprivation is a perceived disadvantage based on some comparison. In the middle of the 19th century, Alexis de Tocqueville studied the question as to why a revolution occurred in France and not in Germany in the late 1790s. What puzzled him was that social conditions in Germany were far worse than they were in France. His answer to this apparent paradox was that German peasants had known nothing but feudal servitude and thus had no basis for feeling deprived. Improving social conditions in France had raised the expectations of its people during the latter part of the 18th century.

Figure 23-2 (p. 596) illustrates the model developed by James Davies predicting that social movements are more likely to occur in a society when an extended period of improvement in the standard of living is followed by a shorter period of decline.

Weaknesses with this perspective include its inability to explain why social movements emerge among some categories of people and not others, and the apparent circular reasoning involved in this approach. This latter point refers to the fact that deprivation is identified as a condition only if a social movement emerges.

➤Mass-Society Theory

This approach, first developed by William Kornhauser, suggests people who feel isolated and insignificant within a broad, complex society are attracted to social movements. Using this perspective, involvement in social movements is viewed as being more personal than political.

Research provides inconsistent support for this approach and it should be recognized that it focuses heavily on psychological origins, and ignores issues of social justice.

➤Structural-Strain Theory

This perspective was developed by Neil Smelser in the early 1960s. In this theory, six social conditions are identified as fostering social movements. These include: (1) structural conduciveness, (2) structural strain, (3) growth and spread of an explanation, (4) precipitating factors, (5) mobilization for action, and (6) lack of social control. Each of these conditions is explained in the text especially with respect to the pro-democracy movement in Eastern Europe.

This approach is identified as being distinctly social, rather than psychological. This theory however contains the same circularity of argument as found in the relative deprivation theory. Further, it fails to incorporate the important variable of resources, such as the mass media, into a formula for explaining social movements and their relative success or failure.

➤Resource-Mobilization Theory

Resource-mobilization theory argues that social movements are unlikely to emerge, and if they do, are unlikely to succeed without necessary resources.

This theory's dual focus on discontent and available resources for the success of a social movement provides critical insight for researchers. However, critics argue that powerless segments of the population can promote successful social movements if they organize effectively and have strongly committed leaders. It is also pointed out that power struggles within the status quo of society itself must be taken into account. For example the Native movements in Canada were more successful when provincial premiers did not present a united front (e.g. participation in negotiations leading up to the Charlottetown Accord.

➤"New Social Movements" Theory

This approach attempts to explain the distinctive features of more recent social movements which deal with global ecology and Native rights among others. These movements focus upon the state itself, recognizing that governments now set policies that affect entire populations. The focus then is national or international in scope and the primarily middle class adherents make effective use of the mass media. Table 23-1 (p. 600) summarizes the five theories.

Gender and Social Movements

While women have played leading roles in many social movements many are denied access or given perfunctory roles. Patriarchy dominates the operation of most social movements.

Stages in Social Movements

While recognizing each social movement is unique, four stages are identified which most move through. These stages include: *emergence, coalescence, bureaucratization*, and *decline*. Figure 23-3 (p. 601) illustrates the stages.
A social movement declines for several reasons, including the accomplishment of its goals, poor political leadership, inability to counteract forces from the status quo, repression by leaders of their followers, and finally, some social movements may eventually become an accepted part of the system.

Social Movements and Social Change

Social movements either encourage or resist social change. Social change is both a cause and a consequence of social movements. Many past social movements, though taken-for-granted by most people today, did much to affect our social lives.

LOOKING AHEAD: SOCIAL MOVEMENTS IN THE TWENTY-FIRST CENTURY.

Social movements have always been a part of our society and are likely to continue to shape our lives. Excluded categories of people will continue to find their voice and information technology can spread that voice dramatically. As well, as suggested in the **Controversy and Debate** Box (p. 602) taking a stand can make a difference. McLuhan's "global village" is upon us, social movements can indeed become international in scope.

KEY CONCEPTS

Define each of the following concepts in the space provided or on separate paper. Check the accuracy of your answers by referring to the text as well as by referring to italicized definitions located throughout the chapter.

collective behaviour	mob
collectivity	new social movements theory
convergence theory	panic
contagion theory	propaganda
crowd	public opinion
deprivation theory	relative deprivation
emergent-norm theory	resource-mobilization theory
fad	riot
fashion	rumour
gossip	social movement
mass behaviour	structural-strain theory
mass hysteria	
mass-society theory	

STUDY QUESTIONS

 True-False

1. T F   Much collective behaviour is transitory.

2. T F   A conventional crowd results from deliberate planning.

3. T F   Crowds share no single political cast; some call for change and some resist it.

4. T F   Rumour thrives in a climate of ambiguity.

5. T F   The creation of the Bloc Québecois serves to legitimate a revolutionary social movement.

6. T F   Mass society theory suggests that social movements are most likely to occur in areas with close social ties.

7. T F   According to structural-strain theory, people form social movements because of a shared concern about the inability of society to operate as they believe it should.

8. T F   "New social movements" tend to focus more on economic matters than on the quality of life.

9. T F   Although the women that join social movements may be more qualified than the men who join, they are mostly assigned to clerical positions.

10.T F   New information technology tends to separate people from each other and reduce the possibility of joint global action.

✎ Multiple-Choice

1. Which of the following is not identified as a difficulty in researching collective behaviour using the sociological perspective?

   (a) the concept of collective behaviour is broad
   (b) collective behaviour is complex
   (c) collective behaviour is often transitory
   (d) all are identified as difficulties

2. Herbert Blumer identified several types of crowds based on their level of emotional intensity. Which of the following is not a type of crowd identified by Blumer?

   (a) casual
   (b) conventional
   (c) expressive
   (d) acting
   (e) emergent

3. A theory of crowds which claims that the motives which drive collective action do not originate within a crowd, but rather precede its formation if called _____ theory.

   (a) contagion
   (b) reactive
   (c) convergence
   (d) subversive

4. A theory which argues that crowds are not merely irrational collectivities is:

   (a) consensual theory
   (b) emergent-norm theory
   (c) structural theory
   (d) reactive theory

5. The essential characteristics of rumour include the following:

   (a) thrives in a climate of ambiguity
   (b) it is unstable
   (c)it is easy to stop
   (d) a and b above
   (e) b and c above

6. An unconventional social pattern that people embrace briefly but enthusiastically is called a(n)

    (a) rumour
    (b) fashion
    (c) fad
    (d) panic
    (e) all of the above

7. What type of social movement seeks limited social change for the entire society?

    (a) revolutionary
    (b) redemptive
    (c) deprivation
    (d) alternative
    (e) reformative

8. The pro-democracy movement in Eastern Europe is used to illustrate which theory of social movements?

    (a) mass society
    (b) structural-strain
    (c) resource-mobilization
    (d) "new social movements"

9. Which of the following is not identified as a stage in the evolution of a social movement?

    (a) emergence
    (b) coalescence
    (c) decline
    (d) realignment
    (e) bureaucratization

10. Which of the following are reasons for the scope of social movements to increase?

    (a) Women and other excluded categories of people gain greater political voice.
    (b) Information technology spreads information quickly.
    (c) Globalization unites people throughout the world.
    (d) All of the above
    (e) a and b above

✎ Fill-In The Blank

1. Riots, crowds, fashions, fads, panics, mass hysteria, public opinion, and social movements are all examples of _____ _____.

2. A _____ is a large number of people who interact little, if at all, in the absence of well-defined and conventional norms.

3. A(n) _____ crowd forms around an event with emotional appeal.

4. _____ was responsible for the belief by many in 1969 that Paul McCartney was dead.

5. Thorstein Veblen defined _____ _____ as the practice of spending money with the intention of displaying one's wealth to others.

6. Running naked in public in the mid-1970s was called _____.

7. The three major dynamic sources of social change in Canada are _____, _____ and _____.

8. Using mass-society theory, social movements are viewed as more _____ than _____.

9. Resource mobilization theory points out that no social movement is likely to succeed without substantial _____.

10. According to a 1995 survey by Bibby, _____ percent of Canadians feel that the financial lot of the average person is getting worse.

Definition and Short-Answer

1. What are three basic characteristics which distinguish collectivities from social groups?

2. Differentiate between the four types of crowds identified by Herbert Blumer on the basis of level of emotional intensity.

3. Differentiate between contagion theory, convergence theory, and emergent-norm theory in terms of how each explains crowd behaviour.

4. Differentiate between the concepts rumour and gossip.

5. Describe four types of social movement.

6. Using structural-strain theory, Smelser identifies six social conditions that help foster social movements. What are these social conditions?

7. What are the five theories of social movements? Compare and contrast each of these in terms of how they help us explain social movements.

8. What are the four stages of social movements?

9. What is the relationship between social change and social movements?

Answers to Study Questions

True-False

1. T (p. 586)	6. F (p. 596)
2. T (p. 587)	7. T (pp. 596-597)
3. T (p. 589)	8. F (p. 599)
4. T (p. 591)	9. T (pp. 599)
5. T (p. 595)	10. F (p. 603)

Multiple-Choice

1. d (p. 586)	6. c (p. 593)
2. e (p. 587)	7. e (p. 595)
3. c (p. 589)	8. b (p. 597)
4. b (p. 589)	9. d (p. 600)
5. d (p. 591)	10. d (p. 603)

Fill-In

1. collective behaviour (p. 586)
2. collectivity (p. 586)
3. expressive (p. 587)
4. rumour (p. 590)
5. conspicuous consumption (pp. 592-593)
6. streaking (p. 593)
7. class relations, regional identity, bilingual/multiculturalism (p. 594)
8. personal/political (p. 596)
9. resources (p. 598)
10. 70 (p. 602)

ANALYSIS AND COMMENT

Go back through the chapter and write down in the spaces below key points from each of the following boxes.

SOCIAL DIVERSITY

" The Rumour Mill: Paul is Dead."
Key Points:

_____

_____

_____

_____

_____

CONTROVERSY AND DEBATE

"Are You Willing to Take a Stand?"
Key Points:

_____

_____

_____

_____

_____

SUGGESTED READINGS

Classic Sources

Gustave Le Bon. 1960; orig. 1895. *The Crowd: A Study of the Popular Mind.* **New York: Viking Press.**
One of the first studies of crowd behaviour, this classic stimulated the investigation of collective behaviour and sparked debates that persist even today.

Jo Freeman, ed. 1983. *Social Movements of the Sixties and Seventies.* **New York: Longman.**
This collection of essays, with a useful introductory essay by the editor, investigates social movements in terms of four processes: mobilization, organization, strategy, and decline.

Contemporary Sources

Clark McPhail. 1994. *Acting Together: The Social Organization of Crowds.* **Hawthorne, NY: Aldine de Gruyter.**
A review of the research about crowds, this book also critiques various theoretical approaches.

James M. Jasper and Dorothy Nelkin. 1992. *The Animal Rights Crusade: The Growth of a Moral Protest.* **New York: The Free Press.**
Here is a survey of the organizations and politics that make up the animal protection crusade, one example of a new social movement.

Canadian Sources

S. D. Clark, J. Paul Grayson, and Linda M. Grayson. 1975. *Prophecy and Protest: Social Movements in Twentieth-Century Canada.* **Toronto: Gage.**
This collection of articles deals with the development of Social Gospel movements. Social Credit, the Cooperative Commonwealth Federation (CCF), unions, and Quebec nationalism.

Stanley R. Barrett. 1987. *Is God a Racist?: The Right Wing in Canada.* **Toronto: University of Toronto Press.**
This book takes a close look at the people involved in several right-wing organizations in Canada. Based on interviews, it gives a real sense of the beliefs and commitments behind organizations such as the Western Guard and the Ku Klux Klan.

Global Sources

Hanspeter Kriesi. 1993. *Political Mobilization and Social Change: The Dutch Case in Contemporary Perspective.* **Brookfield, Vt.: Avebury.**
Many social movements have swept across Western Europe in recent decades; this book assesses what has changed and what has not.

Gao Yuan. 1987. *Born Red: A Chronicle of the Cultural Revolution.* **Stanford, Calif.: Stanford University Press.**
This personal account of one teenager's experiences during the Cultural Revolution in China between 1966 and 1969 explores the causes and consequences of a mass movement that spun out of control.

CHAPTER 24

> Social Change: Traditional, Modern and Post-Modern Societies

- To know the four general characteristics of social change.

- To explain the five sources of social change.

- To understand the four general characteristics of modernization.

- To compare and contrast the explanations of modernization offered by Toennies, Durkheim, Weber, and Marx.

- To explain modernization through the structural-functional and conflict theories.

- To understand how mass society and class society explanations account for social change.

- To explain the relationship between modernity and progress.

- To comprehend the social patterns of postmodernity in postindustrial societies.

- To understand the differences between the modernization and dependency theories.

- To imagine how information technology will affect social change.

III CHAPTER REVIEW

The transformation of the Kaiapo culture in Brazil's Amazon and the Inuit in the Northwest Territories is discussed with reference to the impact of external culture through the medium of television. The Inuit people now have their own network which can be seen by many non-Aboriginal Canadians. How, one might ask, is culture changed, and are the consequences positive or negative?

WHAT IS SOCIAL CHANGE?

Social change, is the transformation of culture and social institutions over time. Four general characteristics represent the process of social change:

1. Social change is inevitable but the rate of change varies between societies;
2. Social change is both intentional and often unplanned;
3. Social change is often controversial; and,
4. Social change has important and unimportant consequences.

CAUSES OF SOCIAL CHANGE

It can be argued that the causes of social change are found both inside and outside of a given society.

Culture and Change

Cultural change results from three basic processes: *invention, discovery*, and *diffusion*.

Conflict and Change

Tension and conflict within a society can be a source of social change. Marx saw that inequality would cause conflict and lead to change.

Ideas and Change

Max Weber's thesis concerning the influence of the Protestant work ethic on industrialization in Europe reflects the influence of ideas on social change.

The Natural Environment and Change

European settlers in North America set about controlling the natural environment in an adversarial way. We continue the same path today, gobbling scarce resources while inflicting the environment with solid waste and water and air pollution.

Demographic Change

Demographic factors are related to how societies change. Changing fertility and mortality rates along with migration can dramatically affect the nature of life in a society or globally. By 2031, for example, almost one quarter of the Canadian population will be seniors.

MODERNITY

Key Dimensions of Modernization

Modernity refers to patterns of social life linked to industrialization. *Modernization* is therefore the process of social change initiated by industrialization. Peter Berger has identified four general characteristics of modernization:

1. The decline of small, traditional communities;
2. The expansion of personal choice;
3. Increasing social diversity; and,
4. Future orientation and growing awareness of time.

Sociology itself began as an effort to comprehend the process of modernization.

Ferdinand Toennies: The Loss of Community

Ferdinand Toennies' classic book Gemeinschaft and Gesellschaft focuses on the process of modernization. Essentially, the Industrial Revolution weakened the fabric of community tradition and led people to associate mostly on the basis of self-interest.

One feature of gesellschaft is geographical mobility of a society's population. Table 24-1, (p. 612) shows that the rate of moving in Canada is high up to the 25-34 year category and drops thereafter.

While synthesizing various dimensions of social change, Toennies's work did not clarify cause and effect relationships between the variables he studied, and he ignored the persistence of close relationships in urban areas.

Emile Durkheim: The Division of Labour

Central to Durkheim's analysis of modernity is his view of the increasing division of labour in society. Durkheim did not see modernization as the loss of community, but rather as a change in the basis of community from *mechanical solidarity*, or shared sentiments and likeness, to *organic solidarity*, or community based on specialization and interdependence. These two types of solidarity are similar in meaning to Toennies' concepts of gemeinschaft and gesellschaft.

Durkheim was more optimistic than Toennies about the effects of modernity, yet he still feared anomie (little moral guidance) could result given the increasing internal diversity of society. The increasing rates of suicide in Canada, fits with Durkheim's expectations.

Max Weber: Rationalization

For Weber, modernity meant increased rationality and a corresponding decline in tradition. In this process bureaucracy increased as well. Compared to Toennies and Durkheim, Weber was pessimistic and critical about the effects of modernity. He was concerned that rationalization would erode the human spirit.

Karl Marx: Capitalism

While other theorists were concentrating on social stability, Marx focused on social conflict. He agreed with Toennies' analysis of the changing nature of community. He was concerned with Durkheim's sense of the increase in the division of labour. His position also supported Weber's view about increasing rationality and declining tradition. However, for Marx, these processes were all changes which supported the growth of capitalism, and of this he was very critical. Such changes, he suggested, would eventually lead to social revolution where egalitarian socialism would allow technology to enrich the many instead of the few. Marx apparently, however, underestimated the significant impact of centralized bureaucracy in socialist, as well as capitalist states.

THEORETICAL ANALYSIS OF MODERNITY

Modernity is a complex process involving many factors. Table 24-2, (p. 615) summarizes the characteristics of traditional and modern societies along the dimensions of cultural patterns, social structure, and social change. Seventeen different variables are used to compare the two types of societies.

Structural-functional Theory: Modernity as Mass Society

One approach to the study of social change views modernization as a process which creates mass societies. A *mass society* is a society in which industrialization proceeds and bureaucracy expands while traditional social ties grow weaker. Two points are stressed. First, the expanding scale of social life leads to impersonality and cultural diversity which overwhelms most individual's attachment to community. Second, the expanding role of the government dominates the regulation of people's lives through a complicated and impersonal bureaucratic structure. Critics suggest that the theory romanticizes the past and ignores inequality.

Social Conflict Theory: Modernity as Class Society

This approach is largely derived from Karl Marx's analysis of society. A *class society* is a capitalist society with pronounced social stratification.

➤Capitalism

For Marx, it was the growth of capitalism, not the industrial revolution which caused the growing scale of social life. He saw the profit motive promoting self-interest and greed, which broke down social ties that bound small-scale communities.

Marx saw science not only as a source for greater productivity but also a justification for the status quo.

➤Persistent Inequality

While many theorists argue that modernization began to break down rigid categorical distinctions, proponents of the theory of class society see a greater concentration of power and wealth occurring. Statistics Canada data, for example, has shown that the top 20 percent of individual earners get 46.5 percent of all income in Canada.

A criticism of this approach, however, is that it tends to underestimate the ways in which egalitarianism has increased in modern societies. The mass-society theory and the class-society theory are summarized in Table 24-3, (p. 619).

Modernity and the Individual

While mass-society theory and the theory of class society have been discussed to this point as perspectives focusing on macro-level issues concerning patterns of change, they also offer micro-level insights into how modernity affects individuals.

➤Mass Society: Problems of Identity

According to this view, establishing an identify becomes more difficult with the social diversity, isolation, and rapid social change which modernization brings about. As Lipset suggests identity is the quintessential Canadian issue.

David Riesman developed the term *social character* to mean personality patterns common to members of a society. He views preindustrial societies as promoting *tradition-directedness*, or rigid personalities based on conformity to time-honoured ways of living. This would be associated with Toennies' gemeinschaft and Durkheim's mechanical solidarity. In culturally diverse and rapidly changing industrial societies, another type of social character emerges. This type, called *other-directedness*, refers to highly changeable personality patterns among people open to change and likely to imitate the behaviour of others.

374

➤**Class Society: Problems of Powerlessness**

According to this view, individual freedom is undermined by the persistence of social inequality. Herbert Marcuse, using this perspective, challenges Weber's contention that modern society is rational. For Marcuse, because society is failing to meet the basic needs of many people it is actually irrational.

Modernity and Progress

Generally, people view modernity as progress, but this conception ignores the complexity of social change. The Kaiapo of Brazil, highlighted earlier in this chapter, illustrate this point.

While basic human rights have been advanced the issue of individual choice and freedom versus duties and obligations toward one another is not resolved. Science and technology is supported in North America (See Figure 24-1, p. 621) but all change is clearly not progress.

Modernity: Global Variation

Most societies are not either traditional or modern; they maintain characteristics of both types of society.

POST MODERNITY

Postmodernity refers to social patterns characteristic of post-industrial societies. Postmodern theorists suggest that:

1. Modernity has failed
2. "Progress" is fading
3. Science does not hold the answers
4. Cultural debates are intensifying
5. Social institutions are changing

While modernity has generally increased the quality of life the **Controversy and Debate** Box (pp. 622-623) suggests that the U.S. is in decline, can Canada be far behind?

LOOKING AHEAD: MODERNIZATION AND OUR GLOBAL FUTURE

Modernization theory and dependency theory, discussed in great detail in Chapter 11, are seen as relevant. Modernization theorists see modernity as increasing the standard of living among the people of a society.

Dependency theory, on the other hand, suggests that social change brought on by modernization victimizes the poorer nations while further enriching the wealthy of the rich countries.

Whatever theory one supports the study of Canadian society cannot be isolated from the interconnections of global relationships since interactions between countries are technically more feasible today than discussions between neighbouring towns a century ago.

Canada is also experiencing an internal revolution, from deference to defiance (See **Exploring Cyber-Society** Box pp. 624-625) which is probably related to the immense flow of information in the post-industrial world. The Internet is power.

The **Cyberscope** Box (pp. 628-629) examines the impact of information technology on cities, social movements, and social change.

KEY CONCEPTS

Define each of the following concepts in the space provided or on separate paper. Check the accuracy of your answers by referring to the text as well as by referring to italicized definitions located throughout the chapter.

class society
mass society
modernity
modernization
other-directedness
post-modernity
social change
social character
tradition-directedness

STUDY QUESTIONS

 ### True-False

1. T F   In any given society, all cultural elements change at the same speed.

2. T F   Max Weber argued that technology and conflict are more important than ideas in transforming society.

3. T F   By the year 2031, it is estimated that almost 25% of the Canadian population will be seniors.

4. T F   According to Peter Berger, a characteristic of modernization is the expansion of individual choice.

5. T F   According to our authors, Durkheim's view of modernity is both more complex and more positive than that of Toennies.

6. T F   A characteristic of traditional societies is women's lives centred in the home.

7. T F   According to mass society theory geographical mobility, mass communications and exposure to diverse ways of life erode traditional values.

8. T F   Class Society theory suggests that elites have essentially disappeared from capitalist societies.

9. T F   Marcuse labels modern society irrational because it fails to meet the needs of so many people.

10. T F   Peter C. Newman suggests that deference to authority is no longer an appropriate characterization of Canadians.

✎ Multiple-Choice

1. Which of the following are key characteristics of social change?

   (a) The rate of change varies from place to place
   (b) Social change is always intentional.
   (c) Some social change is of only passing significance

   (d) a and b above
   (e) a and c above

2. Which of the following is not a source of social change?

   (a) ideas
   (b) population
   (c) genetic heritage

   (d) the natural environment
   (e) social structure

3. The process of social change initiated by industrialization is called

   (a) individualization
   (b) alienation
   (c) rationalization

   (d) gesellschaft organization
   (e) modernization

4. Critics of Toennies' conception of modernization suggest that:

   (a) he ignores the personal relationships which are maintained in modern societies.
   (b) he romanticizes traditional societies
   (c) his cause and effect linkages are overstated
   (d) all of the above
   (e) a and b above

5. Which of the following is most accurate?

   (a) Durkheim's concept of organic solidarity refers to social bonds of mutual dependency based on specialization
   (b) Toennies saw societies as changing from social organization based on gesellschaft to social organization based on gemeinschaft
   (c) Peter Berger argued that modern society offers less autonomy than is found in preindustrial societies
   (d) Durkheim's concept of mechanical solidarity is very similar in meaning to Toennies's concept of gesellschaft.

6. Durkheim's concepts of mechanical and organic solidarity are similar to the notions of:

   (a) mass-society and class-society
   (b) tradition-directedness and other directedness
   (c) anomie and progress

   (d) gemeinschaft and gesellschaft
   (e) none of the above

7. Factors driven by the Industrial Revolution, such as _____ changed the relationships between individuals and how they came to know one another.

(a) a surge in population
(b) the growth of cities
(c) specialized economic activity
(d) a and b above
(e) all of the above

8. Class-society theory suggests that:

(a) power rests primarily in the hands of those with wealth
(b) there is a persistence of inequality in capitalist societies.
(c) discrimination is disappearing because of the intervention by the state.
(d) a and b above
(e) b and c above

9. Mass-society theory suggests that social diversity, isolation and rapid social change make it difficult for many people to establish a coherent _____.

(a) identity
(b) social character
(c) receptiveness
(d) modernity
(e) deference pattern

10. _____ theory explains global poverty as the product of economic domination by rich, capitalist societies.

(a) modernization
(b) rationalization
(d) mass society
(d) alienation
(e) dependency

Fill-In The Blank

1. _____ refers to the transformation of culture and social institutions over time.

2. _____ traced the roots of most social change to ideas.

3. _____ is the process of social change initiated by industrialization.

4. Despite Durkheim's optimistic view of the future he feared that societies might become so internally diverse that they would collapse into _____.

5. Weber feared that _____, especially in bureaucracies, would erode the human spirit.

6. In traditional societies formal schooling is limited to _____.

7. _____ is a society in which capitalism has generated pronounced social stratification.

378

8. A rigid conformity to time-honoured ways of living is what Riesman calls _____.

9. _____ refers to social patterns characteristic of post-industrial societies.

10. By _____ science we can see that this system of ideas has been widely used for political purposes.

11. Control in the post-industrial world means access to _____.

Definition and Short-Answer

1. What are the four general characteristics of social change?

2. Five general domains which are involved in causing social change are identified and discussed in the text. List these and provide an example for each.

3. Peter Berger identifies four general characteristics of modern societies. What are these characteristics?

4. Differentiate between Toennies', Durkheim's, Weber's and Marx's perspectives of modernization.

5. What factors of modernization do theorists operating from the mass-society theory focus upon?

6. What factors of modernization do theorists operating from the theory of class society focus upon?

7. What are the two types of social character identified by David Reisman?

8. Evaluate our global future using the theories of modernization and dependency.

Answers to Study Guide Questions

True-False

1. F (p. 608)
2. F (pp. 609-610)
3. T (p. 610)
4. T (p. 611)
5. T (p. 613)

6. T (p. 615)
7. T (p. 616)
8. F (p. 617)
9. T (p. 620)
10. T (p. 624)

Multiple-Choice
1. e (p. 608)
2. c (pp. 609-610)
3. e (p. 610)
4. e (p. 612)
5. a (p. 613)
6. d (p. 613)
7. e (p. 616)
8. d (pp. 617-618)
9. a (p. 619)
10. e (p. 623)

Fill-In
1. social change (p. 608)
2. Max Weber (p. 609)
3. modernization (p. 610)
4. anomie (p. 613)
5. rationalization (p. 614)
6. elites (p. 615)
7. class society (p. 617)
8. tradition directedness (p. 619)
9. postmodernity (p. 621)
10. deconstructing (p. 622)
11. information (p. 625)

ANALYSIS AND COMMENT

CONTROVERSY AND DEBATE

"The United States: A Nation in Decline? Will Canada Follow?"

Key Points:

_____

_____

_____

_____

_____

EXPLORING CYBER-SOCIETY

"The Canadian Revolution Through the Information Revolution: The Point of 'No Return'."
Key Points:

_____

_____

_____

_____

_____

CYBER.SCOPE

"How will cities, social movements and social change be affected by the Information Revolution?"
Key Points:

SUGGESTED READINGS

Classic Sources

Emile Durkheim. 1964; orig. 1895. *The Division of Labour in Society*. New York: The Free Press.
This is the classic account of social change by one of the founders of sociology.

Derek Sayer. 1991. *Capitalism and Modernity: An Excursus on Marx and Weber*. New York: Routledge.
This recent book examines the limits of modernity and assesses the prospects for postmodernity through a review of the ideas of two seminal sociologists.

Contemporary Sources

Amitai Etzioni. 1993. *The Spirit of Community: Rights, Responsibilities, and the Communitarian Agenda*. New York: Crown Publishers.
In what might be called the "handbook of the communitarian movement," Etzioni suggests ways to fuse individual rights with collective responsibility.

Peter Berger, Brigitte Berger, and Hansfried Kellner. 1974. *The Homeless Mind: Modernization and Consciousness*. New York: Vintage Books.
Peter Berger. 1977. *Facing Up to Modernity: Excursions in Society, Politics, and Religion*. New York: Basic Books.
Highly readable, these books are filled with interesting insights about the modern world.

Canadian Sources

Philadelphia: Temple University Press.
This collection of essays surveys the link between women's social standing and economic development in two rapidly changing Asian nations.

Wendy Griswold. 1994. *Cultures and Societies in a

David Taras, Beverly Rasporich, and Eli Mandel, eds. 1993. *A Passion for Identity: An Introduction to Canadian Studies*. Scarborough, Ont.: Nelson.
This collection of articles by an unusually wide range of authors takes a fascinating look at the question of Canadian identity from national and regional perspectives.

Wallace Clement. 1990. "Comparative Class Analysis: Locating Canada in a North American and Nordic Context." *Canadian Review of Sociology and Anthropology* 27 (4).
This article looks at class formation in Canada in comparison with the U.S., Sweden, Norway, and Finland, taking gender into account.

S. D. Clark. 1978. *The New Urban Poor*. Toronto: McGraw-Hill Ryerson.
This very readable study deals with the experience of people, long caught in impoverished rural areas, who are finally forced to migrate to urban areas to seek a livelihood.

Ralph Matthews. 1978. *There's No Better Place Than Here: Social Change in Three Newfoundland Communities*. Toronto: Peter Martin Associates.
This book is about those "other Canadians who refuse to accept the urban dream and goal" and are left behind in the retreat from rural areas.

Global Sources
Joyce Gelb and Marian Lief Palley, eds. 1994. *Women of Japan and Korea: Continuity and Change.*

***Changing World*. Thousand Oaks, Calif.: Pine Forge Press.**
Close-up examinations of various countries, including Nigeria and China, illuminate this discussion of culture change.

NOTES

NOTES

NOTES

NOTES